SACRED DIVORCE

SACRED DIVORCE

Religion, Therapeutic Culture, and Ending Life Partnerships

KATHLEEN E. JENKINS

RUTGERS UNIVERSITY PRESS
New Brunswick, New Jersey, and London

Library of Congress Cataloging-in-Publication Data
Jenkins, Kathleen E.
Sacred divorce : religion, therapeutic culture, and ending life partnerships /
Kathleen E. Jenkins.
    pages   cm
Includes bibliographical references and index.
ISBN 978-0-8135-6347-3 (hardcover : alk. paper) — ISBN 978-0-8135-6346-6
(pbk. : alk. paper) — ISBN 978-0-8135-6348-0 (e-book)
1. Divorce—Religious aspects—Christianity. 2. Divorce—Religious aspects—
Catholic Church. 3. Divorce—Religious aspects—Judaism. 4. Divorce—United
States. I. Title.

BT707.J46 2014
261.8'3589—dc23

2013027196

A British Cataloging-in-Publication record for this book is available from the British
Library.

Visit our website: http://rutgerspress.rutgers.edu

Manufactured in the United States of America

CONTENTS

ACKNOWLEDGMENTS

This book was made possible through the support of many family members, colleagues, students, funding agencies, and especially the people who were willing to share their stories with me. I thank my respondents for talking with me about painful memories. One of the joys of qualitative research is getting to know a wide range of people and being invited, if sometimes only for a couple of hours, to sit and listen to their stories. I feel privileged to have been trusted with their accounts. I thank all of the clergy and ministry leaders who took time from their busy schedules to talk with me; I hope that my sociological perspective offers some insight as they engage in the important work they do with congregants and their family issues.

Early in the research process, I received a fellowship with the Congregational Studies Project Team, a program funded by the Lilly Endowment that brings together researchers and scholars. The fellowship came with research funds and exceptional mentors. Penny Edgell, Stephen Warner, and Nancy Ammerman offered critical feedback during Congregational Studies group meetings and throughout the research process. Through this program I met Lawrence Hoffman, who brought a critical eye and inspiration for my analysis of divorce experience in synagogues. A Joseph H. Fichter Grant from the Association for the Sociology of Religion and a Summer Research Grant from the College of William and Mary also allowed me to travel and conduct interviews with clergy and divorced persons, and to attend services, support groups, and religious conferences.

The sociology department at the College of William and Mary has been a constant support. Kathleen Slevin, Tom Linneman, and Jennifer Bickham-Mendez read chapters and related articles over the last five years and offered valuable feedback. Exceptional students at the college played a part in the evolving research process. My student Danielle Wingfield conducted fieldwork with me and gathered a number of the interviews in the Church of God in Christ (COGIC) case. Her constant energy and enthusiasm was inspiring. Margaret Clendenen worked as my research assistant when I put the first draft of this book together to send for review; the book is what it is today because of her careful attention to editing details and endnotes, and her brilliant sociological imagination. Students from my ethnographic methods class in the sociology department at the College of William and Mary and my Sociology of Religion course motivated me as I witnessed their sociological imaginations taking shape. Diane Gilbert offered assistance as I was collecting data. Debbie Eck has allowed me to find time to focus on the book while chairing the sociology department, and solved many administrative and technology puzzles.

I am grateful for the time this manuscript spent with the Family in Focus series editors at Rutgers University Press. Although the book eventually found its home on the religion list, Karen Hansen, Anita Garey, and Margaret Nelson gave helpful feedback as I thought about the importance of this book for sociologists of the family. Karen Hansen read an early draft of the book and encouraged me to emphasize links between religious emotion and management of contemporary family experiences. Margaret Nelson, in particular, offered invaluable and detailed feedback at a critical stage, and I am thankful for her guidance and careful eye. Margarita Mooney offered comments during the review process that pushed me to think more deeply about organization and voice. Debbi Osnowitz spent many hours thinking with me about the central arguments in this book. Me'irah Iliinsky offered comments on major ideas and inspired me with her artwork. Gerardo Marti and Lynn Davidman read drafts of chapters and offered helpful feedback. I would also like to thank the anonymous readers and editors who have encountered this manuscript at various points in its publication process and who have given helpful advice and direction. Thank you to Paula Friedman for her careful editing and to Peter Mickulas for his energies and editorial wisdom as the book took final shape.

My family has been a constant support. My mother, Beverly Olsen, is my dear friend and a sharp editor. My stepfather, Dr. Richard Olsen, also edited multiple drafts of chapters and related articles over the years. My husband, Mark Lerman, read and edited chapters. He also allowed space for me to talk, a great deal, about divorce and religion, and took the lead on driving our daughters back and forth, back and forth, back and forth . . . from school and activities so that I could devote time to interviewing, analyzing, and writing. My daughter Kathryn's fashion sense made me presentable on mornings when I was exhausted from teaching, writing, and administrative work. My youngest daughter Jackie gave great shoulder and back massages. Her passion for cooking, combined with my father's advice on the best red wine deals, was a great asset. My son, Marty, and I have shared creative passages and found lost time as I wrote this book.

Finally, I want to thank Dr. Carol Landau, who I worked for, years ago, as an assistant before returning to get my undergraduate degree at Brown University at age thirty. Carol instilled a sense of confidence and love of research that brought me to my sociological imagination, and I am forever grateful.

SACRED DIVORCE

INTRODUCTION

Divorce is a true passage. If we do our work, nothing remains
the same. Our traditions are resources, enabling us to break
through the numbness, to travel, across the painful transition,
safely to the other side.

—Rabbi Hollander (1994, 204)

I was shaking like a leaf. When I put on the Tallit, it was like
suddenly being nestled under the wings of the Shechina; this
calm just totally took over me, and I felt totally enveloped, and I
just knew it was going to be okay. I felt the sense of God's presence and God just embracing me.

—Conservative Jewish woman

It's hard, painful, grueling work. . . . you must be willing to lean
into your pain. Face it head on, or as Father so graphically says,
"We have to vomit it up."

—Catholic woman, support group participant and lay leader

Not that long ago, it would have sounded quite strange to speak
to one of divorced Catholics as a gift to the church. But certainly, over this last decade, that is what you have become.

—Father James Young, 1983 speech at Notre Dame

In the midst of going through counseling, I was made a deacon
in the church, and you could hear the whispers, "He is divorced,
not stable," but you don't give up, you keep pushing.

—Associate pastor in black Baptist church

I found myself writing songs about marriage, divorce, and love. . . . Music was helping me get healed. I was getting it out on paper, instead of holding it in and wanting to kill someone.

—Divorced Pentecostal man, Church of God in Christ

The majority of marriages in the United States begin through religious ceremony (Whyte 1990, 165).[1] Marriage rituals affirm, in the presence of clergy, family, friends, and community, deeply held religious and secular values associated with life partnership. But what about divorce? How might religious traditions and congregations be important as people end these relationships? We likely expect the work of divorce to take place in courtrooms and psychologists' offices, less often in churches. Nonetheless, the United States is home to over 300,000 congregations; researchers have found that a majority of citizens say they believe in God or a Universal Spirit; and sociologists argue that people who identify with a religious tradition often turn to familiar religious beliefs and practices as they face challenging family issues.[2] Given the importance of religion in many individuals' lives, what is the experience of practitioners in faith traditions as they end life partnerships? How might religion shape how people navigate family relationships through divorce? How do congregations respond to or provide resources for members who are separated or divorced? The quotations above are just a few of the voices I encountered during five years of interviewing divorced individuals and religious leaders as they told me stories about managing emotions and making divorce a meaningful, even sacred, process.

Sociologists often study subjects that resonate deeply with our own lives—especially those experiences we recall as fracturing our familiar social worlds. My interest in how people experience divorce in religious community can probably be found in my own encounter with loss of a normative family life: in the mid-1970s, when I was twelve years old, my mother, an elder in a southern Presbyterian church, and my father, active in the church youth ministry, divorced. I remember our minister calling me into his office to talk with me about the separation. I felt intimidated sitting in a chair in front of this thoughtful man with an enormous desk separating us. He told me I could talk with him whenever I wanted to. What would I say? I was embarrassed, ashamed, and frankly more interested in discovering social life as a teenager. I never took him up on his offer. When I was seventeen, my boyfriend's mother, a child therapist and wife of a local Baptist minister, summoned me to her bedroom. I sat with her on the side of her bed as she asked me how I felt about my parents' divorce. Whatever her intention, the encounter produced shame, humiliation, and a certainty that when her son ended our relationship it was because I came from a "broken" home. That was the late 1970s; the divorce rate had been on the rise, children of divorce experienced more stigma than today. Fifteen years later, in a hardened divorce culture and as a convert to Judaism, I experienced life as a divorced woman with a young son, feeling both drawn to and pushed away from my faith community.

My questions were born from personal experience and from professional grounding as a sociologist of religion and family. In my first research project, I conducted fieldwork in a tightly bound religious group, the International Churches of Christ (ICOC), named a cult by many outsiders yet revered by members as saving family relationships (Jenkins 2005). Interviewing and attending religious events in the ICOC, I was struck by church leaders' assertions that there was no divorce in their movement. Of course, as I looked deeper and spent more time with members, I found that there were indeed divorced people among them, it was just that one spouse had left and the other had remained loyal. The church's front-stage performance, claiming a lack of divorce, fascinated me. As a professor who teaches about religion and family, I was also struck by the lack of ethnographic and qualitative work addressing divorce and religion; my students could read research that tried to determine rates of divorce in different denominations, and studies that correlated participation in congregations with mental health benefits during family trauma, but there were few empirical studies that could help them think about religious processes or meaning-making as life partnerships ended.

Many might find a priest's statement, such as Father Young's (above), naming the divorced as *gifts* to the church, puzzling—Catholics don't believe in divorce, right? The nuclear family ideal and marriage as a sacrament for life are the vital beliefs associated with conservative religious bodies. We link these religious traditions to discouraging divorce, not elevating the divorced to a revered status. Yet in all of the religious traditions I explored—Jewish, Catholic, black Baptist, black Pentecostal, evangelical and mainline Protestant, and Unitarian Universalist—from liberal to conservative, there were remarkably similar individual and institutional approaches to enriching divorce experience. This book demonstrates how these religious attempts made divorce meaningful through distinct rituals and symbolic worlds, and at the same time embraced and enhanced essential elements of Western therapeutic culture.

Like religious worlds of old, our therapeutic culture is persuasive and composed of widely accepted beliefs and practices: individualism, constant and creative individual pursuit of self-betterment, expression of inner feelings as the key to growth and recovery, and reliance on expert knowledge and/or intervention.[3] It profoundly shapes individual and group identity, impacting how we understand ourselves, others, and the stories we tell about our lives (Illouz 2007, 48). In this book, I demonstrate how religious understandings of divorce experiences are shaped by this grand authority, an essence that permeates our social structure, an essence so everyday that it becomes taken-for-granted knowledge. The people I interviewed told stories that show the omnipresence of therapeutic narratives of self-realization, individual moral stories of emotional suffering performed and realized through religious beliefs, symbolic roles, and practices (Illouz 2007, chapter 2).

Core ideas and strategies for self-improvement, managing challenging emotions, and expression of feeling in contemporary therapeutic culture are found in seed in religious traditions. Religious emphasis on expression of emotions through prayer, music, confession, and other ritual practices have acquired new importance and form in modern therapeutic methods like psychotherapy, support groups, and self-help media mechanisms. Kathleen Lowney (1999) demonstrates how television programs like Oprah Winfrey's promote expression of "sins" and the taking of time to focus on self-improvement, exemplifying a "religion of recovery." Religious constructions of how to make divorce a meaningful and moral process are deeply influenced by this religion of recovery, shaped by a complex system of therapeutic discourse and of beliefs and practices that promote accepted strategies for handling contemporary family issues.

When people lose life partners, parents, extended kin, health, or time with children, they may challenge or reject therapeutic strategies, but they will still feel the power of these forces in concrete ways. A central argument in this book is that religious efforts to render divorce a sacred process are driven by a commanding culture that understands both marriage and divorce as largely individual emotional work performed for self and family. Individuals who end life partnerships are expected to manage multiple cultural contradictions for self and these significant others through focused emotional labor. For example, divorced or separating parents are faced with gendered expectations of mothering, fathering, and learning to co-parent with an ex-spouse. At the same time they are expected to improve self through work, education, emotional growth, relational skill building, and other paths. Therapeutic culture promotes singlehood post-divorce as deeply meaningful, yet ultimately a time when people are expected to work hard to construct selves that are better able to do the emotional work necessary for managing family emotions and succeeding in another life partnership. In this book, I illustrate how religious approaches to divorce endow the contradictions inherent in our marriage and divorce culture, and thus multiple family forms and new identity, with sacred meaning.

Rates of singlehood may be on the rise, but people who challenge or reject monogamy still live today in a culture where dominant social forces uphold life partnership and its supporting institutions.[4] They live in a society where the beliefs that idealize life partnership and those that legitimate ending a marriage are both strong. Karla Hackstaff (1999, 2) well articulates the resulting cultural tension. She notes that divorce exists as "a set of symbols, beliefs, and practices that anticipate and reinforce divorce and, in the process, redefine marriage: marrying is an option, marriage is contingent, and divorce is a gateway." At the same time, marriage culture exists as a "cluster of beliefs, symbols, and practices, framed by material conditions that reinforce marriage and deter divorce." Hackstaff addresses the management of this marriage/divorce cultural tension in the context of religious attempts to save marriages, but the sociological literature lacks ethnographic focus on religious efforts to confront divorce experience.

Sociologists have called attention to various contradictions of family and kinship in contemporary U.S. society, but religion as an active force in addressing these conflicts is virtually absent in the literature, leaving the impression that, as a cultural resource for balancing ideological and practical tensions, it is marginal. Researchers have identified social values that support involved parenting through emotional, financial, and "concerted cultivation" of children in a society with increasing workplace demands and economic challenges,[5] yet little research addresses how religion might shape parents' experiences as they face these forces. Nevertheless, understanding the place of religion in managing contemporary family expectations becomes even more pressing as more women gain status and power in labor markets, and women and men from multiple socioeconomic statuses face lack of full-time work and/or excessive work hours as they strive to make ends meet and/or achieve professional goals (Gerson and Jacobs 2004). Changes in child custody arrangements post-divorce, and wider acceptance of gay and lesbian unions also bring new parental dilemmas, for instance, how women without custody may find strategies for constructing motherhood through religious communities, or how religion may serve as a resource for gay parents seeking to affirm parental identity post-divorce in a society undergoing significant shifts in legal recognition of same-sex unions. My exploration of religion as a cultural resource for divorced individuals as they balance parenting expectations and the dynamic nature of contemporary family structure speaks to these gaps in understanding.

In general, there is limited understanding from a qualitative or ethnographic perspective about identity construction through divorce and how people who end life partnerships may make transitions meaningful. Existing qualitative studies addressing divorce and uncoupling in U.S. society are dated and lack serious consideration of religion as an institution through which people may transition from marriages.[6] For example, Diane Vaughan's 1986 book, *Uncoupling: Turning Points in Intimate Relationships*, provides ground for thinking about the ways people move through separation and divorce. She talks about endings as transitions that involve redefinition of self, a turn to new social relationships, and efforts to make sense of the failed relationship. Still, her work is largely about individual experience, and in the end she calls attention to the need for more exploration of "the connection between particular social, economic, and cultural environments and the individual lives within them" (7)—the sort of path I pursue in this book.

Sociologists of the family spend a great deal of time measuring the effects of divorce on families and children, predicting the likelihood of divorce, and debating whether or not the institution of marriage is failing.[7] Despite the importance of many of these questions, their dominance in the literature inhibits conversation regarding how prevailing cultural ideas and institutional structures like religion might deeply shape experiences of divorce transitioning. Andrew Cherlin (2009) has called attention to the importance of religion in an individualized seeker culture where those ending relationships find social support and individual spiritual growth in communities of faith. Penny Edgell (2006) notes in her study of family and congregational life that family disruption can lead "people to a renewed sense of importance of religion in their lives," writing that religion is "uniquely suited to address" the questions of "meaning, purpose, and direction" as people experience divorce (53). We know that many religious institutions play a key role in promoting normative family structures and gender ideology, but we know as well that religious worlds must adapt to shifts in gender, employment, and a divorce culture that legitimates ending marriages. In this book, I capture the active nature of religious adaptation through an ethnographic lens, illustrating how people find strategies in religious worlds for making sense of the dynamic nature of identity, moral selves, and family relationships through contemporary transitions.

Some may think that religion provides a buffer against ending life partnerships. Group prohibitions against divorce and the family focus of many congregations may sometimes curb divorce, but research indicates that the relationship between instance of divorce and religion is complicated. Such complications might include, for instance, whether spouses are members of a tightly bound religious community that rejects divorce and exerts strong social pressure, whether both are active in their religious community and how often they attend services, and whether they are members of the same faith. The particular norms and expectations for marriage in congregations add another layer of complexity, for example, how religious ideology that encourages marriage at an early age, may raise the likelihood of divorce?[8] Divorce rates among religious traditions are disputed and complicated, but what sociologists know for sure about religious people in U.S. society is that they begin and end relationships at high rates. The national divorce rate may have decreased slightly over the last decades partly because of higher rates of cohabitation and rising age of marriage; still, people begin and end relationships in this country with a higher frequency than occurs in most other Western nations, and religious people are no exception.[9] What role religion plays in divorce processes, and what the practices and beliefs in religious communities are through which individuals experience endings—these are the questions that lit my sociological imagination seven years ago when I began interviewing divorced congregants and their clergy in churches, parishes, and synagogues.

As a sociologist of culture, I pay careful attention to my respondents' encounters with beliefs about divorce, and to how social actors, institutions, and practices reproduce power and knowledge. I want to know how people who identify as religious understand and confront strategies for managing divorce. Thus, while this book is primarily about divorce and religion, it inevitably makes visible larger dominant cultural expectations faced by many individuals as they confront ending a life partnership. The interviews I conducted for this study, and the time I spent over five years in congregations, in small groups, and in gathering documents from religious divorce resources suggest overwhelmingly that formal religious discourse advocates larger cultural understandings of individuals as responsible for serious emotion work that involves controlling and using their feelings to better the self and manage family relationships. Coping with and exorcising dangerous yet valuable feelings is at the heart of divorce discourse in both secular and religious approaches.

The idea that divorce produces hazardous emotional aftershocks that may cause people to make rash decisions that could harm self and others is kept alive in part through social media and the social sciences. Researchers in psychology and sociology warn about the dangers of divorce for children, and of children being caught in parental battles and suffering mental health issues well into adulthood.[10] Visions of contentious divorce and volatile emotions fill popular media. For example, *Time* magazine (February 11, 2008) published an article highlighting suggestive divorce products, such as a knife rack called the "ex" that looks like a human figure and "comes in six different colors." Other products include "Voodoo Dolls: a safe way to stick it to an ex-lover," a "wedding-ring coffin," and a "wheel of wisdom: advice ranging from meditating to calming down to signing an ex up for junk mail." Divorce self-help books perpetuate the idea that divorce is an explosive emotional time with the potential to cause people not only to act out in dangerous ways, but to hold emotions inside and thus produce ongoing pathological states requiring serious attention. At the same time, ending life partnership is understood in this divorce culture as a period of self-growth, transformation, and discovery.

The religious people I encountered talked about divorce as a charged and auspicious time, even as their beliefs and practices affirmed divorce as a painful process and potentially pathological condition. Their narratives of religious approaches to divorce reflect a dominant cultural strategy that I articulate in detail in this book: *divorce work*, a merging of *grief work* and *marriage work* expectations. Divorce work reflects entrenchment in a grief work discourse born from medical psychology that understands grief as a mourning process that takes place through "stages." The divorced people I interviewed expressed working through grief and understanding this as difficult labor and a moral responsibility to self and family. In medical psychological literature, grief is a troublesome condition that involves "work"—or basic duties that must be "systematically approached" through the help of mental health professionals.[11] Popular self-help literature echoes the seriousness of the labor associated with divorce emotions. For example, journalist Abigail Trafford warns in her popular divorce book, *Crazy Time* (1992, 63):

> Divorce puts you right on the edge of sanity. Some people go over the edge and destroy themselves and their families. They are like kamikaze pilots in a marital war where the death of their shared past can be the only victory. Although most people manage to get through this period of stress, a significant number of divorce casualties are the victims of murder, suicide, and madness. Other times, it's a slow inner death. The weapons are softer, less crude, more socially acceptable, but just as deadly to your psyche. There is a little bit of kamikaze craziness in all divorces.

One might dismiss Trafford's amplification of divorce danger as overly dramatic and empirically unsound; still, several of my respondents identified strongly with her book and some of the religious resources I analyzed recommended the text. In books like *Crazy Time* and other secular and religious divorce resources, weighting potential divorce pathology through harsh metaphor is not uncommon. The Divorce Detox website (http://divorcedetox.com/), with its program drawn from several therapeutic practices, describes its approach as the road to "successful divorce recovery that detoxes the harmful residues that [the] emotional toll of divorce (and a dysfunctional marriage) leaves." Much of divorce work discourse is about processing grief to eradicate destructive feelings, ease kamikaze-like impulses, and make good use of emotions.

Grief, despite its seeming aloneness, is a deeply social and culturally determined experience. In some cultures, crying, wailing, touching, or washing a body after death is expected and gendered. In others, mourners may sit silently in a reserved manner with little body contact with the dead.[12] My respondents talked about loss, rejection, guilt, and anger as emotions connected in profound ways to social bonds within kin and religious worlds. The creators of that religious divorce work that I present in this book are clear that people must manage their grief in efficient ways. In the words of one evangelical divorce program, DivorceCare (http://www.divorcecare.org/): "You need to have a strategy for coping. You need to understand what you are doing and why you are doing it." Recognizing grief as culture-bound is not easy. Most of us have suffered some loss of social bonds, some more extreme than others, and have stories about body and emotion that we might only describe as excruciatingly painful. Body experience and emotions, however, are always felt through our understandings of self in relation to others. Uncovering how culture profoundly shapes the way people talk about and experience feelings does not negate the empirical truth of physical and emotion sensations that may drive one to curl on the floor in a ball and sob; rather, it demands an understanding that tears and sharp body pains are not detached from the social emotions that fill our encounters of loss.

In this book, respondents' social emotions come to life in their stories of serious threats to family and religious identity and the moral task at hand in the emotional labor of grief. As they searched for strategies to fend off threats to core social identities, they found dominant cultural scripts in divorce work resources that reflected rules for managing feelings: emotions must be confronted, expressed, and controlled in an appropriate manner and context; trust should be placed in the advice of professionals who have the expert knowledge and skill to turn potentially dangerous emotions into opportunity and self-growth; and an assessment of feelings and behaviors that occurred during the marriage must be undertaken to insure future success in life partnership. These emotion work rules and guidelines hold great social power and are built from well-established institutionalized beliefs and practices in our therapeutic culture.

I use the terms emotion-work, emotional labor, and intimate labor throughout this book to call attention to dominant feeling expectations that shape cultural scripts of grief work and marriage work active in divorce work. Much of the literature on emotion-work concentrates on emotional labor as relational work and/or as a commodity.[13] Some studies have also called attention to emotion work as a religious or therapeutic strategy for creating group commitment, solidarity, and promoting new identity construction.[14] Eileen Boris and Rhacel Salazar Parreñas (2010) articulate the concept "intimate labor" as a distinct form of work that can involve various forms of personal body/health or emotion work. Much of the literature on emotion work and intimate labor highlights the gendered nature of these expectations and the dominance of women in occupations and family roles that demand emotion management. Gender and other social factors were salient in how my respondents encountered and spoke about the emotional labor of divorce work, and had implications regarding social power. Still, the essential cultural expectation of using painful emotions to promote new self and care for children and family was similar for all.

Secular and religious divorce work strategies promote marriage work as an essential task, alongside grief work. Contemporary life partnerships harbor deep contradictions: we are private beings socialized to respect a therapeutic ethos that expects us to perpetually shape new and better selves, yet that same cultural world encourages us to improve these selves through intimate relationships. These contradictions are facilitated through companionate marriage, a model that took shape in late-nineteenth- and early-twentieth-century Western society as patriarchal marriage gave way to marriage based on love, intimacy, and the idea that spouses should be friends. Marriage work thus involves emotional management of the relationship through development of communication skills, creative management of romance and friendship, and the sharing of religious/spiritual orientation—strategies that manage the "alone together" nature of contemporary life partnership (Amato 2007). Contemporary companionate marriage has been further shaped by the rise of dual-wage-earning households, increasing acceptance of LGBT life unions, higher rates of cohabitation, rising age of marriage, and high rate of termination of life partnerships, all shifts that intensify the notion that people make a deliberate choice to enter into marriages. This emphasis on choice has given rise to a historically specific and highly intentional form of marriage work constructed largely by psychologists and social scientific "experts." In the dominant discourse, marriage work is chronic intentional emotion work meant to build competence in life partnership skills.

Divorce is presented by secular and religious marriage experts as a time to assess and retool for future relationships, to build on and learn communication skills, to create a stronger spiritual self who can succeed in future relationships, and to labor to acquire relational skills for parenting with ex-spouses. As found in wider culture, the marriage work of divorce in religious constructions often sustains gendered notions of women as essentially emotional or better equipped for relational work and men as resistant to such work. Still, most important is that, for all genders, marriage work expectations involve a steady retooling, an endless unraveling and evaluation of self and relationship.

Religious renderings of divorce work have constructed this labor as hard, individual work facilitated largely through strengthening personal engagement with religious practice, belief, symbolic roles, and, for many, relationship with religious community and/or a divine power. The people I interviewed engaged in prayer, participated in support groups and conferences, sang, wrote in journals, meditated, and shaped new rituals from old religious practices—all strategies that legitimated their ideas about and performances of divorce work. Most believed that, if they did not get rid of dangerous emotions and analyze failed relationships, they might hurt themselves, their children, or others, and would never be capable of sustaining healthy life partnerships. They talked a great deal about how religious practices and beliefs gave them meaningful tools for learning to express and use emotions as they transitioned from married to single selves, strategies they used to articulate new identities and self as on a moral path. As I show in this book, congregations were, even though respondents often felt a disturbing shame and silence around their divorce experience in these communities, essential spaces where many could tap into religious emotion that helped make sense of the social feelings surrounding this significant life transition.

Sociologists are well aware that religious and family life in the United States is shaped in deep ways by a culture that promotes expressive individualism and cultivation of self. But they have only begun to uncover the complexity of social and individual power embedded in therapeutic assumptions and processes as individuals face changes in family structure over time. Sociologists have yet to consider in depth how class, race/ethnicity, family structure, and particular religious traditions might come together to shape encounters with therapeutic culture. This book is an ethnographic treatise of the convergence of religious and therapeutic discourses—a blending of models that others have noted as ripe for understanding (Ammerman et al. 2006). I work to reveal the taken-for-granted assumptions of this deep cultural convergence, the significance it holds for individuals as they interpret and construct meaningful lives through family transitions, and the implicit social control underlying basic cultural assumptions about self and intimate relationships.

SACRED DIVORCE—METHODOLOGICAL APPROACH

In sociological parlance, my sample is purposive—meaning that I chose to interview, conduct participant observation, and gather documents based on a research question about a particular kind of individual and institution. I wanted to talk with people who participated in religious communities, who identified as religious and/or spiritual practitioners, and who also engaged religious processes as they sought to make divorce meaningful. Many people do not turn to religious beliefs or practices to make sense of endings, and some of these may still identify as religious—they are not my research participants here. My respondents' stories are also somewhat shaped by my research topic and my role as listener and researcher, an inevitable dynamic in ethnographic data collection, and one that I address throughout the book and at length in my methods appendix.

I have purposively collected narratives of individuals at differing distances from initial points of ending. Some of my divorced research participants had been separated for only a few months, others up to twenty years. This diversity allowed me to explore the multiple relationships that shape divorce experience over time, and to consider how the telling of divorce narratives may change with length of time since divorce. Within religious traditions, I also sought out innovation and creation of divorce practices. I made sure to interview individuals involved in divorce ministries and small groups, and also those who did not participate in, or were not aware of, such groups.

Given my interest in how religious communities differ in approach, I pursued a diversity of religious traditions, acknowledging some differences that may vary by race/ethnicity and class. I included the black Baptist tradition (primarily National Baptist Convention, USA, Inc.), black Pentecostal (Church of God in Christ), Jewish communities (Reform, Reconstructionist, Conservative, and Jewish Renewal), as well as white evangelical (primarily nondenominational), mainline Protestant (United Methodist, Presbyterian), Unitarian Universalist, and Catholic (primarily Roman Catholic) cases. Most traditions promoted heterosexual marriage, but the Unitarian Universalist (UU) and Jewish communities (Reform and Reconstructionist) openly affirmed same-sex life unions. In the methods appendix, I go into more detail regarding the data collection process that I followed in each tradition.

I use the terms *marriage* and *life partnership* interchangeably, my criteria being that both words denote a commitment to a monogamous lifelong union. Thus, my use of the term *divorce* includes the ending of legal life partnerships and of marriages not accepted by states. I recognize that there are serious consequences for disenfranchised LGBT individuals and that the larger political debate over marriage deeply affects these families (consequences of which surface at times in the stories I tell here), but my interest here is in the experience of ending life partnerships in a culture that highly values coupling for life. Although some may argue that people should challenge the institution of marriage and its sexist and gendered institutional practices,[15] the empirical reality is that many LGBT life partners are invested in monogamy, many religious congregations have welcomed same-sex marriage ceremonies, and religious symbols and beliefs have provided passionate arguments for same-sex marriage rights.[16] Many LGBT partners desire a life companion and lover and a spouse with whom they can raise children, and see such relationships as spiritual and/or God-given. Further, LGBT individuals build and then sometimes break social bonds with life partners, children, kin, and church relationships just as heterosexual couples do. In analyzing the dominant forces at work in managing the social emotions of divorce, my work ultimately speaks to similarity of cultural encounters regarding same-sex and heterosexual life partnerships.

I used several types of data collection to gain a more nuanced understanding of divorce experience. I conducted open-ended conversational interviews with seventy-five religious practitioners who had ended life partnerships. I interviewed thirty-one clergy members, eleven other pastoral and lay leaders in congregations and divorce ministries, and three counselors working with Jewish support groups. The people I interviewed varied in age from their early thirties to their mid-sixties. They were broadly middle class, although a handful came from poor households and several told stories of downward economic mobility caused by divorce. I interviewed more women than men, which is not surprising, given that women participate in religious communities in higher numbers. The majority of people I interviewed considered their divorce a difficult life disruption that brought threatening social emotions, although, as I address in the concluding chapter of this book, the stories of those few who experienced joy and happiness as their relationship ended adhered to dominant divorce-work scripts in interesting ways.

Overall, finding religious people who had been divorced and were willing to participate in interviews was a difficult task. These are the stories of those who were ready and willing to tell me about their experiences. My sample is skewed, then, toward religious people who considered their story of divorce and subsequent meaning-making important enough to share with a researcher, and felt able to do so. I asked many who refused. Although some may have refused because of time commitments in their busy contemporary lives, or because they felt that their story of religious experience and divorce was not substantial, I talked with several potential interviewees who indicated that the topic was too raw or personal, as well as religious leaders who told me about congregants who had gone through divorce but were not ready to tell their story. In one evangelical Christian case, a church leader told me that a man going through a divorce would not talk to me because I was a woman. The silences of those not ready to talk, and the limited conditions under which some were willing to tell their stories, represent an absent voice in this book. This silence offers some validation of the private nature of endings and the profound impact of the social grief and threat of shame that still presents when individuals end life partnerships in a culture where divorce is commonplace.

I crossed the lines of normal social interaction when I pressed people about details of what many assume to be private: grief, shame, intimate kin relationships, and religious/spiritual identity and practice. In many cases, I could feel the person's pain and grief getting in the way of articulating experience—tears, silence, physical gestures that indicated discomfort, eyes staring full and pained, eyes closed and lids shaking. To ease tension and fear of judgment, I often let respondents know that I had been divorced and suffered associated relational losses.

I also conducted participant observation in support group meetings in the evangelical Christian case and regional conferences for the divorced in the Catholic case. I was denied access to support groups in other traditions because of leaders' perceptions of their confidential nature. I attended services in each religious tradition and, when possible, attended services in my respondents' congregations. I also analyzed hundreds of pages of religious divorce literature and media referenced by my research participants, as well as popular secular divorce self-help texts. In the Catholic case, an older leader of Catholic Divorce Ministries gave me cassette tapes of major addresses given by ministry leaders at regional conferences since the mid-1980s, and offered me a large box of newsletters and support group handouts and leadership training materials to copy. My research design evolved over five years, and represents both the fluidity and the rigor of a qualitative design. Sampling choices were shaped by my ongoing collection of data, identification of prominent themes and concepts, and review of existing sociological research.[17]

This book, like all ethnography, is an interpretive text. The story I tell of my respondents' experience of making divorce sacred is shaped by who I am, my own life experience, and how these translate into my role as a research instrument. In many ways, my experience of divorce and religion was very different from that of most of my respondents. I was only married for a couple of years, initiated the divorce, and, unlike most of my respondents, was not a member of a religious community as I ended my marriage. I remarried and spent six years co-parenting with my ex-husband as he fought, and won, several battles with cancer. I experienced most of my divorce trauma when my ex-husband remarried and custody battles followed. During that period of my life, I turned away from religious community to individual spiritual practice, and I have since found community in a small, unaffiliated synagogue. I have known the power of prayer and scripture, and have felt both embraced and rejected by religious community. I have turned to therapeutic professionals to help with divorce dynamics and felt empowered, deeply frustrated, and betrayed. I consider my position a strength that helps me understand and gain the trust of my research participants; at the same time, I accept that it demands a constant awareness of stepping back to achieve sociological perspective.

CHAPTER CONTENT

In the first chapter, Social Shame and Religious Tools, I introduce key respondents whose narratives represent dominant types of social emotions that resulted from threats to parental bonds and challenges to religious identity. I illustrate the significance of religious tools as my respondents told stories about becoming stronger in their family roles and affirming religious bonds. Parents who were distanced from children because of custody issues, and those who suddenly felt like single parents when spouses left the home, all faced challenges in redefining what it meant to be a parent through and after divorce. Respondents whose core identity in church communities revolved around their position as part of a couple experienced radical shifts when their spouse left the home or congregational space. Similarly, people who felt their marriages as sealed by God through a sacred vow searched for ways to protect their religious/spiritual status as their relationship ended.

Chapter 1 also introduces how religious tools emerged more formally in congregations and religious traditions. I describe Catholic Divorce Ministries (CDM), whose approaches well represent the kinds of strategies and symbolic tools that members across traditions encountered in religious designs of sacred divorce. Religious resources like those produced by CDM provided efficient practices and moral paths through which respondents understood themselves as developing into better parents and potential partners, emotionally healthy and well able to sustain family and church relationships. Such an approach speaks to cultural assumptions of individual responsibility for growth through tragedy, and of changing family forms, reflecting larger understandings and the prevalence of divorce work in our society.

In chapter 2, Divorce Work as Accepted Cultural Strategy, I take apart the concept of divorce work as it emerges in respondents' stories, formal religious divorce resources, and popular divorce self-help and psychological texts. I show how grief-work and marriage-work discourse combine to promote divorce as an experience of death that demands grieving through stages. Grief work assumes that, if handled well by the individual, divorce can lead to better, new intimate relationships, spiritual growth, rebirth, and authentic identity. Handling grief work well is also understood in larger therapeutic discourse as protecting children and developing healthy family and relationship habits and skills. I show how psychological models of grief work provide a basis for understanding the divorce experience as potentially pathological, and argue that, though divorce may no longer be a stigma in U.S. culture, grieving understood under such a medical model continues to render considerable potential for stigma.

In this chapter, I also illustrate common themes and therapeutic approaches to divorce work found across religious traditions, and how divorce work, through its grief- and marriage-work components, legitimates companionate marriage and life partnership as normative. Most important, I show how religious worlds have powerful emotional resources and symbolic roles that give therapeutic tenets added, sacred status: for example, the use of pilgrimage as a symbol for divorce experience in Catholic resources, sacred passages and sacrifice in Judaism, and God and Jesus as physician and ultimate healer in evangelical voices—religious concepts that turn divorce work into sacred labor.

In chapter 3, Solitary Work through Community, I tell respondents' stories of engaging in sacred divorce work through congregations and community rituals, demonstrating the emotional power of community practice. As they participated in services and small groups, they pulled from religious ideas of solitary journey or pilgrimage, focusing on individualized practice in collective space. My illustration of solitary journey through community highlights the power of religious emotion in narratives of divorce work. My respondents embraced religious symbol, story, and practices that resonated with long-familiar sentiments capable of motivating action. In their stories, congregations and group practices emerged as valuable backdrops for the private emotion work that affirmed religious identity and the betterment of self for children and future life partnerships. Music, for example, brought some further into the collective's worship, but was also a vehicle for movement to an exclusive individual realm of therapeutic experience. Although they might use community spaces for sacred divorce work, most respondents, in their stories, revealed feeling judged by others in their congregations and a general silence around discussion of divorce. A constant weight in their storied endings was the individualism and the solitary nature of divorce and marriage in contemporary U.S. culture. Theirs were narratives of togetherness in collective ritual eclipsed by self-work imperatives.

In chapter 4, Cautious Clergy, I explore the careful efforts of clergy to respond to divorced congregation members. All of the rabbis, priests, and pastors I interviewed talked about the concealed nature of divorce in their congregations. Clergy generally described numerous demands on their time, and most felt removed from the private relational lives of members. Still, a significant number of my respondents did turn to clergy at some point during the years surrounding their divorce as they pursued strategies for managing their emotions and affirming their religious status.

I demonstrate how clergy cautiously assembled meaningful symbols and practices as religious tools for members of their congregations transitioning from marriages and facing challenging relationships with children. These clergy told stories of being compassionate listeners, delivering careful sermons, refitting such existing practices as annulments in the Catholic case and *gets* [Jewish divorce documents] in the Jewish case, and even working with members to construct new and individualized rituals. Each of these approaches shows the highly private nature of sacred divorce work and the difficulty of constructing public community rituals that simultaneously hold marriage and divorce sacred.

As I have conducted research for this book, I encountered many religious folks, primarily from conservative traditions, who argued that creation of new rituals for divorce was dangerous because it would validate divorce. My analysis of sacred divorce work, in this chapter, builds on arguments made in chapter 2 that demonstrate how divorce rituals and religious strategies in many ways supported, rather than undermined, marriage and life partnership as ideal, and provided approaches for caring for the emotional lives of children. Most clergy and formal creators of sacred divorce work engaged in a careful discursive balancing act, embracing marriage and divorce culture to the extent that they could within the boundaries of their traditions. The clergy/member dynamics reflected in this chapter underscore the privatization of religion and the limited moral authority of contemporary religious communities to intervene in family dynamics.

In chapter 5, Rich Lived Practice, I call attention to the importance of understanding my respondents' approaches through a lived religious lens. Such a focus on lived religion inevitably illustrates the relationship between class and therapeutic pursuits. Listening to my respondents' stories, we hear a strong emphasis on the individualism that drives religious and therapeutic culture as these respondents narrate efforts to work hard and to take control of their lives and move forward. I illustrate the distinct and multiple religious instruments that surfaced in their stories as they managed emotions associated with transitions to new family, religious roles, and for some, serious physical challenges. I turn to Nancy Ammerman's (2007; 2014) and Meredith McGuire's (2008) works on lived religion to stress the importance of recognizing subjective definitions and bodily experiences of religion and spirituality in everyday life.

I show how my respondents were grounded seekers, generally identifying with a single religious tradition or congregation, but turning to a greater variety of religious and spiritual beliefs and practices to fashion creative divorce strategies for managing their emotions and those of family members. For example, they found creative expression in music—listening, performing, and writing songs in private and community settings. Creative expression worked to prepare some for future relationships; for others, such practices controlled emotions that they described as threatening to their children and/or to their relationships with ex-spouses. Most talked about prayer and/or meditation as a central and private practice. Reading secular and religious texts, writing fiction, appealing to saints, journaling, doing yoga, and dancing were some dominant forms of daily practice as well. These respondents' stories demonstrate the multiplicity of religious identity and practice in American society, the ubiquity and social power of therapeutic culture in managing self and family relationships; and they suggest the importance of socioeconomic position for the performance of narratives of self and family betterment through divorce.

In chapter 6, Religious Emotion and Multiple Family Forms, I argue that congregations across traditions found ways to adapt to divorce culture, and that through religious emotion and through other practices they were well able to balance multiple family forms. Congregations are thus a strong institutional link fueling a society that both begins and ends life partnerships at high rates. I discuss the global implications of this power and suggest avenues for future research. I also highlight variation in encounters with religious emotion. The salience of gender, class, and race in how people activate and experience therapeutic discourse highlights social relations of power. I stress that people are both empowered and disempowered by relgio-therapeutic strategies that can produce constructions of pathology and exclusive practice, and that religious leaders and congregations should continually assess this potential. I suggest that ethnographers turn attention to religious emotion work in the face of family dissolution and disruption on the part of those embedded in other cultural knowledges—for example, new immigrants' experiences of family and encounters with congregational worlds. I also underline the importance of future research that may further unpack religious emotion and therapeutic approach as cultural tools for balancing dynamic and multiple contemporary family forms.

There are many self-help and divorce guidebooks that address the emotion work of divorce. This is not one. Such books are a component of the larger forces in U.S. society that I analyze here. We may hear that divorce is no longer a stigma, but such a statement does not begin to capture the potential for social shame when family and religious identity is challenged through ending life partnerships. This book is about how individuals who identify as religious people talk about experiencing these breaks in core family and religious bonds, the associated social emotions, the spiritual tools available to them, and the larger cultural strategies and approaches in institutions that shape their stories of restructuring family and religious identity. That said, I suspect that listening to the narratives of my research participants—to the songs they wrote, the prayers that comforted them, the strategies they employed, and the ways they talked about and made sacred their deep loss, may help people who seek to make divorce meaningful. Whether we choose to oppose or activate dominant ideas, there is great power in simply understanding our most intimate relationships and emotions through a sociological lens.

1 ✳ SOCIAL SHAME AND RELIGIOUS TOOLS

When we think of divorce and grief, we may imagine a deeply psychological and private experience, yet grief is a core social emotion; social interactions and cultural expectations deeply influence our beliefs, practices, and experiences of loss.[1] All people do not experience ending life partnerships in the same way, or search for religious strategies to make divorce meaningful. Still, every divorce has the potential for some type and level of social shame. When marriages end, people may feel embarrassed, guilty, a sense of failure or rejection or disgrace, caution, fear, excitement—a range of emotions related to the social relationships that may be in jeopardy or changing.[2] My respondents had, to varying degrees, been deeply invested in marriage bonds cemented by religion, children, kin, and friendship networks. Most talked of having internalized the idea of self as part of a sacred union, and remembered well the religious ceremonies and spiritual hopes that marked this union's creation. Divorce left them full of questions, as roles and identities like daughter-in-law, stepfather, religious leader, or married congregant were in flux.

It comes as no surprise that most of my interviewees, as people who strongly identified with religious traditions, turned to individual spiritual and community practices to help guide their transitions and ease feelings associated with social shame. Familiar religious beliefs and practices, as well as new practices crafted by divorce ministries and clergy, held powerful emotional sway in their stories. Ann Swidler (1986) argues that culture shapes a "repertoire" or "took kit" composed of certain skills, habits, and approaches through which individuals create "strategies of action" for approaching social relationships and identity. Swidler (2001) names divorce as a prime example of what she calls "unsettled lives," where people are actively searching for "cultural tools" and "strategies" to find order. The people I interviewed, as narrators of their life story, spoke from moral positions and told stories that reflected processes of self-evaluation.[3] They talked about themselves as actively searching for religious tools to better themselves and care for their children as they faced painful emotions related to their divorce; in doing so, they claimed a highly respected therapeutic identity as seekers of effective self work.

They were persuaded by larger social forces to do this therapeutic emotion work. Anthony Giddens (1991, 3) writes: "In the settings of what I call 'high' or 'late' modernity—our present day world—the self, like the broader institutional contexts in which it exists, has to be reflexively made. Yet this task has to be accomplished amid a puzzling diversity of options and possibilities." Divorce brings on "an acute version of a process of 'finding oneself'" which the social conditions of modernity enforce on all of us," a process that demands "active intervention and transformation" (12). My respondents mined through religious and wider therapeutic cultural tools as they confronted various types of social shame and actively sought to transform into stronger members of family and religious community.

Each of the people I interviewed told a distinct and multiple story of social shame. Loss of children and loss of religious status were the most dominant contributors to the threatened shame; still, their stories represented other upsets such as loss of financial security, home, or employment status; illness; and the decline of physical health. Todd, a former Catholic and self-identified evangelical Christian who had been divorced for five years, told me: "I call myself a broken sinner who is recovering from losses—the loss of my marriage, the loss of my financial security, the loss of my concept of family, the loss of a mother, a brother, a Christian brother. I'm in that point of recovering from not only my divorce, but a whole bunch of losses."

Individual life history and related social losses deeply shaped respondents' stories of *contemporary liminal experience*—a sense of being somewhere between social roles, highly vulnerable, standing on variable social ground. In his classic *The Ritual Process* (1969), building on the earlier ritual theorizing of Arnold V. Gennep (1960), Victor Turner describes a liminal state as an ambiguous condition of self associated, across cultures, with rites of passage (95). Liminal states are met with community rituals that work to guide transitions. In more tightly bound cultures, the primary focus of both Gennep and Turner, rites of passage meant to order and guide individuals through liminality and to reincorporate them into new social roles seem more straightforward than the multiple practices and feasible relational identities at work in contemporary Western society. For example, when a woman or man leaves a life partnership, he or she may live life as a single person, chose to live with a sexual partner, find a life partner of the same or another sex, and/or take on the identity of a part-time or full-time mother or father. He or she may (or may not) maintain kin ties with the ex-partner's family of origin or take on a new spouse's children. The options and paths for new family construction are many, as are the types of self-help mechanisms one can pursue, but how people work to achieve and legitimate these new family positions is limited by society's dominant therapeutic culture.

Social values and prevailing institutional worlds acknowledge that ending a life partnership is painful, but that it should be an occasion for working on self. Diane Vaughan's (1986) research on uncoupling suggests that people whose relationships are ending see themselves as in processes of transition and of redefinition of self. Anthony Giddens (1991) begins his work on modern identity with the example of divorce, commenting on Judith Wallerstein and Sandra Blakeslee's (1989) book, *Second Chances*, "Divorce, the authors point out, is a crisis in individuals' personal lives, which presents dangers to their security and their sense of well-being, yet also offers fresh opportunities for their self-development and future happiness" (1991, 10). Every person I interviewed, whether or not he or she could tell stories of achieving this goal or not, embraced the idea that the death and pain of ending a union should bring the potential for new life or purpose and thus stronger family and spiritual selves.

In this chapter, the stories of three respondents illustrate this overarching narrative and the two dominant themes of social shame that surfaced in my interviews: feelings related to loss of parental position and feelings related to threatened religious status. These stories introduce how *religious tools* came to bear as the respondents repelled and/or repaired social statuses. Some were divorced for years and others only a few months, but the narrative of each portrays religious strategies that activated the character of therapeutic seeker, a role that, like that of a patient pursuing diagnosis and treatment, has the power to provide meaning and to ease social shame.[4]

THREATENED SOCIAL BONDS

The majority of my respondents were parents, and so their stories were in large part about shifts in their role as mother or father. Several women and men told stories of suddenly having their children all the time and struggling to manage children's emotional and physical needs alongside their own—of being suddenly thrown into the role of single parent. Most of my respondents told stories of being separated from their children through custody, whether by not seeing them so frequently, or through not seeing them at all. One woman noted the emptiness and pain resulting from the unexpected loss of time with her children: "You expect to have your children for eighteen years and then they go to college. That's the expectation and now that time has been cut, shortened. I don't know if that pain ever goes away." All interviewees who were parents were left to shape new roles in a culture in the midst of defining what it means to be a good mother or good father through and after divorce.

In spite of our divorce culture, divorce is still a social death and a deviant action, especially when children are involved. This is true even though research indicates that divorce does not always lower child well-being, and that the effects of divorce on children are shaped by numerous factors like level of marital and divorce conflict, and quality and circumstances of remarriage.[5] Regardless, when children are involved, divorce is often understood as creating a "broken home," and divorced individuals are left to save face in the eyes of others.[6] Thus, the stories my respondents told about how they managed their children's lives after divorce was an important social performance. Several men and women I interviewed talked about staying in their marriages for longer than they would have if they had not had children. Others told stories of turning to religious practices and beliefs to help manage their new roles as divorced parents. There are few, if any, acceptable social performances for mothers and fathers who are not active in their children's lives, and even fewer norms for how stepparents should approach stepchildren post-divorce. Even in my small ethnographic sample, at least five respondents experienced long years where they did not see their children. In these cases, threats to parental bonds took up considerable space in their narratives, as did their construction of selves as searching for religious tools to heal, move forward, and manage emotions for self and family.

Lenny

When I first spoke with Lenny on the phone to schedule our interview, he told me that his divorce papers were just being processed and that he was having difficulty facing the finality of ending this marriage, even though he had been separated from his second wife for two years. He was a forty-three-year-old black salesman with a college education. We met in a quiet coffee shop. He paused several times during the interview, overcome by emotion, and struggled, at points, for the words to describe his emotions. He depicted himself as a private person and expressed surprise, at the end of our interview, that he had enjoyed our conversation, revealing that he had "never talked to anyone in depth like that about the divorce."

Lenny was a member of a large (2000–3000 members) black Baptist congregation, although he had grown up in a small (100–150 members) rural southern black Pentecostal church. He married, the first time, in his early twenties, a union that lasted five years and gave him one daughter, now in her early twenties, with whom he had had a distant relationship. After his first divorce, he felt strong judgment from his Pentecostal congregation: divorce was proof that "you didn't work hard enough with God, or listen to God." He described his relationship with the congregation as damaged, seeing gossip as eventually pushing him from the church and away from his hometown: "It was just so hard because a hundred people pretty much knew your story." Lenny said he wanted to keep his feelings and family experience private, so he prayed alone for hours at a time, opening up to only a couple of close relatives who tried to help him, ultimately relocating to a town hours away to start a new life; in this town, he met and married a woman who had children from a previous marriage.

Lenny spent most of our interview talking about the circumstances and feelings surrounding his second marriage—understandably, given that he saw himself as in the midst of "grieving" this ten-year partnership. He repeatedly questioned what he might have done to allow what he saw as the core problem, this second wife's temper and physical and verbal abuse, to continue: "She was just acting out violently. . . . How much can I handle in that case? . . . I couldn't keep doing it. It was wild. And, um [*finding it hard to tell me about this, he pauses several times*], . . . verbal, physical, you know, and you think back and say, okay, what did I do to get to this point, what did I do for this to happen?" Lenny presented himself as having worked hard on his marriage, going to counseling sessions with the pastor at the couple's church and trying to work on communication with his wife. In the end, he decided the abuse, which took place alongside several deaths in their families, put too much pressure on the marriage: "I had been going for four or five years to the sessions, and it wasn't helping us. . . . I just couldn't see—at a certain point people were actually dying and things were not better. Relatives were leaving and it was still the same. . . . Death in my family, in hers, and things were still bad between us."

Living in what he described as an "unhealthy" marriage became too much for him to bear, and eventually gave him what he saw as the ethical grounds to leave: "I'm somebody who is always saying I'm going to help somebody else as I help myself. . . . I'm not helping anybody. I'm actually causing pain here." He turned to his minister for help in working through his problems. The minister told Lenny that he might have religious grounds for divorce, given the abuse, but still advised him to "see it out" and to pray, and that his wife might change. Lenny presented two long years of "seeing it out," giving him time to weigh his commitment to his wife, to her children, to God, and to himself. He saw a pattern of destructive marital behavior hurting his family and his own health. Prayer, together with his pastor's validation, gave him the religious grounds he felt he needed to pursue a legal divorce.

Lenny did not have any biological or adopted children with his second wife, yet his story of ending and coming to terms with the divorce was very much shaped by the role he played, and now didn't play, in her children's lives. He talked about spending a significant amount of time raising her two children, a stepparenting relationship that had always been a source of some friction:

> I raised them from the ages of about eight and ten; some of those hurt feelings [are] from that too, because they never really appreciated the sacrifices I've made for them; . . . their Dad was actually locked up in prison all their lives. . . . I can understand why they are acting out like that, but it's kind of hard to tell a kid why you are acting like that. You know what I'm saying? Okay, okay, he has a father, he can't accept you as his father because he misses his real father and wants to know what happened to him, and why did this happen to him, and things like that. . . . I tell people I can only just do the best job of being a father and hopefully one day they can look and say, well, okay, this guy did this.

Lenny presented his role as a father in his biological daughter's life as limited, and expressed his desire to be a good father and make a difference in his children's lives. In his story, his status and authority as a stepfather in his second marriage had always been challenged and he had worked to provide his stepchildren with material and emotional support. As his life partnership was ending, his status and social contract with his stepchildren was changing in radical ways. He imagined himself remembered by the children he tried to parent as "this guy."

At the end of our interview, Lenny searched for the words to communicate the depth of ambiguity surrounding his divorce, and the battle going on in his private world:

> It is grief, but more than that. The most challenging thing is in doing it . . . ; going in, I made this serious vow to myself, not only to myself, but I made it to God, that I wasn't going to get divorced this time. So, I was going to do what I had to do to make everything work, and so that was a problem for me. . . . Crazy as it might sound, if I hadn't gotten to a breaking point in my head, I would still be there right now because of that vow, fighting to make it work, and, to me, that I have to reduce myself. . . . [*He has a hard time speaking, his eyes fill with emotion*] It's crazy because I remember when I made it, and . . . I remember the feeling of making it, so breaking it was a constant thinking about when you did it and how you did it, circular thoughts . . . crazy. It definitely hurt; . . . the grief thing is actually it. But the big thing that I have with it now . . . I just think back and it's like, could you still do it? Could you have gotten through that? And sometimes I still think, yeah, I can.

His divorce papers were signed, but Lenny still presented himself as questioning the decision, working to understand what went wrong in the marriage and how, at the very least, he might still be a presence in his stepchildren's lives. Prayer became an important practice that he could access throughout the day to try and understand how he had come to this point of divorce after having made such a serious commitment to himself and to God.

Lenny's story was of disruption of fatherhood and the breaking of multiple social bonds, a condition that left him confused, uncertain, and experiencing a particular kind of social shame that intensified the private nature of his divorce. He was in the midst of struggling as his status as parent radically changed. To be a man who succeeded in marriage and parenting seemed an essential religious and family identity for Lenny. He had been raised by his stepfather and believed strongly that his presence in his stepchildren's lives could help them succeed in life. As he thought about his recent signing of divorce papers, he was faced with the reality that he was a man who had not succeeded in reaching these ideals of fatherhood, and a man who had experienced the ending of a second marriage, an act that he saw as "reducing" himself.

He ended our conversation with "I'm still going through it. I haven't gotten to the end of this divorce, so it's crazy. . . . I don't know. . . . [*Again, he stops and finds it hard to speak.*] I probably won't ever get over this, . . . just because I put so much into it. I probably put more into this than I put into the first relationship. Breaking my vow even put me to a point where I feel less spiritual." He saw his divorce as a failure to keep a deep promise to God and to himself, and wanted to feel the spiritual energy he remembered having had as a younger man.

Lenny's narrative is fresh, and his resolution of divorce experience not yet complete; thus there is a heightened sense of liminality represented when he talks about the "circular nature," or "crazy" place he occupied. Still, he understood the task at hand and described his emerging role as a self in pursuit of a position that would allow him to be successful in future relationships: "I say to myself, I would never get married again. I know that's kind of strong but I'm not at a healthy place to even think about it." To pursue this healthy place, he went to church services when his work schedule allowed, and listened to contemporary gospel and jazz music at home and in the car to help tame his emotions, longing for the emotional connection to God he remembered having as a young man, to help him deal with his "crazy," "circular" feelings.

May

May's narrative of religion and resolution of family and religious position was more complete. She was a fifty-four-year-old white evangelical Christian and, like Lenny's, her divorce narrative had a focus on loss of children. Early in my research, I spent six weeks conducting field studies in May's church, a conservative nondenominational evangelical New England congregation. I attended services and women's groups, interviewed people who had been divorced, the church staff, and clergy who ran support groups and counseled people who were ending marriages. I met with May one afternoon at the church, where she worked part-time; she proudly noted her position as the Sunday morning "greeter"—a job in which she strove to "make divorced people feel welcome as they enter the sanctuary." In the time since May's divorce, six years before our interview, she had fully changed her status and position in the church, from that of wife in a founding congregation couple whose marriage was failing, to a woman restored through exiting an abusive marriage.

May was married when she was twenty-one. After twenty-seven years of marriage she packed her bags and left. Her story was of searching, for years, for a way to stop an abusive relationship, and of looking for a "biblical" way to end that would not damage her contract with the church community and her promise to God. May and her husband's front-stage performance was of happily married founding members of the church; backstage, she described his abusive actions as furtive. She was a featured vocal soloist at church, and he would often disgrace her after she received praise from congregants. For example, one Sunday morning he whispered in her ear, as she stepped down from singing a solo, "You looked like a slut up there." Her story was of being psychologically abused and of growing fears of physical abuse: at one point toward the end of their marriage, her husband took away her car keys and gathered all his rifles and shotguns and put them under their bed.

May did eventually, after much prayer and finally talking about the abuse with others at the church, secure a restraining order and got him out of the house, but the children went with him. Their absence brought a deep emptiness. She described in detail the moment when she seriously considered suicide. When she finished telling me about how she planned to end her life, she said: "I think that, when you come to the end of yourself, when you get to the place where you are going to take your own life—I don't think there is any worse place." She turned to private prayer as sacred strategy for finding strength, and, in true evangelical Christian fashion, she believed the transformative grace of God felt through prayer helped heal her "brokenness" and allowed her to manage dangerous and out-of-control emotions.

May's story of managing feelings post-divorce was centered on the absence of her children in her daily life. She framed the cost of leaving: "So, in the divorce, I gave up all four kids." Her ex-husband's lawyer made a case through the courts that her ex-spouse should have full custody. A guardian ad litem (lawyer advocate for the children) was assigned to the case, but May said the advocate could accomplish little, as her ex-husband worked to "alienate" the children from her: "He had been working the kids against me. He turned them totally, totally against me." May's accusations of spousal abuse further fed her children's resentment: "so, with his alienating combined with the restraining order I got against him, the kids were all angry at me, and his brother was a psychologist and his brother really worked the kids, told them what to say to live with him." Her children were in their teenage years, so the court had to take their wishes into consideration and May was left to negotiate motherhood from a distance. Her religious community and ministry role in the church became even more central in her life as she lost parental status. Reaching out to others in church and working with the singles ministry became a religious practice that helped manage the social shame of a mother not allowed to care for her children. Freed from the bondage of an abusive marriage, she understood her daily religious practices as making her into a stronger "servant of God," better able to manage the pain and difficult relationships with her children.

As we talked, six years after her divorce, she emphasized the extreme nature of loss of children, and her reconciliation with some: "My youngest daughter came back first. . . . It didn't take long for him to start treating her the way he had treated me." Her younger daughter then "really worked on" her second oldest daughter to have a relationship with their mother; she succeeded, but only after four years of coercing this older girl to call her mother. The oldest daughter got married but did not invite May to the wedding. Regarding her relationship with her son, May said, "I used to call my son once or twice a week. I did that for about six months [after the divorce], but he was treating me like his father did." May did not see him for six years. She recalled a dream that haunted her for weeks: "I dreamt that my son had died and my husband wouldn't tell me . . . everybody else kept saying, 'He's dead, he's dead,' and every time I called my ex-husband he would say 'No,' and he wouldn't tell me where the wake was, and I couldn't even get to him in death." May did not see her son until two months before our interview, at her second daughter's wedding: "He was icy, but I went up and told him it was great to see him, and said you are tall, you are handsome. I told him I loved him and I was glad he was there, and he said he was glad I was there. . . . It had been six years. [*May and I are crying*]. The last time I saw him he was a boy, and I just needed to absorb the presence of him."

Attending school functions, taking children to doctors' appointments, and being home for children after school are examples of "doing motherhood" in our culture (Garey 1999). May could not do the central work of mothering if her children would not see her. As she narrates her story, she emphasizes the deliberate efforts she made to put herself back in her children's lives, the importance of not letting her son treat her badly, and the significance of religious practices of prayer, attending services, and caring for others in need. These actions together represented a moral performance of managing motherhood in the wake of divorce.

I would be remiss not to mention at this point that my subjective experience of divorce and grief involves loss of children. Respondents' stories involving similar loss were difficult for me to listen to, yet they were also the most understandable and so I sometimes shared my loss with respondents at the end of interviews. An excerpt follows, from my interview with May, one year before I saw my sixteen-year-old son for the first time in almost eight years:

MAY: How old was your son when you saw him last?

KAY: He was nine.

MAY: I dream that I see my son somewhere, and I even go up and talk to him, but I can't ever see his face; and then I have nightmares where he is hurt and I can't get to him.

KAY: I have that one too.

MAY: I have that one a lot.

KAY: I have one where I touch him, and he is a boy, and he kisses me.

MAY: I have even held him as a baby.

KAY: I haven't gone back that far.

May and I were very different—I had not been in an abusive relationship, I was not an evangelical Christian, and at that point I was not active in a synagogue—yet our experiences of social shame related to mothering were similar. We both felt the unsettled position that came from being a divorced mother not able to be present in our sons' lives. We both had stories that we told others about the efforts we made to try and see our children, and we both understood that this interview conversation was a rare social interaction where we could talk about the depth of our emotions without social shame.

May had lost time with her children and felt the loss in a deeply physical and emotional manner. Her feelings were related to a radical fracture in a social bond of mothering, a change in status and identity. Her story was also of a woman who found the courage to end an abusive relationship through appeal to religious tools, and of a person redefining herself post-divorce through her outreach ministries at the church. She proudly noted that when, on Sunday mornings, she would greet people at the sanctuary door, she could "spot from a distance" guests who were "suffering" from endings, and that she made it her job to let them and all singles feel welcomed and loved. Her story was of religious beliefs and practices that had enabled her to care for others, to build a stronger self, and to be a patient mother from afar.

Divorce generated serious questions, for most of my respondents, about how they were to love and care for their children and/or reshape family relationships. May ultimately encouraged her children to sustain a relationship with their father, the man who had abused her and who kept them apart for many years. Other respondents struggled to cultivate relationships with former in-laws and stepchildren. There was a strong sense in my respondents' stories that they had important choices to make about how they would detach from or affirm kin status, and that controlling and using their emotions in appropriate ways was crucial to this task. With divorce, they had to work harder on their feelings, to find the strength to negotiate new family structures and relationships.

Loss of time with children is central in these respondents' stories, but also present are threats to religious status and related social shame. Lenny felt that he had let down God and himself, and several of the Catholics I interviewed talked about staying away from the Eucharist because they imagined they were no longer "good Catholics." May stayed in what she described as an abusive relationship for similar reasons, feeling that she would disappoint God, that "God hates divorce." Religious status in church communities was threatened in other ways as well. Some women respondents talked about how they felt unwelcome at couples' gatherings in congregations and hated feeling that they were now seen as sexually suspect—single divorced women on the prowl. May's preceding core involvement in the church community with her husband led to a type of religious social shame that I saw manifest in several cases: people feeling that they were letting down their congregation by ending a marriage that was highly valued by the community.

Sandy

Sandy was a white, fifty-year-old lesbian and artist who had been an active member for ten years in her small (150-member) New England urban Unitarian Universalist (UU) congregation. The ending of her relationship was deeply shaped by the social bonds that she and her partner had made as a couple who were active in congregational leadership and small group ministry. Her story was also tied to loss of her parental role and its associated status in the congregation. She and her partner had been thought of in this congregation, whose members worked to promote same-sex marriage rights, as a model lesbian family. Familiar religious ritual and beliefs helped her manage intense emotions after her partner left, and aided in her affirmation of new status as a single in the congregation.

Sandy contacted me a few months after I finished what I thought was my last interview at her church. My number had been on her desk for months: "When I first saw the notice in the church paper, I thought, I don't want to talk about this. As soon as I noticed that, I knew that I should talk about it because it's three quarters of a year later and I still have that immediate 'arggg!' reaction." Sandy and Teva had been part of what Sandy described as a group of eight couples, a "really tight bunch of lesbians." They had met at church, "happy to find a religious community that was also gay and particularly lesbian." In Sandy's words, "We made our own kind of neighborhood within the church." Teva had also been involved in church leadership and was on the board. When Teva left, Sandy said it was "like she just, like, dumped the church. . . . People would ask me how she was or what was going on. I had just been thrown out and was really mad, was really hurt, didn't want to be the voice of her." Sandy was embarrassed that Teva had joined her congregation, became involved in church leadership, formed deep friendships, and then abruptly left everything. It hurt her to sit in the sanctuary where she remembered sitting with Teva and their daughter Rachel. And so she decided to take some time away: "I wasn't at church all that much, but that isn't so unusual for Unitarians anyway, when there is a change. . . . I wasn't cut off from people entirely, but it made me sad to be there and to sit where we sat and to have a service where the kids are involved . . . and not having Rachel. I remember going for one service and having to leave. I had to go out and cry in the car."

Teva and her previous partner had a daughter, Rachel, and, even in the few years they were together, Sandy had come to think of herself as a parent, to love and care deeply for the girl. Similar to Lenny's situation, when Teva left Sandy, she took access to Rachel with her. Sandy's visitation rights were like those of stepparents who face family court systems where biological family ties largely determine custody and visitation. I asked if she had seen Rachel, and she said: "It's kind of hard; she has a busy social life. She's in third grade but she's with the one mom some weekends and the other mom the other weekends and goes to camp so that's been not so great." She had managed to see Rachel for her birthday.

When the relationship first ended, Sandy stopped attending services regularly for a few months. By staying away, she avoided painful questions and the threat of social shame. Members asked her where Teva was, why she had not spoken to anyone, and how Rachel was and whether Sandy had been able to see her.

Sandy also worried about disappointing people at her church who supported LGBT family and marriage rights. "There were a couple of people that I wanted to tell personally and I waited until after church and just met them in the aisle and just told them. . . . It was hard, it was really hard . . . they were really saddened." She recalled how people used to say to her: "How could people not support gay and lesbian couples? Look at your family. Look at the three of you together and look at how happy and in love you are." Sandy felt they had become the congregation's "poster girls, and there was another level of . . . hoping these kinds of families would be different or something. . . . It was hard." When Sandy's and Teva's relationship ended, Sandy's status in the church as part of this ideal lesbian family ended.

Sandy described feeling lost when Teva broke off with her: "I was so drifty and lost when she asked me to leave." Sandy was an artist and so suffered loss not only of a home, but of her studio as well: "I had my studio in the house so I kind of lost everything at once." Her studio represented a large part of her identity as an artist, and she wondered how she would find and afford another space large enough to accommodate her work. Not wanting to be alone and undergoing major shifts in relationship, occupation, parenting, and congregational status, she stayed with another church member for two months, even though she could afford to rent her own apartment: "I was going through stages that I had no clue about. I was about to turn fifty and was going to be single, and I had just lost this whole thing, and I just felt like I had no idea what was next." Living with a close friend from the congregation gave her some sense of social connectedness and consistency, and gave her the space to find renewed direction.

Services reminded Sandy of deep loss, but, even when away from the congregation, she said she carried the power of its collective energy with her and used its power to heal herself. In particular, she stressed the healing power of "Spirit of Life," a song from the Sunday morning service: "I tried for a while in the morning and at night, the first thing I'd do, is sing that, at least say the words." She sang: "Spirit of life, come unto me. Move in my heart all the stirrings of compassion. Roll in the wind. Rise in the sea. Move in the hand, giving life the shape of justice. Roots hold me close. Wings set me free. Spirit of life, come to me, come to me." Singing this song reminded her that she was connected to what she called a larger "web of being" and "life spirit," a religious tool that helped her in coping with negative emotions. She presented the power of this congregational bond, born through song, helping her ease feelings of rejection, anger, and the pain of losing a child. It also helped with the physical effects of hand surgery in the months after Teva left: "I work with my hands as an artist, so it hits a real place. . . . I'd try to get the whole way through [Spirit of Life] without having my thoughts interrupted. Use it as a meditation, . . . like calming my brain down . . . and to kind of be present." The interconnected web of life assured her that she was "not alone in whatever is going on. Other people have had it happen, too. . . . It's just a big, comforting kind of feeling. It helps me think that what I do with myself is going to affect other people, so, you know, how long do I want to be angry with someone? It won't help and it's hurting me to be angry." She talked about this song as helping her slowly return to services, let go of anger, and move forward.

When Sandy finally returned to services, she lit a candle during the "joys and sorrows" part of the Sunday service, saying a few general words to the congregation that affirmed a belief in change as positive: "I said something about how big changes in your life leave room for other things to happen. . . . That's what change leaves you with, new opportunities." Lighting this candle, together with her use of "*Spirit of Life*" and meditation on the UU principle of a web of being, were essential beliefs and practices in her story of reestablishing status in the congregation as a single member.

Lenny, May, and Sandy all had access to familiar religious beliefs and practices that emerged as important in their strategies for moving forward. Given that I was looking for innovation in divorce practices, I interviewed a number of individuals who were also active in divorce ministries (see Appendix on Methods for details in each case).

Respondents active in small groups for the divorced and divorce ministries told stories of becoming stronger post-divorce that were profoundly shaped by these associations. Sue was a white Catholic woman in her early sixties who had one adult son and was divorced for ten years. Like May's, her narrative had a strong sense of completion and moral resolution, and was deeply influenced by her involvement with Catholic Divorce Ministries (CDM).

Sue

Sue and her husband had been high school sweethearts and dated as teenagers, believing in true love that was supposed to last a lifetime. As a Catholic, she also understood her marriage as a sacrament, a bond sanctified by church and by God, meant to produce children and last forever. When she decided to end the marriage, she felt her position as a good Catholic at risk. She related her decision to leave her husband as one that took place over time, describing him as growing more and more selfish and irresponsible over their twenty-five years of marriage: "He wasn't happy about the divorce. But there were no affairs. I decided that I had had enough. I was married to a man-child who loved credit cards, and I just couldn't take it any longer." She wanted to spend more time volunteering and working to help others in the community, and described her husband as getting in the way of these religious efforts, as a man who needed a woman to be "joined to his hip." She described her marriage as inflicting a deep-rooted sense of loss of self over time, and as keeping her from the life God wanted her to live. Her understanding of the marriage as inhibiting her religious purpose, and her narrative of working hard on the marriage through secular counseling, mitigated threats of Catholic shame and mirrored central ideas at work in Catholic Divorce Ministries (CDM).

Interviews with priests, Catholic Charity organizations, and divorced Catholics like Sue early in my research indicated that the North American Conference of Separated and Divorced Catholics (NACSD) was a significant force in U.S. Roman Catholicism, and a provider of religious tools for those who encountered the ministry. The organization, as of 2007 renamed Catholic Divorce Ministries (CDM) (http://www.nacsdc.org/), was founded in 1974 by Paulist priest James Young and by Sister Paula Ripple Comin. Young writes in 1979 that the CDM had grown to be a "vital, growing ministry by and to separated, divorced, and remarried Catholics," with "over 500 support groups, official diocesan ministries, and a national organization" (3). In the early years, James Young inspired divorced Catholics with assurance of their religious status: "The threads of divorce experience are not golden; its threads often tell of human frailty, poor judgment, self-inflicted injury. But when these poor, human dramas are given to the Lord, he transforms them into gold" (1983 National CDM conference speech). Change as Christian Identity and Divorced Catholics as the Church were core strategies in CDM. The idea that change was an essential characteristic of Christian Catholic identity emboldened those divorced Catholics, like Sue, who had participated in CDM.

CDM draws from multiple religious tools in attempting to make divorce a meaningful Catholic experience for participants, but particularly persuasive in defending divorce as sacred process and position was the early founders' use of Catholic liberation theology: God as a God of the oppressed, who endeavors to free people from the pain and suffering of social injustices.[7] Divorced Catholics as suffering and as thus in a special condition supplied a key theological justification for removing social shame and bringing about sacred individual change. CDM's discourse provided Sue, then, with religious legitimation for her journey from suffering in marriage to finding herself through serving others in ministry. Young (1984, 102) writes: "Our faith tells us that for some unknown reason God invites some to walk more closely, to know more pain, to be put more clearly to the test. . . . Could it be in our time that many of our divorced brothers and sisters are invited to mirror the suffering and death of Christ in their own lives, and to come to new life afterward, as a sign that God is present to our suffering?" During a 1985 conference, he noted that the divorced know best the "Paschal mystery," what it is like "to pass from death to life."[8] They "are the people who understand immediately what the mystery of Christ is all about because they have lived, they have suffered, they have known death, they have also known resurrection." CDM gave Sue and other Catholics tools to tell stories of their divorce as a highly sacred process.

CDM authors and speakers also used traditional Catholic pilgrimage as a symbolic tool. Paula Ripple told hundreds gathered at the 1990 National Conference at Notre Dame, "Some make their pilgrimages to sacred shrines and some of us make our pilgrimages to places like Tarrytown for divorce conferences in search of wisdom and life." James Young (1984, 81) writes that the Second Vatican Council[9] described the "Church today as a pilgrim people on a journey to the Kingdom of God. . . . We are drawn through time and history over unfamiliar terrain to God's home; we are challenged to invite others to join us on this exposed, perilous trip, promising them only the hardship of travel but ultimately a great heavenly feast." Divorced Catholics like Sue are contemporary pilgrims: "A Pilgrim people on a journey seems to be a much more helpful way of describing us as a Christian people in today's world. We know where we're going, but we're not always sure these days how we are going to get there. . . . We seem to need new resources of reconciliation and maturity if we are to manage the stresses of journey and persevere" (81–82). Embracing the hard work of change through difficult emotions *becomes* Christian identity work: "For the believer then there are no real endings, just changes. . . . Being able to change means that one has grasped this basic truth" (42). Young reminds readers that "the end of a marriage can be the prelude to a new human existence and a new Christian identity" (42–43).

CDM, while legitimating divorce as a sacred process, also balanced marriage as a sacrament and so not to be ended without much consideration and grounds; loss of self, abuse, and infidelity emerged as legitimate reasons. Alongside valuing marriage as sacred, CDM stressed the welfare of children through the divorce processes. Highly significant in Sue's narrative of Christian identity work was her serious contemplation of leaving and making sure to first care for her son's emotional life. She described, that is, wanting to leave the marriage at an earlier point but staying because of her son: "I realized I couldn't do it to my son at eight years old. He needed his father, whatever kind of a father he was, . . . so I stayed. Shoved it down a little bit more and kept on going as if nothing happened. And that was okay, because today he will tell you that he had a wonderful childhood. Absolutely wonderful and he is very close to his father."

She presented part of her journey as caring for her ailing parents for several years, as well, and feeling lost when left alone with her husband: "My mother and my father were both ill, chronically, when my son was in his teenage years. So I had my mother dying, my son turning thirteen and going into high school, and my father suffering. . . . When my son graduated from high school, and after the death of my parents, I lost my identity. I was not a daughter, I was not a mommy. I was like, who the hell am I? And I turned and looked at my husband and I said, 'Who are you?'" Sue described feeling especially alone in this liminal space: "It wasn't recognized, no one recognized. I'm really only now recognizing that I was actually having a breakdown and there was no one there to help me." Even as she was making the decision to leave, most of her family rejected her feelings' seriousness, attributing them to "menopausal hormones" and continuing to plan a twenty-fourth wedding anniversary party as she packed her bags.

While still living in, and invested in, the marriage, Sue experienced a range of emotions as she actively searched for a space that would validate her feelings and provide some direction and purpose in life. Diane Vaughan (1986, 20) suggests that some people reach a point where they "no longer" find a "relationship compatible with sense of self," and so "turn to alternatives that supply the self-validation they seek." Visiting the chapel in the hospital where she worked, combined with other distinctly Catholic sacred practices like devotion to saints who intervened in her daily life, helped her to leave her husband and find strategies for creating a stronger self with renewed Catholic and spiritual status. A major chapter in Sue's story was discovering that she could support herself financially, seeking out people who would listen to her and validate her concerns.

In her story, CDM became a major source for religious tools to help manage feelings of guilt related to her son's resentment, and to find her religious purpose in ultimately helping others confront loss of marriage, family, and other forms of grief and loss. Sue's son was angry when she left, which made her feel guilty, depressed, and fearful about being on her own. She made clear: "I knew right away I needed a support group. Being Catholic, I was going to go to a Catholic support group." But the first one did not live up to her expectations; it was more of what she described as a "social group." Sue needed a "serious" space to "work" on her emotions, so she became involved instead in a DivorceCare group at a local Presbyterian church, a support group she described as "absolutely awesome." "You would go through that week and, boy, when that night started to come you knew you had to go back for support because you were going crazy with what you were going through." In the Presbyterian DivorceCare group she received mailings from other singles groups and conferences held in the area, which is how she came to attend a CDM conference: "I went because it was the Catholic group and, while I was with the Presbyterian group and they were very fine, they were also being more Presbyterian. I was ready to move to the next stage and I went to the Catholic group and I've been with them ever since." In fact, Sue became an active volunteer with CDM, working registration for the conferences, leading support groups, and coordinating retreats.

The major source of marital decline in Sue's story was her husband's continuous draining of her emotional energy, a dynamic that kept her from being her "true self"— which to her meant the person God wanted her to be. Although the CDM group leaders I interviewed used varying practices and resources, a dominant theme in the materials I analyzed was that a person was to reject victim status, accept oneself as a "person of value," and take responsibility for making "healthy" decisions. CDM small groups like the ones Sue and several of my Catholic respondents attended were places where people were expected to confront and work on destructive feelings, which in their stories helped them discover true self and manage family relationships post-divorce. Sue faced the challenge of an adult son who was at first angry with her for leaving his father and then distant. CDM seminars and support groups creatively combined resources from mental health professionals with religious beliefs to teach participants how to best take care of children's feelings through divorce. One workshop guide, "Divorce Etiquette for Parents," gave general and specific guidelines that began with "Do unto others as you would have them do unto you." Participants were reminded that they were divorcing the "other parent, not the children," and to recognize that divorce "doesn't terminate grandparent-hood, or cousin-ship. . . . severing the legal bond between parents does not dissolve the genetic bond, or the relationships established over one's childhood." Developing the emotional ability to help children maintain respectful kin ties with ex-in-laws and other relatives was cast as God's will, as was allowing children to "love the other parent and step-parent." Learn to "be honest about the other parent's problems, but encourage the parent-child relationship." In addition, divorcing parents should "provide opportunities for children to express their anger and grief, and help them cope with feelings appropriately."

Sue's narrative was one of turning divorce into a gift for herself and others—a story of sealing religious bonds and caring for her adult son's relationship with both of his parents. She described complete fulfillment in having developed her position as a CDM volunteer and a bereavement counselor in the wider community. In this presentation of self, she exemplifies the words of CDM's founder, James Young, "Divorce, as a gift, is not something to be hoarded and kept under a bushel measure. If it's just my personal growth, my special experience, it will remain brittle and frail" (1984, 88). One 1990s CDM regional newsletter talked about the kind of reward that, Sue understood, came from leading small groups: "Long after facilitating days are over, their hearts will still feel those special accolades that only support group facilitators can feel, especially that ultimate accolade—the opportunity in one's lifetime to imitate, in our human way, Christ's lifetime practice of loving thy neighbor as thyself. This 'gold medal' is not hung around one's neck; God takes this one and hangs it around our soul." In Sue's story, such a gold medal around the soul brought new identity and removed all remnants of social shame.

RELIGIOUS THERAPEUTIC SEEKERS

Despite the differences in my respondents' positions and crafting of divorce narratives, they all spoke of seeking therapeutic strategies through religious means. May and Sue had been divorced for many years and so told more complete narratives of divorce as rebirth of self and reconciliation with family. Lenny has not yet escaped his "crazy" emotional position, but he presents his exit from the marriage as fueled by a desire to help self and family members. He longs to reignite his "spiritual" self and connection to God so that he can claim a healthy life. Resurrecting authentic Catholic self was evident in Sue's story: her husband had slowly, over the years, kept her from being the person she thought God wanted her to be, but through a slow and painful journey out of the marriage, she emerged a more ethical person.

Like Sue, some respondents had spent years contemplating divorce. Others told stories of shock and deception as their husbands or wives abruptly broke off all affection and commitment. Respondents were not always clear about who initiated the split. Some never detached. My respondents came from varied social locations and pulled from different religious beliefs and practices, but their understandings of how they should confront contemporary liminal position were remarkably similar. Even respondents like Lenny who described being stuck in a liminal state, or the few I interviewed who described elation on ending marriages, understood that they should tell stories of advancing or journeying, that they should be constantly changing, moving forward, working on their emotions and growing stronger for self and family. In their stories of divorce they were seeking resources to become better parents, potential partners, and emotionally healthy family members, and to fortify religious identity.

Consider the informal social sanctions that would result if their stories of ending were about rejecting these beliefs. What would happen if they talked about their divorce as being "the end of me," or lamented "I'm broken for life"? Last summer I was with my two girls in a souvenir shop in front of a display of kitchen magnets. I stared at one for several minutes while they riffled the tee shirt racks; it read, "What does not kill us makes us stronger." More recently, their phones play Kelly Clarkson's popular song "What doesn't kill you makes you stronger." This well-known quote, attributed to nineteenth-century German philosopher Friedrich Nietzsche,[10] is deeply embedded in our cultural discourse, representing a time-honored belief in many cultures and grounded in symbolic religious worlds, all of which endows the pursuit of the idea with a particular kind of emotional energy.[11] When sociologists employ the sociological imagination, they do not deny that such adages hold some truth, nor do they assume that all individuals encounter them with equal force; rather, they strive to make their institutional life, their everyday power and social meaning, visible. The therapeutic assumptions embedded in the command that what does not kill us makes us stronger, profoundly shaped my respondents' narratives of the emotional labor of divorce.

To make sense of their attempts to construct divorce experience as sacred, we must first unpack this dominant cultural strategy positioned deep within our social structure, divorce work, and understand how religious manifestations of sacred divorce had the power to fortify and complement therapeutic approaches to ending life partnerships.

2 ✳ DIVORCE WORK AS CULTURAL STRATEGY

Grief work must be done with great thoroughness or there will remain the danger of constantly living in the presence of the open casket of a dead marriage.

—Reva Wiseman, "Crisis Theory and the Process of Divorce," 1975

Formal creators, the *religious architects* of the sacred divorce strategies I explored, are the lay leaders, pastoral counselors, and clergy who produced divorce programs, small groups, and published books or online resources. As they constructed sacred approaches, they employed and enriched a dominant cultural strategy, *divorce work*. Divorce work draws from larger therapeutic cultural scripts[1] that communicate that emotions must be confronted, expressed, controlled, and explored in an appropriate manner and context so that potentially dangerous feelings can be transformed into self-growth and used to foster what these scripts would term healthy family relationships. These emotion-work rules and guidelines hold great social power and are built from therapeutic beliefs and practices of *grief work* and *marriage work*. Religious architects assembled persuasive tools, pulling from religious symbols, theology, scripture, ritual, and story, fashioning a collection of familiar emotional routines and practices that my respondents understood and felt in profound ways.[2] The core beliefs and practices they used from their traditions merged effortlessly with therapeutic tenets of grief and marriage work, endowing this emotional labor with religious energy and purpose.

44

"GRUELING *WORK*"

Laurie was a white Catholic woman who lived in a wealthy California town and attended a parish that served thousands of families and ran a number of small-group community programs. She was married for almost eighteen years before her ex-husband, four years before our interview, announced that he was in love with another woman and then walked out the door. She described his withdrawal from the marriage as bringing an acute type of gendered social shame: "I was filled with shame. I was the woman who was rejected, left behind without even a second glance. . . . My shame caused me to hide out for months. . . . I was devastated, taken to my knees." She talked about feeling, during those first months, as if she had a "Scarlet S" on her chest; she worried that their teenage child would suffer and was concerned about future ties with her adult stepchildren that she loved and had cared for over the years. She felt anger toward her husband and his girlfriend. She found a way to address these feelings and relationships in a divorce group that her parish priest founded.

The small group started by this priest operated first and foremost under an ethic that the work of divorce was painful and hard emotional and spiritual labor. Laurie explained: "We don't call it a support group on purpose. . . . What we are not about is coddling each other to say, oh, I get this. We are very focused on it as hard work . . . we are there to encourage each other to work on your pain. So we focus on the work. It's a workshop. It is work. It is hard. It is painful. It is leaning into your pain. Yes, it's a supportive environment, and of course you go in for support, but it is about work."

She described the power of seeing the group space for the first time, a room where tissue boxes and a circle of chairs signaled the expectation that feelings would surface: "I was an emotional case, and I remember walking into the room for the first meeting, and the chairs were sitting in a circle, and they had prayers printed and sitting on the chairs, and I just looked at the space, and I think, the first eight weeks, every time I just stepped into the room I cried. There were tissues between every chair. It was always very painful, but I always knew I had to be there."

After she progressed through the workshops, Laurie, like others who came back to tell their story to people in early stages of separation, became a witness to recovery and, as lay ministry leaders, they helped to build an emotive space in a familiar religious room through the creative retelling of their own stories. They became "team leaders" who routinely read their carefully crafted recollections to conjure feelings. She explained: "For each group, there is a topic. . . . We start with denial. We do family of origin. We do trust, fear, acceptance, forgiveness, loneliness and rejection, anger, all those kinds of things." Then the "team leader will do some opening or Father will do some opening about the topic, and one of the team leaders has written their stories that are typically twenty to thirty minutes long on that topic, and they are very gut wrenching." Laurie gave me several she had composed as part of her own "journey" of healing: "It is gut-wrenching to write them. . . . Everyone is very well-prepared; they will have gotten together and heard each others' stories and critiqued them. This is Father's thing, they need to be oozing with pain because the purpose of it is to evoke that in someone else; it is to have them resonate so that we are surfacing people's stuff so that they can deal with it." The following is an excerpt of her story on anger (caps and format for emphasis are hers):

> I am just like you. Three years ago . . . I was devastated and in pain like I had never known before. . . . I think I cried my way through my first 10-week work-shop. I now know that my tears were my soul's way of letting me know that I was getting ready to tap into the truth.
>
> . . . This journey some of you are just beginning and others of you are con-tinuing is about the telling of YOUR truth. . . .
>
> Father [*priest's name*] often speaks to us about this work being about find-ing the spring after the harsh winter of our Divorce. . . .
>
> So the first thing I will share for you that belongs in the WHAT I KNOW TO BE TRUE category:
>
>> It's hard, painful, grueling WORK
>> It takes as long as it takes
>> There is no hurrying to get through it or ways to get around it. If what you want is to live your SPRING and glorify God by being FULLY ALIVE.
>> You must be willing to LEAN INTO your pain. Face it head on, or as Father [*priest's name*] so graphically says, 'We have to VOMIT it up.'
>
> The next thing I want to say about truth is that it is an awakening.
>
>> It's about being gentle with yourself and letting the truth behind your pain and your wounds expose themselves
>> It requires an acceptance of your emotions, even when they show them-selves to be ugly and "un-Christian like."

Laurie then recounts a more detailed history of her marriage and how she worked to uncover "mistakes." A "milestone" in her "healing journey" came when she took off "blinders" to see that it was not the affair that had broken her marriage, but that "it had been hemorrhaging for years." She was then able to see the "truth" about her part in the "death" of the marriage.

Laurie's narrative, which I have interpreted from our interview and the written documents she gave me, stunningly demonstrates the divorce work script. It is a story of journey and discovery of self that puts high value on expressing and embracing emotions, accepting fault, and carefully assessing the marriage. Even though she had "graduated" from the divorce group the year before our interview, she understood that her "journey" was not over. The group had given her a "safe place" to do her "grieving and step back into life as a single person." Serious divorce work had also repaired her position in the church; she now had status as a lay leader in spiritual ministries. In addition, she had made a commitment to a new professional career that demonstrated her new relationship skills, expertise, and belief in life partnership: "I am a family and relationship coach now. I use my own experience. I hope people can find the way inside their marriage instead of having to discover that piece of them outside of their marriage to do that." Soon after our meeting, she was headed to the East Coast for an extended visit with her adult stepchildren, a trip that signified success in affirming the significance of her family position in their lives.

Sacred Grief Work

The strategies in Laurie's parish group reflect dominant approaches found in popular psychology self-help books and programs that suggest divorce demands grief work.[3] For example, journalist Abigail Trafford's (1992 [1982], 65) popular book, *Crazy Time*, describes divorced persons as in the middle of a painful transition "equivalent to the mourning period after death and catastrophe." Therapeutic counselor Mel Krantzler (1974, 1) writes in his book *The Creative Divorce*, "The death of a relationship is the first stage in a process in which the death is recognized, and the relationship is mourned and then laid to rest to make way for self-renewal." In popular psychology and self-help books the grief work of divorce can be done well or badly, but most important, as seen in Laurie's group, it is hard work that must be completed; there are, in this view, no shortcuts.

Divorce grief work is demanding and brings danger to those who do not put in enough effort. Therapeutic professionals Bruce Fischer and Robert Alberti (2008 [1981], 5–6) warn of hazards in their book, *Rebuilding When Your Relationship Ends*: "Some people don't have the strength and stamina to make it to the top . . . they miss the magnificent view of life that comes from climbing the mountain. Some withdraw into the shelter of a cave, . . . another group . . . never reaches the top. And sadly, there are a few who choose self-destruction, jumping off the first cliff that looms along the trail." In *Crazy Time*, Abigail Trafford writes: "Most people go a little crazy when their marriage cracks open. . . . You are rarely prepared for the practical or emotional turmoil that lies ahead. You swing between euphoria, violent rage, and depression" (1992, 2). Religious architects echo these concerns, adding the force of scripture and divine intent. The founder of CDM, James Young, in his 1984 book, *Divorcing, Believing, and Belonging,* uses the biblical story of Jacob and Esau to illustrate: "How often is the divorcing person tempted to give in—to wallow in self-pity, to escape into martinis or tranquilizers, or just drop out. . . . God who wrestles with us invites us to hang onto the uncertainty of the recovery process—to hold onto one's values and one's faith amid the stress and strain, and to be confident one is gaining strength" (93–97). People either take such anger and turn it into an "engine which drives them to put together a new life situation for themselves, get in better physical shape, go back to school, make new friends, take a more challenging job," or they bring it back into themselves: "Such anger turned on oneself can be like a corrosive acid eating away at the potential of recovery, blinding one to one's own gifts, immobilizing one's energies and gifts" (29).

The emphasis in Laurie's group and in secular grief—work texts regarding the difficulty of the emotional labor that must be completed reflects historical constructions of the divorced as somehow damaged and in need of professional help. Kristin Celello (2009, 27) notes early twentieth-century marriage and divorce experts who introduced the idea that the divorced were "psychologically damaged." For example, in Willard W. Waller's (1930) study *The Old Love and the New: Divorce and Readjustment,* "the divorced needed the public's empathy because they were profoundly unhappy individuals who rarely had the wherewithal to cope successfully with the end of their marriages" (Celello 2009, 27). Waller made a strong argument that the divorced lived in a serious chaotic state and were "psychologically fragile and in need of mental 'reorganization.'" To get through this chaos "required a great deal of hard work and self-knowledge; the road to being 'saved'—psychologically, not religiously—was arduous indeed" (27).

Leeat Granek (2010, 46) demonstrates how grief itself evolved in psychology as a "pathology to be privatized, specialized, and treated by mental health professionals," noting Freud's (1917) prominent essay on mourning and melancholia: "Freud (1917/1963) proposed that the mourner had the task of detaching their libido/emotional energy from the deceased and sublimating it into other areas of their lives" (2010, 51). Over the years, others have built on Freud's model, suggesting that people who fail to do grief work properly may "end up with a psychiatric illness resulting from pathological grieving" (51). Granek calls attention to Helene Deutsch's introduction of the idea that "unmanifested or repressed grief, will resurface in other ways if not brought into consciousness and treated." In Deutsch's words (1937, 21), "the process of mourning as a reaction to the real loss of a loved person *must be carried to completion*" (Granek 2010, 54). Her work gave birth to the idea that "all grieving people are potentially ill and need to be monitored for the process of their 'grief work.'" The strong individualism is noteworthy in this early theorizing: "'grief work' must be done or else it will resurface somewhere," which "puts the onus of responsibility on the grieving person to self-monitor or risk becoming ill or psychologically unbalanced" (54).

Religious divorce scripts illustrate, and add power to, therapeutic notions of individual responsibility for grief work. Laurie's parish priest and Sue's CDM groups described the hard emotional work of divorce as a Christian journey and as becoming the person God intended one to be. Working through loss and grief prompted familiar religious ideas of change as Christian identity, and of pilgrimage as sacred path, for these and other Catholic respondents. Unitarian Universalist architects, grounded in a rational humanism and, more recently, spirituality and seeker religious practices that adhere to "religious piety as a *journey* and a *process*,"[4] stressed the divorced as creative rational selves, an approach that fused effortlessly with grief work's expectations of individual effort. Black church authors drew from core understandings of liberation theology and womanist theology, where God becomes a constant source of strength and healing for the marginalized and oppressed that ask for help.[5] In the Jewish resources, I found architects combined themes of sacred passage and individual journey in the Jewish calendar cycle with the idea that grief work involves deliberate emotional labor. In the evangelical Protestant case, focuses on brokenness (of mind, body, or relationship), the transformative grace of God, and free-will individualism were religious tools that reflected and further charged expectations of grief work.

Blending spiritual with medical psychological approaches to grief can be found in popular strategies, as well, and my respondents sometimes turned to these sources as they engaged in sacred constructions. In *Crazy Time,* Trafford draws from psychologists and theologians, and throughout her text introduces various phases, stages, and steps of divorce, arguing that "the decision to separate is like Martin Luther nailing his theses to the door. You stand up with your list of past grievances and new expectations. You break with your past. You start on your own emotional reformation" (1992, 58). Swiss-born psychiatrist Elizabeth Kübler-Ross, a public figure in the death awareness movement and author of the widely read *On Death and Dying* (1969), provided fuel for religious architects.[6] This book introduced the widely known and often quoted stages of the dying process: denial and isolation, anger and resentment, bargaining and attempts to postpone death, depression and feelings of loss, and acceptance of death. In her book with David Kessler (2005), *On Grief and Grieving,* she applies these stages to those left to grieve. Feeling stages are interconnected and take much time, and it is sometimes hard to determine whether a stage has ended (18). Still, Kübler-Ross stresses that one must engage them and uses religious language to argue that the "grace," "miracle," and "gift" of grief waits for those who put in effort (231).

Religious architects drew directly from therapeutic notions of grief work as recovery and as taking place through stages. Rabbi Perry Netter, a member of the Conservative movement of Judaism and author of *Divorce Is a Mitzvah,* writes: "Divorce is a little death—or, more accurately, a series of little deaths. . . . Deciding to end a marriage is like deciding to amputate a limb. You know there is enormous pain in store for you. You know there will be a long period of recovery" (2002, 7). The seriousness of such a death requires process. Netter turns to Kübler-Ross, listing her five stages of grief and noting anger as a functional emotion that can serve a "valuable and necessary purpose" (85). Other Jewish authors stress the emotional labor of letting go and of working through "stages." For example, in *The Outstretched Arm,* published by the National Center for Jewish Healing, a page of text is devoted to divorce emotions and "Stages of Divorce Recovery:" denial, shock, depression, rage, terror, shame, revenge, grief, loneliness, reflection, reassessment, forgiveness, and moving forward.

Grief work can take place with the assistance of family, counselor, or small groups, but ultimately therapeutic professionals understand it as a solo enterprise. Kübler-Ross writes, "Your loss stands alone in its meaning to you, in its painful uniqueness" (2005, 29). Mourning is "internal work," it is "a process, a journey," and "as individual as each of us" (115). Such an emphasis reflects the individualism active in medicine and therapeutic culture: individuals have the power and the strength to change their lives for the better if they engage expert assistance and muster up the will. This "health and wellness" movement places even greater focus on individuals choosing preventive medicine and lifestyle, and small group, self-help, and twelve-step-like movements are omnipresent.[7] This type of individualism has deep Protestant roots but reflects contemporary expectations across religious traditions that individuals will take responsibility for bodily and spiritual health.

Appeals to individual effort resonated well with religious architects. Laurie tells group members their journey is about "the telling of YOUR truth" and that, if they want to live their "SPRING" and "glorify God by being FULLY ALIVE," they must "LEAN INTO" their pain and "face it head on." Co-founder James Young appeals to contemporary Catholics with an emphasis on Christian journey and pilgrimage, "The Lord did not promise us a detailed road map but only a destination and some principles to guide us on our journey." Charting individual roads through injury to new life was a central CDM message: "He makes us fill in the details ourselves and shape our own path. He is with us always, but it is truly our journey, and the getting there is worked out by our own trial and error" (1984, 82). Rabbi Netter (2002, 4–5) stresses divorce as a *mitzvah*, an obligation on the part of those ending a marriage, that contains "all the weight of God's commanding voice." The "central question governing divorce," he argues, is "to seek the holy and the sacred," the "ultimate question of every aspect of personal life: What are my obligations as an individual, as a spouse, as a parent, as a child? What does God expect of me as I struggle with the seemingly infinite decisions that surround divorce? How can I go through this crisis without destroying my soul in the process?"

Expressivity, feeling emotions and then getting them out of the body, is a core tenet of grief work that reflects and enhances core religious tools. Kübler-Ross writes: "Tell a counselor how angry you are. Share it with friends and family. Scream into a pillow. Find ways to get it out without hurting yourself or someone else . . . any type of exercise helps you externalize your anger. Do not bottle up anger inside. Instead, explore it" (2005, 16). In medical therapeutic culture, dangerous feelings, like sins, exist deep inside physical beings and "recovery" takes place when one chooses to get them out to rid oneself of the danger.[8] Emotions can be dangerous, in this view, but are valuable raw material for growth and healing. Such ideas are born from religious worlds. In the evangelical fervor of the Second Great Awakening, which swept through the American landscape (1800–1830), individual expression in revivals through collective group spirit worked to purge sin. Anyone who has been to a high-spirit Pentecostal service can attest to such religious expression of feeling through dancing, speaking in tongues, and verbal releases. The idea of emptying oneself to allow God to fill you up is a theme in Christian theology. Even the quiet air of grave emotion through group prayer, Buddhist meditation, or Quaker silences reflects the activation and expression of feelings. A CDM support group handout stresses that "memories, past trauma, unexpressed emotions, plus old worries and fears still live with us. Left unmended, they can make us physically ill later in life. Repression of emotions like anger, sadness, and joy makes matters worse. Real healing begins when old wounds are addressed and released." Formal architects across traditions advised that people ending sacred life partnerships find religious spaces where they could accomplish this essential task of grief work assisted by divine and/or collective group energies.

Religious architects also have echoed therapeutic assumptions of the benefits of expressivity through measured practice. For example, Rabbi Netter underscores calculated and controlled expression of emotion when informing children of a divorce: "I knew that if I had not scripted my statement the words would have stuck in my throat, which would be contracting while I was trying to stifle a flood of tears. . . . emotions of the moment would cripple my thought process. . . . if I left the choice of words to chance, to a sudden spasm of prophetic inspiration, the poverty of my language might cause me to say a wrong word that could wound my children deeply" (2002, 97). Active naming and release of emotions through controlled ritual practices in support groups legitimated the release of emotions through careful practice. For example, small-group leaders across traditions used guided meditation, prayer, and spiritual music to bring about emotional release. One Catholic group leader put a glass of water on a table and each person added a drop of a food coloring to represent a feeling. The glass turned a murky brown color. She put in a drop of bleach and the group, she stressed, watched the negative feelings fade away, reminding them that God can wash pain away. A Jewish support group leader asked members to bring an item that represented a feeling related to the marriage and its ending; they walked together one night to a local pier and threw these items in the water. Such deliberate refitting of symbolic practice for release of emotions is an age-old religious strategy and figured prominently in religious architects' approaches. For example, the rabbi's visual release of emotions into the water reflects the ritual of Tashlich where, on the afternoon of Rosh HaShanah (Jewish New Year), the words of Micha 7:19 are performed, throwing *tashlich* (sins), for some symbolized by bits of bread, into a body of water.

In an on-line resource, *Let's Talk about Divorce and Broken Relationships* [hereafter: *Let's Talk*],[9] its principal author, the Rev. Colleen M. McDonald, reinforces expressivity through UU principles of fostering creative selves and rituals as instruments for growth and ethical reflection. She recommends several resources to help in the creation of personalized rituals that will help control and use emotions—for example *A Healing Divorce* (2001), written by Phil and Barbara Penningroth, a couple who created their own healing ceremony and provide strategies and resources for others who wish to do the same. McDonald also notes journaling as "a wonderful way to release emotions and deal with loneliness," or constructing a "private place in your home where you can place symbols of your inner state—symbols of grief, loss, forgiveness, anger, memories, etc." (*Let's Talk*, 14–15). She invites families to come together to support these individual expressive efforts: "gathered family members" can "place a candle among the symbols and then light the candle . . . sit quietly, pray silently or aloud, or share when the spirit moves them to speak what is in their hearts." She suggests creating a mandala, a "circular piece of art that radiates from the center." Grieving family members can again support individual expressive efforts: "each person takes a large sheet of paper and crayons, pastels, or paints," and adds to the ring patterns one by one: "There is no theme or purpose; everyone should do what feels good, appropriate, and healing" (15).

Most important in therapeutic prescriptions for divorce work is the idea that feelings are functional, a belief to which sacred approaches add a sense of mystical force. In Kübler-Ross's model of grieving, anger can be used as a tool to persuade useful emotions to emerge (2005, 12), and even denial works in an almost mystical way: "There is a grace in denial. It is nature's way of letting in only as much as we can handle" (10). Depression is one of many "necessary steps along the way" (21) that makes us "slow down," and "take real stock of the loss" so that we can "rebuild ourselves from the ground up." As Laurie's account pointed out, and as suggested by CDM's founder regarding sacred Christian journey, emotions are instruments for discovering authentic self, for finding a "deeper place in our soul that we would not normally explore" (24). In *The Pain of Death When There Is No Funeral: It's Called Divorce*, author Edith L. McGrew (2008), a supervisor of the Women's Department of the Central Georgia Diocese of Church of God in Christ (COGIC), tells readers that she was able to "recover" because "God . . . delivered" her from a "sad and painful" time; she presents her writing about divorce as a calculated exercise that worked to clean out her "closet," a means for "evicting the ghost out once and for all," a "total cleansing" (37). Rabbi Vicki Hollander's chapter, "Weathering the Passage: Jewish Divorce," in *Lifecycles* (1994, 201) emphasizes that "one must actively navigate this most crucial passage, this time of death, of leave-taking, of crisis, of potential cleansing, of unprecedented possibility for deepening and growth." The task is challenging because it is the undoing of the holy: "Divorce is like rewinding a tape, going backwards to the marriage ceremony. We unwrap the bonds that bind and relinquish vows of holiness." In her own experience of divorce, she "sought ritual, enactment, to break through the numbness" of her "passage." She knew that "with the shattering" of her "world, feeling could emerge; feeling, the crucial prerequisite for healing" (202). DivorceCare, a thirteen-week video and support group evangelical series that I attended, makes clear that emotions like depression can be used to advantage through "stages" of grief that are sometimes hard to distinguish. Once the initial stages are completed, individuals labor to make sense of why and how a relationship ended; thus, painful feelings are deeply associated with religious identity and purpose.

To not engage in improving the self through working on feelings, in secular and religious constructions, was a deviant path and potentially crippling for self and family. In religious and therapeutic constructions, Rabbi Hollander stresses, emotions are there to push one through to a higher state of self and ability to care for children: divorce "invites one to plumb and work through layers of feelings; provides an opening to break through to new levels of being for oneself, and if a parent, for one's children" (1994, 204). In the UU divorce resource *Let's Talk*, the tradition's investment in rational and creative reflection propels interpretation of the labor of the "psychological divorce" as working through "residual feelings of anger, guilt, shame, blame, or betrayal that may interfere with the divorced person's ability to learn from the past and move on."

Religious tools also reinforce therapeutic demands for avoiding distractions while engaging serious grief work. Grief work demands full attention as it fatigues and refreshes. Kübler-Ross warns, "Support groups may bring new people into your world," but "be careful not to take on new relationships with lots of emotions. You may not be ready, and they can often complicate things. Your emotions, just like your body, need to repair" (2005, 37). *Crazy Time* warns: "Falling in love is your emotional midwife. . . . You just lose yourself for a while"; it is "avoidance strategy," a temporary retreat from painful emotions (1992, 206–207). Matthew McKay, Peter Rogers, Joan Blades, and Richard Gosse (1999, 29–49) warn too that divorced people can fall into traps that include self-blame, blaming others, clinging to an ex-spouse, living for others, escaping from oneself by burying pain, or entering into "Don Juanism—a period of 'promiscuity'" (47). Grieving weakens physical defenses. The task is to give grief its proper time and maintain healthy body and mind. Kübler-Ross readers are reminded to "eat a bit better or do a little more," yet be careful to "go slowly" and not "take on more than you can handle" (2005, 127). Religious architects draw from tools in their traditions to bring mystical force to focused grief work. Rabbi Hollander turns to religious themes of passage and sacred journey to emphasize the importance of hanging "on tenaciously to your emotions, for it is your *passage*; it is not a time to take care of others" (1994, 204). Religious architects from Christian traditions have drawn from familiar themes to present singlehood as a sacred time when individuals should pause before entering into intimate relationships and use the opportunity to focus on their emotions and find God's love and guidance.

In the DivorceCare video, participants were warned: "Another relationship is like Novocain for the heart . . . it is sort of like having a broken foot and you can take a shot of Novocain . . . and you can still walk . . . and you can look around and say I am fine really . . . and one day you look down, you see this white bone sticking through the skin, . . . and you realize that you have done a lot more damage to yourself with the Novocain than if you would have, you know, put a cast around it, protected it, gave some structure to it." Avoiding work on emotions can also lead individuals to divulge bitter feelings about ex-spouses and thus hurt children, whose emotions divorced parents need to carefully guard and manage: "In Proverbs 12:18 we find these words: Reckless words pierce like a sword, but the tongue of the wise brings healing. . . . Those are your feelings. It does not help the child if you try to drive a wedge between your child and its departed parent." Even if an ex is "behaving in ways that are inappropriate and the child witnesses . . . , you want to let them know in an objective way, which means again without the emotion, without the frustration . . . point out this behavior is incorrect." DivorceCare made clear that a healthy single-parent home post-divorce is one where the parent is in control of his or her emotions: "A family is when there is a single parent home that is in control. That is not a broken home."

In divorce work, children require special attention and emotional labor; a divorced parent who has his or her own feelings under control can then facilitate the child's grief work. Religious and secular architects of divorce work recommend that parents carefully encourage their children to talk about their feelings. DivorceCare advises: "You have to just be there and maybe three or four hours into a very innocent evening they will really come out with some feeling and concerns, and sometimes that is three in the morning. . . . you have to change your lifestyle a little bit to be available for them." Noncustodial parents have a different kind of emotional work: "It's very difficult to stay involved in the life of your child when you don't live with them. In fact it is so hard you may be tempted to give up trying. . . . But please don't. Your kids need you." Another DivorceCare voice confirms: "I blamed him [the father] because he wasn't making an effort to make contact with us, and of course that just harbored and built on the anger I already had for him." The task demands controlling your emotions: "Stay active in that child's life, but active without confusion. No comments about your ex—uh, no negative statements." Secular and religious authors of divorce work made clear that you should not let your children do your emotional labor or ask children to carry hostile messages or report on an ex-spouse's behavior. Religious and therapeutic texts warned not to force a child to hide positive feelings about the other parent or to keep secrets. Architects from all religious traditions reinforced the danger of emotions (parent's or children's) left unexpressed and untamed. CDM founder James Young warns, "Divorcing people can get into a lot of personal trouble—make rash decisions about finances and family obligations, stay away from friends and possible sources of help, getting involved in new relationships for which they're not emotionally ready" (1984, 14–15). Grief work itself can also become pathological. DivorceCare cautions: "We have also seen people get stuck in their grief by becoming recovery junkies. . . . If you don't grieve or if you get stuck in the grieving process you will end up hurting yourself and those around you."

Religious constructions, like secular approaches, promoted an appeal to "experts" to heal and move through stages of grief. Mel and Pat Krantzlers' (1998) revised text, *The New Creative Divorce,* suggests that you may need to "seek out a good professional divorce counselor to assist you in getting unstuck from the first stage of the mourning process" (142). Don't think of this as a failure, the book adds; "it is the strong person who recognizes the need for professional help when he or she is too close to the problem to see it clearly" (142). Religious architects named both medical therapeutic experts and religious therapeutic professionals as wise to see, and valuable in guiding one through grief. In evangelical Christian resources like DivorceCare, the concept of *brokenness* fueled images of individuals as needing specialized attention. Pages xiii–xv of the DivorceCare workbook lists "DivorceCare Experts" including: a professor of psychology at Fuller Theological Seminary; a practicing clinical psychologist; a licensed clinical social worker who speaks at seminars, workshops, and retreats on spiritual growth, marriage, and divorce recovery; and a pastor at an evangelical church. In the DivorceCare videos, support of expert intervention was embellished through medical metaphor:

When your life is threatened by serious injury or illness we activate an advanced medical system to help save your life. If your condition is critical you are rushed to an emergency room to be stabilized, to get an exact diagnosis of what's wrong. Once the doctors know what is wrong with you there is an incredible array of medical help that can be directed towards healing you. Highly trained doctors and medical specialists, surgical procedures, intensive care, therapy, and rehabilitation are mobilized to help restore your health. . . . There are a lot of parallels when you compare physical injury to the trauma of divorce. In its own way divorce can be just as traumatic as a medical crisis. The problem is the help system is not as apparent. There are not emergency rooms like this one to come to.

Core evangelical beliefs in the DivorceCare video series propelled therapeutic prescriptions of grief work. God as a transcendent force who intervenes in individuals' lives, and a personal relationship with Jesus fostered through religious community, pushes emotion work: "Your spiritual life gives you the power to overcome the emotional energies that are being drained from you. . . . Be sure that you have asked Christ into your life, that he is the lord of your life, and you have insurance of your salvation that you're stabilized in a church. . . . It's sort of like running your car without oil. You can go you know quite a ways before it finally you know burns up everything. But your spiritual life allows you to smoothly run." Freewill-accountable individualism, a focus on brokenness (of mind, body, or relationship), the Bible as a source of truth used to manage everyday life, and the transformative grace of God are key evangelical tools activated in DivorceCare.[10]

Evangelical Christians have varying beliefs regarding social issues, and can be found in a variety of denominations, but most, like architects of sacred divorce work in the black church and Catholic traditions, have a normative vision of marriage. Evangelicals especially emphasize God as joining a man and woman together as "one flesh."[11] Thus vivid images of skin ripping and bodies breaking apart when divorce occurs represent well the evangelical view of divorce injury and resulting grief. Church Initiatives founder Steve Grissom, who has been divorced, tells DivorceCare viewers: "God uses a medical metaphor to describe what happens when you and your spouse became husband and wife. . . . They become what the Bible calls one flesh." He warns: "When your marriage comes apart, we don't revert to becoming two individuals again. Instead, we become two parts of the same one-flesh marriage torn away with huge, gaping, emotional wounds." A woman in the video shares: "I felt as though there was a part of my arm . . . that was cut to a point that it was dangling and continuously bleeding with no relief." One of DivorceCare's religio-therapeutic experts comments: "You leave these webs hanging, bleeding. I call it the emotional gushing wound of a broken relationship." A DivorceCare video witness testifies: "I had people that I was very close to that thought I was dying. They told me months later that they just knew I had a terminal disease because I rarely spoke. I had lost so much weight. I looked like a cadaver."

Enriching therapeutic understandings of divorce as opportunity for self and family, Christian architects named a state of brokenness related to ending sacred life partnership as efficacious, a "gift" from God. James Young, one of the founders of Catholic Divorce Ministries, endows the divorce experience and its related emotion work with explicit religious purpose and familiar spiritual emotion, stressing that divorce is "a poor gift—so much sadness, so much pain, so much heartbreak. It brings a time of extreme want. One feels empty, without resources; nothing in life seems to have any value. Yet when we give this experience to God, it becomes like gold" (1984, 86–87). A woman in the DivorceCare video explains: "One of the gifts that I was being given was being broken apart, being broken down long enough to be still and listen to the Lord about who I was, who I really was created to be." Another woman refers to that place: "when you can't fight any longer, fall apart, crack apart, break apart, and be desperate before God. There is no better place you can be. Desperation for God can heal you." Brokenness before God symbolizes powerful feelings in evangelical emotional regimes, and is understood as "spiritually invigorating." Still, injury alone is futile; as with larger grief-work scripts, emotion work added to suffering is what generates transformative recovery.

Potential pathology resulting from such weakened or broken condition is enhanced in religious constructions through medical metaphor and religious beliefs about body and sacred character. DivorceCare warns: "It is essential that you stabilize physically to protect your health . . . along the road to recovery there are two huge pot holes that you must avoid. The first pothole is the result of your depleted energy supply. In your weakened state you will find it more difficult to maintain your moral value system." Such a weakened body leads to deviant behaviors: "Everybody just has a different drug of choice . . . some people use drugs . . . some people use alcohol, some people become workaholics." A major danger then is self-medicating and avoiding expression of emotions and the stages of grief.

Religious architects paint care of one's body as religious command drawing from religious tools. For example, in the National Baptist Convention text *Singles: Strengthened, Secured, and Spirit-Filled* [hereafter: *Singles*], Dr. Rosalind Denson draws from biblical images of body-as-temple: "Our lives and our bodies are not our own. We are the temple of the Holy Ghost" (2007, 78).[12] Cyneetha Strong, a black Baptist M.D. and contributor to the same text, writes, "We are to glorify God with our Bodies." Several chapters of this book encourage singles to "be holy" in dating, suggesting that women and men should save sex for marriage. Denson warns of two types of risky dating, "emotion-driven" and "hormone-driven"; these are in opposition to "spirit-led" dating (74–75). Emotion-driven dating is of special concern post-divorce: "A person may be recently divorced, and in an effort to validate his or her worth, will go out with relative strangers just to see if *'I still got it.'* Others use dating to inflict revenge on members of the opposite sex to salve their own hurts. Still others, in an effort to deal with the pain and loss due to death or abandonment, date to fill a void and to keep from dealing with the realities of no longer being part of a couple" (74). Sometimes, "we are not healed from previous relationships and only carry baggage into new venues if dating is out of sync with God's timing" (77). COGIC's McGrew writes: "The rejected one, most cases a woman, is left alone to grieve. Feelings of rejection over-flood the soul. Open shame at having been left. . . . Those in such deep pain will want to show others that they are 'attractive to the opposite sex,' but know that it is not 'wise' to date right after the ending" (2008, vii).

Grief work done well produces a mystical power that leads to new life and more authentic self. Therapeutic authors Matthew McKay and colleagues (1999) write, "As you finish your identity work, you may experience a sense of strength and accomplishment. You've endured an enormous test" (14). You will, they say, have uncovered some authentic self: "Recentering means sculpting your life to fit the person you are" (15). In the end, "The recentered self is different from the married person you once were. You've endured separation, ridden the roller-coaster, and survived" (15). Kübler-Ross writes: "There is wonder in the power of grief," and grief "alone has the power to heal." Grief is dependable and constant: "Grief always works. Grief always heals. . . . grief is the path that returns us to wholeness. It shouldn't be a matter of *if* you will grieve; the question is *when* you will grieve. And until we do, we suffer from the effects of that unfinished business" (2005, 227–229). Religious architects have endowed this mystical essence with particular sacred energy through casting this emotion-work design as originating from a higher source. In the Jewish case, tying grief work to High Holiday passages associated with Yom Kippur and Passover has given divorce work tasks awesome power. In the UU case, religious devotion as self-reflexive process and journey elevated therapeutic stages of recovery. DivorceCare promoted that "God created us to grieve," and its video host, Steve Grissom, conjured evangelical emotional force by casting God and Jesus as ultimate physicians: "I don't think anybody can be healed from this kind of trauma without returning back to God." DivorceCare's therapeutic experts saw themselves as working alongside Divine design and energy to stabilize and heal; for instance, according to Grissom:

> Second Corinthians 5:17 says therefore if anyone is in Christ he is a new creation. . . . If I am brought to an emergency room with a serious injury I want the best doctors, the best specialist, the best care I can get to help me recover. . . . If the doctors tell me I need painful surgery to help me recover I would likely take their advice despite the pain and discomfort. In the coming weeks we are going to introduce you to the best specialists and the best experts of divorce and recovery topics. They'll share some very practical suggestions on how to recover from divorce. Some of the advice might be a little painful but it is designed to help you heal. And ultimately all of our experts are going to point you in the same direction: that the presence of God in your life is the key to your healing.

DivorceCare's message, unlike other religious architects, was blatantly exclusive: there is only one authentic way to truly accomplish grief work. A religio-therapeutic expert, in the video, argues: "People who don't have Jesus Christ can do something. . . . You can whitewash it. It can look clean. It will be presentable. It will seem on the outside that everything is going alright, but just scratch the service and all the brokenness is still there. . . . in the final analysis the only real healing that comes to the human condition is the healing that we see through Jesus Christ." Christian forgiveness merges with medical expertise: "Remember this, . . . Jesus was the great physician, the great counselor, the great psychiatrist. . . . Holding unforgiveness and bitterness is bad on our health, . . . a root of bitterness that poisons everything else." Church membership and group religious ritual hold select healing power: "If you are really serious about maintaining or restoring your value system you will need some help," and the church "can offer the help, the support, the spiritual environment to increase your spiritual life as well and reenergize your life spirituality, which will restore your moral value system."

DivorceCare's attachment to Jesus Christ as physician represents an exclusive position, but an appeal to a divine source as the ultimate sacred power in grief work can be found in other traditions. For example, Rabbi Netter stresses the final words in the Talmud on divorce: "If a man divorces his first wife, even the altar sheds tears." Netter uses the symbol of the Temple in Jerusalem as "the point of contact between heaven and earth." He writes that "God cries about divorce" at the altar "not because God is judging us as sinners, as so many people believe," but because "God, like us, is in pain and cries with us. When we hurt, God hurts. God is present in God's tears" (2002, 77). An appeal to divine presence through particular religious images was a central strategy in the divorce work of most architects. In each case, singlehood develops as a special time for closeness to God as one works on assessing, retooling, and managing relationship with an ex-spouse.

Sacred Marriage Work

Laurie's story at the beginning of this chapter highlights her careful assessment of the marriage that ended, and a retooling of herself into someone who better understood the work involved in life partnerships and in family relationships post-divorce. She related the history of her marriage to those attending the group and told how she worked hard to reveal mistakes that she and her husband had made, recalling that a milestone in her "healing journey" came when she saw that the affair did not break the marriage, that "it had been hemorrhaging for years." Uncovering and analyzing the relationship allowed her to see the "truth" about her part in the "death" of the marriage, efforts that allowed her to move forward, claim authentic self, sustain and build strong relationships with her children and stepchildren, and co-parent in a "healthy" way with her ex-husband. Her narrative demonstrates how marriage work manifests through expectations of the emotion work of divorce as *assessing and retooling* for the next marriage and *managing relationships with a former spouse*. Sacred architects like Laurie stressed the ethical and religious implications of this as blessed work.

Marriage work is not reactionary; it is proactive and constant, and the social pressure to complete this work remains even after a life partnership ends. The gendered nature of today's marital work is constructed from multiple masculinities and femininities, rising ideals of involved fatherhood, mothers and fathers faced with increasing demands of work and family, and the growing acceptance of same-sex unions, but the expectation that people must work hard on life partnership to beat the odds of divorce is deliberate and demanding for all genders and sexual orientations.

Historian Kristin Celello (2009, 3) details the development of gendered marriage work in twentieth-century U.S. society, pointing to the rise of a "diverse group of experts" who "defined and shaped the character of marital work in response to heightened fears about an increase in divorce and family breakdown." College courses for women about marriage developed and "became increasingly popular on college campuses across the United States throughout the 1930s and also spread into high schools in the postwar years" (32–33). Sociologists like Talcott Parsons (1955) further promoted the idea that men and women had separate roles in marriage and that women were largely responsible for managing the emotions of marriage and family life. A genre of marriage advice literature emerged, early- to midcentury, that focused on the importance of mutuality in sexuality and romance; this literature represented the beginning of "the construction of the relationship as a therapeutic object."[13] The countercultural revolution of the 1960s and 1970s brought attention to marriage work fueled by egalitarian relational and work ethics of second wave feminism, men's movements that encouraged male expressivity and rejection of the harsh demands of the workplace, and the same-sex marriage movement.[14]

The extraordinary growth of the marriage therapy and relationship counseling business in contemporary U.S. culture is evidence of the pervasiveness of marriage work, as is a self-help industry fueled by psychological and social scientific putative experts who shape calculated marriage enhancement and divorce prevention efforts. Exemplary texts are: William Doherty's (2001) book, *Take Back Your Marriage: Sticking Together in a World That Pulls Us Apart,* the fourth edition of Merilee Clunis and Dorsey Green's (2005) *Lesbian Couples: A Guide to Creating Healthy Relationships,* John Gottman's (1999) New York Times bestseller, *The Seven Principles for Making Marriage Work,* and Howard Markman and colleagues' revision (2010) of *Fighting for Your Marriage.* Religious communities have also been highly active in efforts to promote marriage work in U.S. society, playing a role in the creation of "hybrid political religious organizations" like the Marriage Movement and producing hundreds of marriage guidebooks and programs.[15]

The dominant scripts in these texts and marriage programs provide strategies for the development of communication skills, creative romance, friendship, and even shared spiritual orientation, but there are differences. For example, gay and lesbian advice books like Berzon's (1990 and 1996) connect building enduring and stable permanent partnerships to social movement goals within the gay and lesbian community; heteronormative Marriage Movement strategies tend to exclude nontraditional families; and some resources promote gendered notions of women as essentially emotionally equipped for relational work and men as resistant to feeling work. Still, for all, marriage work is seen as involving a steady retooling, an endless unraveling and evaluation of self and relationship. Most important, in dominant therapeutic discourse, divorce presents as a time to assess and retool marriage work skills.

The secular text *The New Creative Divorce* (1998) proclaims that divorce "gives us a second chance to rethink the meaning of love and learn why the love you once thought you had forever at the time you married evaporated" (72). Religious architects use religious principles to emphasize a similar call for self-reflexivity. For example, UU architects whose religious community highly values investment in the moral value of self-reflection suggest in *Let's Talk* that clergy encourage people to look at "past relationships that ended in divorce or dissolution," and to discern "what was learned from these experiences" (*Let's Talk*, 6). Black Pentecostal author McGrew recommends accepting "your responsibility in the divorce," learning from past experiences, being "prepared to avoid the same mistake again," taking "inventory of self" and working at "self evaluation" (2008, 31). She awards the task religious purpose: "We must really work at our self evaluation and realize that we are truly fearfully and wonderfully made. . . . We are the marvelous works of God. Psalm 139:14 (paraphrased)" (34). Religious architects from all traditions render singlehood not just a valid life choice, but as a sacred time for learning why endings happened and gaining skills that will make future life partnerships durable. Rabbi Netter (2002, 15) invites complex reflection as religious intent: "The first mitzvah of divorce is to try to understand it—its psychology, its sociology, its ontology. The first mitzvah is to try to understand why this is happening at all. For there is no growth without understanding, no insight without knowledge, no healing without wisdom." Netter then provides readers with tools to think about why their marriage ended, proposing reflection of multiple influences: psychological factors, developmental factors, and economic and demographic forces.

In religious and secular therapeutic texts, divorce also emerges as a second chance to acquire a better understanding of the skills for cultivating authentic love. Ann Swidler's (2001, 114) work speaks to the sustained contradictions in cultural understandings of romantic love; individuals choose partners, yet romantic love is a "mythic love" where people may fall in love at first sight or find a "soul mate." Investment in "prosaic love" is strong in our cultural repertoire: the idea that real love grows over time, that real love is based in mutuality and does not necessarily last forever. Secular marriage authors John Gottman and Nan Silver (1999) maintain that mutual respect through friendship provides a foundation for love and brings more passion to a marriage. Although not necessarily claiming to be the sole arbiter of whether or not love lasts, many self-help books suggest that expressivity, careful listening, and taking partners' concerns as genuine and legitimate can enhance life-long romance, and offer concrete strategies, arguing that romance is thus sustained through communication and creative strategies for lifelong friendship and intimacy.

Prosaic love also demands ongoing management of a spouse's feelings, a constant building of intimate knowledge of his or her desires and emotions. Betty Berzon (1996, 17) writes of sustaining long-term gay and lesbian relationships: "I try to tune my clients into the rhythm of their moves: close, distant, close again. . . . It is the poetry of movement that choreographs intimacy; the rhythms come from inside us and resonate to the inner rhythms of the other." Most religious architects cast this work as sacred, reminding those ending relationships of the idea that a divine entity or pious purpose is an essential part of a life partnerships. In *Let's Talk*, McDonald highlights a section of Nemser's 1966 UU divorce rite (1998, 414) that reminds those divorcing of the serious ethical intent of marriage: "People marry experiencing many of the strongest feelings they have known: feelings of wanting to share, of faith in themselves, of belief in another, of trust in the morrow, of choosing two before one. . . . For marriage is not a moment but a lifetime. Marriage is growth" (*Let's Talk*, 3). Almost all clergy members I interviewed for this research talked about stressing the importance of being in touch with a partner's needs and emotions, and those in more conservative Christian communities stressed that God must be active in this day-to-day marriage work. McGrew writes that "marriages are built on day to day activities with the Holy Spirit as the planner" (2008, 32).

The idea that spouses should strive to be "spiritual partners" achieving some sort of mystical togetherness and individuality through shared moral principles and life purpose is pervasive in secular marriage work and used by religious architects of divorce work to stress an essential ingredient for future success in marriage. Spiritual companionship and deepening intimate connection through love and romance is not a contemporary notion; the Victorians, for example, saw love as a kind of spiritual and transcendent force, albeit precarious and suspicious (Shumway 2003, 64 and chapter 2). In our contemporary therapeutic culture, where individualism takes a central position, spiritual connection has evolved into creative and deliberate forms of relational and self work. For example, secular authors Howard J. Markman, Scott M. Stanley, and Susan L. Blumberg (2010, 27) note that "we hear a lot about the desire to find a soul mate—*the one*—the person with whom all these positive connections spark and explode," and that such a mystical connection involves commitment, effort, and time: "Don't expect to be your beloved's soul mate before you've been there as your mate's soul unfolds. . . . Soul mates evolve as lovers grow together and coauthor their own relationship story." The prescription that love demands constant attention to self and partner and requires demanding emotion work reflects well our seeker–quest culture, where laboring through meaningful life journeys can be a creative group effort (Roof 1993; Wuthnow 1994b). In the UU resource *Let's Talk*, readers are reminded that marriage begins with the idea that "marriage is a milestone along a path of an evolving relationship between two persons who have turned to each other in search and expectation of a greater fulfillment than either can achieve alone" (2). Secular authors Merilee Clunis and Dorsey Green (2005, 22) warn lesbian couples, "You need to establish the psychological identity of your relationship— 'what we want our relationship to be'—and, at the same time, create room for each of you to be individuals." Matthew McKay and colleagues (1999, 319) claim, "The right choice of a marital partner depends very much on how well you know yourself." A CDM support group leadership resource advises that a sustained long-term relationship demands understanding that "Spirituality is a God-connection. It is knowing that each person is called to be a God-reflector. It is recognizing the 'God-in-me,' and the 'God-in-you,' when relating to the other."

Secular authors thus stress the importance of knowing oneself as a necessary task before marriage can succeed, and sacred architects give self-awareness in marriage mystical purpose, fuel for the divorce work of deciphering what went wrong in the marriage. Most Christian architects stress that if individual spiritual growth is stifled, as Sue in chapter 1 indicates in her narrative, the marriage is dysfunctional. Catholic author Antoinette Bosco (2006, 55) uses individual spiritual growth to legitimate ending: "If being spiritual means anything at all, it is to be living in a state of harmony with yourself, with others and with God. There is nothing 'holy' about remaining in an infantile state of 'obedience,'" by hanging on to an intolerable marriage "which ultimately becomes destructive to your spiritual maturity." Rabbi Netter (2002, 22–28) interprets a well-known biblical story, the binding of Isaac, to emphasize the importance of self-development in divorce. He writes that the story is so "compelling, so mysterious, so engaging that it pulls us back into it again and again." In the story God tests Abraham "by asking him to take Isaac—his son, his only son, . . . to an unknown place where he would tie Isaac to an altar, slaughter him . . . as a sacrifice to God." Netter's "favorite reading of the story is by the second-century sage Rabbi Yitzhak, who suggests that Isaac was thirty-seven years old at the time," thus a grown man who "willingly allows himself to be placed on the altar." Netter adapts the story to represent the importance of self-growth through life transitions: "There comes a time in every adult life when we have to go up on that altar and die to our past in order to inherit our future. . . . Often, as adults make the transition through the various stages of adulthood, the relationship that worked earlier in their lives has not developed along with them to accommodate who they have become. Mature love is able to change along with the people in the relationship; immature love dies on the vine."

Religious and therapeutic architects of divorce work stress confronting emotional disturbances in one's sexual past as part of the feeling work needed to ensure a rewarding spiritual marriage in the future. Therapeutic texts connect sex with spiritual expectations of marital intimacy. For example, in *The New Creative Divorce* (1998, 100), Mel and Pat Krantzler advise, "The spiritual component of the sexual experience is also a central value that today's times reaffirm as essential to an enriching relationship." Single status after divorce is an exceptional time to accomplish a deeper understanding of the importance of sexual intimacy in marriage. DivorceCare uses religious tools to further enhance the importance of this marriage work: "the truth is the Bible celebrates sex. All you have to do is read the Song of Solomon to see plenty of evidence of that, but the sex celebrated in the Bible is that between a married couple, and it takes a meaning far beyond the physical." DivorceCare reinforces that "when a couple is having sex they are bonding their bodies and their souls together." Across traditions, support group embrace the idea that people may need to explore the emotions associated with sexual abuse before entering into another relationship. One Catholic support group leader encourages participants to embrace their God-given nature as a "sexual being" outside of marriage before they consider moving into another marriage.

The stifling of spiritual self and/or relationship with God emerges as legitimate grounds for divorce across all traditions. DivorceCare, like other religious architects, offers legitimation for ending relationships in cases of physical and mental abuse or adultery. A woman in the DivorceCare video testifies, "He actually threw me down a staircase and broke my foot and was trying to kill me." And another, "My daughter went into the drawers, got a pair of scissors, and went between him and me; she was going to protect me." A DivorceCare expert then weighs in, "Physical violence is never ever justified." Grissom qualifies: "If you are on the receiving end of violence, you need to get you and your family out of danger immediately and find help in resolving the situation. . . . In the turmoil of your circumstances, it might seem like seeking safety means that you are giving up on your marriage. That doesn't have to be the case." DivorceCare, deeply invested in evangelical recovery discourse, keeps alive the possibility of recovery for abusive spouses, thus promoting intense measures of marriage work.

Most religious architects strongly suggest that serious marriage-work effort should be done before making a final decision to end the marriage. For example, in James Young's book (1984) and in his conference speeches, he affirms that "there may be times when divorce may be the only Christian solution available to an intolerable, destructive relationship" (11), but he does so alongside examples of couples who were able to work on their marriages and get back together (10), and reinforces the ideas of ideal love and the importance of marriage work: "Our Christian instinct is always to say it is better to stay. It is better to rely on God's help to work through problems and conflicts and grow together as husband and wife in the process. The Church will always insist that true love is tested and proven in adversity and suffering." Rabbi Netter (2002) is clear that couples with problems need to first work hard on assessing the relationship before ending it

(58–59), turning to a rabbi and therapist to help if needed. "You have years of your lives invested in each other," he reminds readers; "Do not give up easily. You have traveled a long path together." When endings threaten, the UU on-line resource *Let's Talk* promotes consideration of working to save the marriage and reaching out to therapeutic experts. Still, efforts to save a marriage or reconcile are most commanding and gendered in conservative voices. For example, black Pentecostal author Edith L. McGrew (2008) writes: "I encourage women to fight for your *marriage* [her emphasis] with all that is within you. . . . Women have a specific calling in making marriage work: 'Woman, you were made to be a helpmate' . . . ; if your marriage is in trouble, make sure you have done all you know to do in order to build your marriage. Spend quality time with him as your mate and other times with him as the father of your children. . . . Strive to be friends and lovers in order to cement your relationship" (1–2). In the end, McGrew devotes almost as much time to marriage work as she does to the process of ending (32–33).

DivorceCare puts a strong emphasis on reconciliation through marriage work. The program advises one should go to a "pastor or Christian counselor, someone who is not going to just say end the relationship, but someone sympathetic with keeping the marriage together and reconciliation." One DivorceCare counseling expert advises giving at least six months to work on reconciliation: "I believe that the cycles of reconciliation will occur. That when a person leaves they will at least mentally and emotionally want to reconcile and to come back to the line. . . . I believe that most of them will, not all 100 percent." He has spouses sign "contracts" that say they will not date for six months and commit to reconciliation efforts. A minister names the benefits of reconciliation after divorce: ""You save the heritage of the family" and "[save] the children an awful lot of misery." In DivorceCare's evangelical frame, the divorced are also warned that bringing children into a new marriage is a risky emotional venture: "One of the common misconceptions is if you remarry that you once again have a whole family that's without breaks or fractures . . . , but a blended family is not one cohesive group. It's two single parents working together. . . . There's everything you need for an explosion. It is exhausting. It's tiring and it's difficult." Mending the existing marriage is preferred.

No-fault divorce may be the dominant legal position, but a major task in contemporary divorce work is deciphering blame, to which end authors of divorce work guides suggest one go back and assess and retool, particularly in the area of communication. Affirming one's position as a parent and future spouse involves serious refining of communication skills. Secular authors Markman and colleagues (2010, 106) proclaim, "Communication is the lifeblood of a good relationship; it keeps all the good things flowing and removes blockages that most couples experience day-to-day." In true marriage-work fashion, they teach respectful but assertive communication, using "*I* messages to describe how you feel," stating a solution and pointing out its advantages, and "rehearsing" and preparing in advance for the reader's communication with her or his ex (92–93). Religious architects of sacred divorce work also promote the acquisition of new communication skills to activate a higher purpose. For example, one CDM leader offered a seminar, the "Art of Communication," for participants to learn to "speak with compassion," develop "healthy communication," and "verbalize what is within," in the wake of the "grieving process." UU *Let's Talk* architects have invited couples to think about their upbringing and expectations of marriage, and explore "communication styles and approaches to conflict" (6). A CDM seminar strove to help participants unlearn habits acquired while living in "dysfunctional families" of origin or bad marriages and that kept them from being strong individuals and activating God's gifts. The guide reads, "Time will be spent on developing the skills needed to establish healthy boundaries," which will "make it possible for a relationship (of any kind) to be intimate without being suffocating, controlling, or manipulative." Learning to create "healthy boundaries" will bring, says the guide, "the space that allows the person to continue to discover his/her gifts." The idea that people who get divorced have possibly lived in families where people do not learn how to be full individuals was a dominant theme across Christian traditions, as was fighting "co-dependence."

In traditions that promote heterosexual marriage as ideal, marriage work involves reaffirmation of God-given marriage design and the importance for marriage partners to be equally yoked (both committed Christians) to ease spiritual togetherness and a healthy relationship. DivorceCare makes clear that "Marriage is not a product of society. It is not a product of psychology or psychologists. . . . Marriage is a product of God." Because God made marriage, "It's his product, and if you're going to deal with someone's product it is important for you to follow their specifications; . . . you must submit yourself to God, to His manual, which is the Bible." For example, Genesis 2:24 is used to reinforce the deep emotional and physical bond: marriage is "a committed relationship for life," where a man and a woman are "fused" together, a union where a person actually "share[s] physically with the other person part of your own being." Thus, God intends only heterosexual marriage and "hates divorce." DivorceCare experts combine biblical story and image with contemporary marriage ideals stressing that "marriage requires that you be both intimate friends and have a growing, dynamic relationship actively moving before you choose to marry." Doing divorce work and waiting for the "right" spouse would then make singlehood a sacred position. NBC's *Singles* text (2007, 32) encourages: "We do not need to worry about any societal stigma associated with being single. We are in good company because Jesus Christ, who was single, was the greatest person—single or otherwise—to ever walk this earth. Do not worry about broken relationships or about dates that turned sour. God would have made that relationship work, if it had been meant for you." COGIC's McGrew (2008, 15) writes: "If the marriage fails remember that God never fails." God is not just immanent, but present, touching the person's physical body. Most important, God is in charge "don't seek a mate. Allow God to send someone if it is to be." DivorceCare makes a similar recommendation: "Find the Lord; He'll find the mate." Singlehood is an important stage and a respectable lifestyle, in both secular and religious manifestations of divorce work, but in religious constructions it takes on a sacred life that gives added power to combat social shame.

Another major way that marriage work is active in divorce work is through the expectation that a person will learn how to maintain a healthy relationship with an ex-spouse—primarily when children are involved. This relational labor is undertaken without romantic love and companionship as mitigating forces. Secular authors Matthew McKay, Peter Rogers, Joan Blades, and Richard Gosse (1999, 90) stress developing new communication skills with the ex-spouse: "Healthy conflict resolution depends on three separate skills: the ability to express your needs, the ability to listen, and the ability to generate alternative solutions." Religious architects add a sacred charge to building communication if children are involved. DivorceCare warns that divorce is "like a funeral, but you can never really close the casket because you have . . . to learn how to deal with your children's feelings and your ex being involved in their lives." Rabbi Netter (2002, 158) writes: "The mitzvot of parenting, the sacred commandments driving parents to rise above self-interest and to care for their children, . . . Every decision can be measured against God's standard, which demands: *What's in the best interest of the children?*" A CDM support group handout advises a "divorce etiquette for parents" that begins with the Golden Rule, and advises learning to "communicate clearly and negotiate fairly." Even more, learning how to communicate well with an ex-spouse's family is given moral purpose: "Just as divorce does not terminate parent-hood, it doesn't terminate grand-parenthood, or cousin-ship. Severing the legal bond between parents does not dissolve the genetic bond, or the relationships established over one's childhood."

Secular authors, like religious architects, promote forgiveness as a valuable emotional skill in marriage and post-divorce family health, but religious architects are able to tie this emotional effort to powerfully familiar beliefs and rituals. DivorceCare states, "Making amends with the other person is one of the hardest things you can do in life on your own strength, but with the help of Christ in your life you have extra resources for the process." Jewish group leaders do not use the concept of forgiveness in the same way, but rather stress atonement and the importance of respecting one's ex-spouse, especially when children are involved. Rabbi Alan Lew (2000, 6–7), known for his work in Jewish meditation and in synthesizing Zen Buddhist practice with Judaism, uses the high holiday of Yom Kippur to address atonement after divorce, in a pamphlet published by Jewish Lights: "The Hebrew word for atonement is *kaparah. Kaparah* means 'a covering over.' The idea is not that atonement effaces our sins. . . . They will always be there, . . . When we make atonement, we are covering over our wrongdoings with the will to behave differently. . . . it allows us to move on and let go of the past. . . . We no longer need to feel guilty or angry about it. . . . So it is with divorce. Our marriages never leave us. They cling to us in our dreams and in the names we call up from our unconscious. But the ritual of divorce covers them over with a fresh act of will." In *Divorce Is a Mitzvah*, Rabbi Netter (2002, 177) writes: "If we love our children, we can learn to support that part of our ex-spouse that feeds their souls. If we truly love our children, we won't behave in such a way as to hurt them." Whether interpreted through a Christian or Jewish lens, letting go of negative emotions, forgiving, plays a large role in communicating well with an ex-spouse and purging dangerous emotions like anger and resentment.

SACRED DIVORCE WORK

When we lose life partners, time with our children, parents, homes, or health, we may challenge or reject therapeutic strategies, but we will likely feel the wide-reaching coverage of divorce-work expectations if we turn to institutional worlds for guidance. Our cultural world imposes removal of risky emotions from the body and the pursuit of creative individual and relational practices. If we do not present ourselves as devoted to bettering our relationships through therapeutic practices, of growing stronger after emotional injury, we risk being labeled by intimate others and religio-therapeutic experts as stagnant, stifled, or stuck—even ripe for mental and physical illness and susceptible to irrational acts, in no condition to enter into new life partnerships. When the religious individuals I interviewed adopted divorce-work scripts to tell their stories, they were in touch with social authority born from the intermingling of therapeutic with religious worlds.

Therapeutic culture provides a far-reaching social canopy, a sacred cosmos (Berger 1967) where individualism, constant and creative individual pursuit of self-betterment, expression of inner feelings as the key to growth and new relationships, and reliance on expert knowledge and/or intervention are attributed to a higher omniscient force. Religious worlds have powerful emotional resources that add sacred status to this therapeutic canopy. The use of pilgrimage as a symbol for divorce experience in Catholic resources, sacred passages and sacrifice in Judaism, and God and Jesus as physician and ultimate healer in evangelical voices are examples of religious concepts that turn *divorce work* into *sacred labor*. In UU architects' prescriptions, the sacred character of this emotion work is tied directly to core religious beliefs of self-reflexive process, ethical reflection, and journey. In other traditions—reminiscent of monks, nuns, and priests—the lack of the distractions of sex and marriage is presented as bringing more time for connection to divine energy. Gail Adkins writes in the black Baptist *Singles* resource: free from the "concerns of yielding, catering, and accommodating spouse and family, singles have an awesome opportunity to love on God without interruption" (2007, 40). Singleness becomes a season, "not only a time to 'know' oneself, but . . . an opportunity to know God and develop an intimate relationship with Him."

Individual responsibility for emotional labor intensifies through the emotional energy embedded in religious symbolic worlds. My respondents saw the collective emotion produced in congregations as ritual spaces where they could accomplish divorce work and take on sacred identity as religio-therapeutic practitioners.

3 ✳ SOLITARY WORK THROUGH COMMUNITY

In church you can cry and nobody will ever ask you why. They may assume you are crying because you are happy. They may assume you are crying because you are going through something. They may assume you are crying because you got peace. They may assume you are crying because you got hit by the Holy Spirit. There were Sundays that I cried because I felt like God was there. Couldn't find him in my house. Couldn't find him at work. Couldn't find him at night when I went to sleep, but when I went to church it gave me peace, . . . almost like the Holy Spirit speaking to me: you are going to be all right.

—Natalie, black Pentecostal woman

Several respondents left congregations as they experienced changes in family, but most stayed active in familiar or new congregational spaces even though silence around divorce and the potential for social shame flourished. Some stayed even in the face of intense social stigma. A few supposed what it might have been like in congregations if their spouse had died instead of exiting the relationship; they would have had a clear role as widow or widower, members of their congregations would be bringing them casseroles and cards, and at home, they imagined, there would be more control in their parenting and estranged in-laws still active in their lives. Despite this lack of guided ritual for their loss, the majority continued in seeking strength in familiar spaces through collective worship.

In listening carefully to their stories, it became clear that they found communal religious spaces to be deeply moving emotional worlds for the accomplishment of sacred divorce work. Many, like Laurie and Sue, also found this collective power in support groups and conferences for the divorced. Their narratives present these shared rituals as having tangible body and feeling effects, as persuasive emotional communal space where they accomplished private sacred work through familiar emotional scripts. Performances in these group spaces demonstrated to self and others that they had done the work of recovery, that they had learned how to make life partnership healthy and long lasting.[1] Ritual theorists have long argued that individual connection through group practice can induce subjective sensations of being part of a larger force; for example Rudolf Otto's (1958 [1923]) "the numinous," and Émile Durkheim's (1996 [1912]) "collective effervescence." Randall Collins (2004, 39) reminds us that this "socially derived emotional energy, as Durkheim says, is a feeling of confidence, courage to take action, boldness in taking initiative. It is a morally suffused energy; it makes the individual feel not only good, but exalted, with the sense of doing what is most important and most valuable." In my respondents' moral performances of individual emotion work, there is the echo of divorce-work scripts whose cultural weight is activated through the alone/together nature of communal practice.[2]

"I PICKED MYSELF UP"

Natalie was a pastor's daughter raised in a Church of God in Christ [COGIC] church in a small southern town. Her place as a "first family" member carried great congregational status, a position threatened when she left her husband. I attended services at a church similar in size and character to Natalie's, where the first family had designated seats in the front of the church. During a special meal after one Sunday service, I sat with the congregation, all of us eating on paper plates, while the first family dined at a table in the front of the room eating fried chicken, sweet potatoes, and pies and cakes on china. Natalie had become pregnant at the age of nineteen and, as a first family member, felt the disapproving eyes of the congregation.

The father of her baby was also a pastor's son, a "first family" member at a nearby COGIC church. Without question, they quickly married: "We thought that's what you do if you are pregnant." The marriage lasted thirteen years, and they had two children. When the marriage ended, Natalie felt the eyes of the congregation on her again. Her story, at forty-five years of age, was proudly told. Her narrative was of a completed divorce journey: she had remarried, found a steady job at a bank, and saw herself as "spiritually mature."

Natalie identified as a "private person," especially as she went through the divorce, crediting this to her primary socialization: "We were always taught in my family that whatever goes on in the actual family stays there. So you couldn't go out and say, my mom and dad got in an argument." Her parents kept the children out of their issues; in fact, she had only recently learned that her father, a COGIC minister married for fifty years, had had an affair and she had a brother she had never met.

In her narrative, she talked about engaging in years of serious reflection and Bible study to make sense of what went wrong in her first marriage. "So you've got two preacher kids that have a baby. They got married thinking they were doing right. They don't train you, though. You don't know how to be a wife at twenty. I didn't even know how to be a momma—come on!" She came to understand that she had not been prepared to be a wife as God intended. In Natalie's story, her spiritual stage influenced her decision to end the marriage: "I'm going to be honest and say my faith wasn't where it is now. My walk with Christ wasn't where it is now." The years of transition were also difficult for her, trying to pay her bills, see her children, and find peace with her situation: "I do believe that when you are at your lowest, that is when you can hear God the most. When you are at a point and you've done cried and you can't cry anymore, . . . you say, God help me. . . . my kids always ate. My car note always got paid." She understood God as present, providing for her at every stage and difficult step along the way. God sent "angels," people who helped her, like the manager in the fast food restaurant where she worked who had also been divorced and who gave her a thousand dollars, "no questions," to help her.

Through her most difficult emotional times, Natalie never stopped going to services, even though she felt the threat of social shame, especially as a first family and choir member: "I got out of the choir. . . . It is okay to praise God, it is okay to worship, but I felt like I wasn't the example that a young girl should look at, . . . but I never missed a Sunday unless I was sick because I knew, at some point, that if I pray it hard enough God is going to heal this broken heart that I have." By sitting in the pews with the other members, and knowing that God was always there for her as an unconditional emotional support, she found the threat of congregational shame softening: "I felt like I wasn't looked upon as much out of the choir. I felt like I wasn't talked about as much. When you do things in certain positions, they [the congregation] believe you should sit down." She had hoped that those sitting in the pews would offer some indication that they were praying for her, she craved acknowledgment of healing energy from other congregants' emotion work, but ultimately they didn't know how: "It was a lack of understanding. They didn't know that they can pray for me and still love me. It doesn't mean we have to agree with what she [a woman divorcing] is doing . . . ; they didn't know how to address, didn't know how to come to me, didn't know how to approach it."

Despite their silence, going to church every week provided her with private ritual space where she felt the power of religious emotion that gave her the "strength to go on." Sitting in the pews, listening to the blaring sound of the electric piano accompanied by clapping and singing and swaying bodies summoned emotions from her body in a familiar way. Her story demonstrates a claiming of sacred single position post-divorce as she makes time and claims the space for God to come to her through the music and the preaching. He would "hit" her and "pour" restorative energy into her body, providing fuel for painful emotion work.

KAY: When you say that you found God in services, what did that feel like?

NATALIE: [*Her eyes get teary.*] It felt like somebody was really with me that I knew was with me but I didn't know how to recognize it?

KAY: Like physically with you? [*She starts crying.*] You don't have to go there if you don't want to.

NATALIE: That, even when I don't feel good and even when I'm sad or mad, I had this feeling one day that He was with me. Like this. [*She grabs my wrists with her hand and sort of jolts me.*]

KAY: Holding on to you.

NATALIE: Yea, somebody can tell you it's hot, it's hot, it's hot. Don't touch that, it's hot, don't touch that, it's hot, but his mind is going to keep going there until he actually touches it. He don't know that it's hot. I know God, but until I

actually allowed Him to touch me, remembered He is not going to force him-
self, it was like touch me God but, mmmm, help me God but, mmmmm. . . .
[*She grabs my wrist each mmm with a jolt.*] If you've never really experienced
God, you don't know. Experience Him once and then you will know.

Natalie's emotions during the separation and ending process were a blur of
powerful feelings. She was distracted at first and did a lot of "clubbing," but
presented herself as always coming back to God, finding him every Sunday
in church through music and worship: "I tried to find peace. I tried to find
comfort through other things. Honestly, I'd go to the club until 3 a.m. Saturday night and would be in church at 11 o'clock. I could be out till 3 a.m.,
lie down for a minute, take a shower, go to church. . . . I'd tell people, if I
keep going to church, one day a light bulb is going to go off and I'm going to
listen. One day I'm going to find a real peace and, when I find that, I don't
care what people say about me, and I'm going to come and, God, you love
me for who I am." After months of sitting in the pews letting God come into
her and working through feelings of guilt, disappointment, and fear of how
to move forward, she returned to the choir: "When I got back in the choir,
I picked myself up."

Natalie was willing to tell me her story at this point in her life, perhaps
because she could offer a performance of sacred single journey, of having accomplished the emotion work of divorce, of "picking herself up," of
having moved from pain to purpose, from injury to a new, stronger self
through divine assistance. In fact, she made clear that she did not want to
revisit the divorce, but agreed because she understood that it might help
somebody to hear her story: "If you had come to me a couple of years ago,
I don't know if I could have done this, because I was in an infant stage.
And I'm telling you there is word [scripture] that we are babes. We suck as
babes but, as we grow in Christ, we grow mature, and I saw my point where
I was a babe in Christ." Natalie's religious symbolic world was an important backdrop for the emotion work that pushed her to develop as a more
"mature Christian" and do the marriage work needed to succeed in her new
relationship. At the same time, the perceived gossip and silence she experienced in her congregation produced a heightened sense of aloneness, a
solitary effort to activate divine energy and religious emotion. Being able
to tell a story of repairing social bonds in her religious community and in
family was essential.

Her story featured the development of a strong second marriage, of accomplishing the marriage work of divorce and being able to enter into a healthy partnership. She talked of working hard on her marriage skills after the divorce: "I had to say, okay, God I want to be stronger, I want to move higher. I want to be the best wife I can be. . . . Me and my husband, we don't have fusses and fights. We may have a disagreement, and I'm going to say, Baby, I'm mad, and he says, I'm mad too. And we talk about it." She had even reconciled with her ex-husband: "I was able to finally go to my ex-husband and say I'm sorry. As a matter of fact, we are really good friends. Sometimes when I'm going through something, I have this husband here but I have this other man that loves me, that loves my kids, that, even when I got married to this man here, he [her ex] said, I've got your back, are you okay, are you happy?" Being able to communicate well is a sacred skill: "I'm learning communication is of God. God helps you." Natalie ended our time together with a pledge to keep moving forward, become a better individual: "I am who I am today because of what I had to go through; . . . every disappointment, every struggle made me the strong person I am now. I don't know it all [and] even now I'm still learning. I'm learning who I am at forty-five. Remember I'm not the same person that I was at forty-four. . . . Some of it didn't come from books; it came from fasting, praying, asking God to [make me] be a better person, help me. . . . I know God loves me for who I am. That keeps me moving."

She may have stepped down from the choir, but she did not remove herself from the awe-inspiring potential of music in a Pentecostal service. Music was a valuable religious tool of restoration, across traditions, one that both subdued and incited intense emotion.[3] Music's importance for divorce work in black church settings was unmistakable. Not surprising, given music's distinctive force in African American religious history. C. E. Lincoln and Lawrence H. Mamiya (1990, 346) note that "music, or, more precisely, *singing* is second only to preaching as the magnet of attraction and the primary vehicle of spiritual transport for the worshiping congregation." In the black church services I attended, music was central, constant, and full of emotion. Worship times always began with energetic "praise" songs that prepared sacred space. Even during sermons, musicians worked in harmony with pastors—playing softly under their words, building intensity as the sermon grew more passionate, and then softening again as the ministers wiped sweat from their brows. Black Baptist services had more musical down time than the Pentecostal worship, although some of the Baptist services I attended had adopted what members named a more Pentecostal praise style regarding music and congregational response.

In Pentecostal services, people stood during a great deal of the service, letting the music and prayer move their bodies. Divorced members referred to such energy as facilitating a close, emotion-filled relationship with God that affirmed their sacred single position. Pentecostal women like Natalie were especially articulate about physical union with the divine through group and individual worship. Their stories reflect a distinct Pentecostal idea of individuals' relationship with God that is "first and foremost an experiential" movement (MacRobert 1988, 191). One divorced Pentecostal woman who had attended Baptist services argued, "I'm not going to say we have a stronger belief, but we tend to go into God more, meaning we communicate with Him in prayer and praise, so you know that helps. . . . I would say, when I empty myself before God and once I'm empty, I just feel a presence of warmth and His love, like, you know, I can just feel like He's there. It's almost just like you are loving somebody and you can feel Him there." Another woman described: "It's unexplainable; you can't describe it. It's just that you know that you feel His presence, you feel Him lifting the burden, you feel cleaned, you feel comforted, you feel peace, and you know that He is pouring His spirit into you. . . . It [worship] is where I gained my strength from—releasing my cares, my fears, my concerns over to the Lord. I was given the opportunity to pour out to him and let him pour back into me." In their stories, this familiar exchange of energy with God through music invited calm and the management of painful feelings. Such religious emotion affirmed identity as someone who is loved in an intimate physical manner, which soothed threats of divorce as marring religious status with God and community.

Most of the Pentecostal women, like other conservative Christians I interviewed, used the concept of *brokenness* and turned to major ideas in liberation theology. The divorced came to God through worship and prayer, shattered and feeling marginalized, and in their stories the communal power leads them to accomplish critical private emotion work. As with other conservative Christian approaches, ultimate security does not originate from earthly goods and relationships, but from God's promise of a better world to come and from intimate relationship with the divine in this world. Central to the formation of black church communities is the institution of slavery and subsequent racism and acculturation in a white Protestant culture. Thus, redemption and deliverance are key theological concepts, as is an understanding of God as highly active in individuals' lives and the social world. To be sick, to be broken and need healing, is center stage in COGIC churches where bodies—through physical praise, dance, speaking in tongues–are routinely restored to health. Jeff's story below shows the sacred single script emerging in black church space. Injury does not demean; rather it humbles and pushes a personal path to salvation through collective worship and intimate relationship with God.

"Coming Home"

Jeff was in his late forties and had been divorced three times. The first marriage ended eighteen years before, and the most recent a few years before our interview, which took place at his church after Sunday services. His narrative felt complete, beginning with a story of grief that included loss of children and the death of his grandmother, of being "broken" by these deep kin losses, and then of growing into a stronger person, ultimately finding purpose in a new role as pastoral counselor and active noncustodial father of his teenage children. When I spoke with him, he was making a solid middle-class professional salary and had become an associate part-time pastor in the small southern urban black Baptist church he had attended most of his life. His narrative seemed well rehearsed, a performance of self that I imagined he shared frequently with others. His story was frenetic, moving back and forth between divorces and jumping ahead in time without explanation; it was almost like music itself, it had its own rhythm.

Jeff had experienced several types of loss over the years: spousal companionship, time with his children born from the first two marriages, and the loss of biological kin through death. He talked about each of his marriages, but the climax of his narrative was of extreme emotions and actions when his second wife asked him to leave, which occurred after several relatives had died, and on the night his grandmother died:

> I had six family members die in a seven-month period. I remember going to see my grandmother at the hospital. She said to me, "As long as you are who you are, you will always have a roof over your head." And I did not know what she was talking about. She gave me a kiss and went to sleep and did not wake up. I got home that night and there was a letter on the table from my wife

telling me to get out. And the first thing that went through my head was, How did she [grandmother] know? So I moved into my grandmother's house. . . . Six months passed; I got fired from my job; I sat up in that house and lost track of time . . . did not know the month or day.

The end of his second marriage and concurrent family deaths led to loss of employment and threatened social shame as his social position as parent, husband, congregant, and worker changed. He hid in his grandmother's house in what he described as a long and confusing liminal state. An effort to see his daughter brought a turning point in his story. One night, after seven months of isolation, he came to church to pick up his daughter for a rare visit. As he approached the church, he did not walk in but rather cracked a door and yelled inside for his daughter. A long-time female pastoral counselor walked down the hall to greet him; he entered the church for the first time since his breakdown; and they ended up talking for hours about what had happened in his life—a spiritual and therapeutic conversation that he saw as pivotal in healing and coping with a paralyzing and highly chaotic state of being.

In his narrative, Jeff confronts and works on his emotions with help from a pastoral counselor, but only after intense grieving and emotional trauma that came with the end of each marriage. He draws from a Christian script of brokenness and then rebirth, his recovery facilitated by the power of spiritual music in a familiar religious space that prompted expressivity: "I basically sat in there on the left side and cried, every time I came to the service. No matter what sermon it was, I cried; no matter what song it was, I cried. I cried because I didn't have a marriage anymore. . . . I couldn't get it out of my system. . . . I was crying because my daughter, I was missing her. . . . Coming here and reestablishing my faith, being restored, I was crying because I didn't believe people loved me."

He understood music in this familiar sanctuary as helping him to shed the tears that drove out painful feelings. Still, he was aware of the presence of others, some who judged him harshly. He described people he had known for years, extended kin and close biological family members, "watching him" carefully as he sat grief-stricken in his pew. It was hard for Jeff to have his mother watch him, to witness his breakdowns during services. They both knew that he might move forward, or take steps back: "It's like which way are you going to grow? Do you come out with a hard, tarnished heart or are you going to come out with a heart so vulnerable to love that God can just use you?"

Jeff also tried secular counseling, risking an additional type of social shame with older family and church members who composed the majority of members in his home church: "You're in church, you're in counseling. In the African American society and you're going to counseling—their old way of thinking, you're going to the nut house, . . . you're crazy—so you sneak into counseling," although "it's more open now, we are more educated. It's a good thing now." But ultimately he describes his encounter with a secular counselor as falling short. The counselors "could not understand how to deal with the principles on a spiritual basis." They would ask him, "Why do you feel this way?" He would answer, "Because I'm following Christ." Therapists challenged him, "Do you believe in putting your faith all in one creature or one belief?" He replied, "What's wrong with ya'll?"

Jeff's story moved back and forth in time, describing marriages, losses, and his search for therapeutic relationships, but, throughout his narrative, congregational worship, close relationship with God, and music emerged as the essential instruments for working on his emotions:

> The one that pierced my heart in the ministry was "Consecrate Me." I broke down like a baby when I heard that. And now just about any love ballads, like, "Jesus, Jesus, Jesus . . . Jesus is his name; Healer, Healer, Healer, Jesus is his name . . . Savior, Savior, Savior"—and that was something they had played on the radio too. And I would break down and cry. . . . You get to the point your heart is just so broken, almost anything can touch it and that when you know you are there. Believe it or not He said, 'Seek not thy own understanding,' because, . . . when you are at the point where it's like cut the wrist, turn off the lights and shock me down to sleep. That's when the whole world opens up.

Before and after Jeff's religious awakening, he found himself in and out of court working on custody and financial issues regarding his children. At one point he described, "I was going to court and they [both ex-wives] were tearing me apart and I didn't care anymore." His two ex-spouses became friends and hired the same lawyer. He recalled walking out of the courtroom and his son's mother threatening, "I'm going to destroy you." Jeff expressed great regret for his children's suffering, and feelings of deep loss that came from not fathering. He talked about grasping whatever time he could get with the children, over the years while they resided with their mothers, and described painful years going by when he could not touch or come near them. In his narrative, as he became more mature in his emotional and religious life and the children grew older, forgiveness and reunion ultimately followed: "My daughter will be twenty-one this year. I had not heard from her in seven months. She called me just recently to say, 'I love you.' I asked her if she was okay and she said, 'Yes.' I said, 'You are starting to see some things, aren't you?' She said yes and I told her I was always there for her." Jeff's story culminates with his strong identification as a pastoral counselor and associate pastor, roles in which he routinely helps others manage family dynamics through separation and divorce, and as an involved, noncustodial father who has learned to be present emotionally for his children.

Jeff relied on community worship as restorative space where he could do the emotion work of divorce, even as he felt social shame and heard people gossiping about his ability to let God heal him and to be a leader in the congregation. In Jeff's narrative, as in Natalie's, the collective emotional force of group worship in long-familiar sacred space overcame threats of social shame that might have pushed him away from the community. In fact, he used that force to repair religious bonds, eventually becoming a deacon and an associate pastor in the church, despite the disturbing whispers of disapproval from some members: "He's divorced, not stable." Jeff emphasized, "You don't give up, you keep pushing." A similar claiming of valuable religious space in the face of gossip and shame can be heard in Alice's story.

"My Church"

Alice, a black Baptist respondent, continued to attend her home church after her husband of twenty years left her for a younger woman. Alice was an administrative assistant with a BA in sociology, and her ex-husband was a successful local business owner. They had one daughter, who was seventeen when they separated. Alice's story culminated in an emotional outburst at church that risked additional social shame but in the end seemed to further secure her bonds with the congregation.

Like most of my respondents who identified as having been left, Alice made clear that she had a profound commitment to companionate marriage as sacred. People are supposed to "stick to marriage," she told me, even in the hardest of times. Still, in telling her story, she admitted that there had been problems in her marriage, but she had not suspected at first that her husband was cheating on her. She turned to her pastor so that she could do the marriage work needed to save her relationship, but she found the pastor's advice unreasonable: "I'm an aggressive person, assertive, and he told me that to save my marriage I had to become more submissive!" This made little sense to Alice: how could she become "submissive" since this wasn't who she was, and since, besides, she saw marriage as mutual and egalitarian.[4]

She described herself as a "basket-case," "shocked," someone feeling like her whole world was coming apart when she discovered her husband had been seeing a woman who was not a church member. Alice was embarrassed; the congregation was a close community, she was in the choir and spent a lot of time helping at the church, and almost everyone who attended services knew that her husband had left her. Music and prayer were familiar religious emotion work tools that brought tangible results in the first weeks and months after her husband left: "I prayed all the time, I had to hold onto something." In fact, she made up her own personal prayer for strength to keep herself together. She prayed in the morning and night on her knees; she prayed at the office at her desk. She demonstrated for me: her palms came together, her eyes closed, and she took a deep breath. She prayed for strength, reciting, as many respondents did, the Serenity Prayer[5] to help calm feelings of loss of control.

Music helped hold her emotions in check, for awhile. For example, in the choir she sang a song that signified she was not alone in experiencing her feelings of anger and betrayal: "The Battle Is Not Yours, It's the Lord's" (lyrics by Michael McKay). She listened to McKay's song on the radio as well; the lyrics read, in part: "There is no pain Jesus can't feel, no hurt he cannot heal. . . . No matter what you're going through, remember God is using you. For the battle is not yours, it's the Lord's." Another song she found powerful was "Stand," with lyrics that read, in part: "How do you handle the guilt of your past? Tell me, how do you deal with the shame? And how can you smile while your heart has been broken and filled with pain? . . . When there's nothing left to do, you just stand. Watch the Lord see you through." To Alice, God was her immanent provider, the receptacle for her feelings and troubles, whose power she felt intensely as she sat in the choir, staring at the stained glass and pews in front of her, where as a child she had first felt divine force.

Soon after her husband moved out, he started showing up for services with his girlfriend. Alice became increasingly bitter and angry as she and the whole congregation watched him walk in and worship beside his new love. She did not want to see them on Sunday mornings as she worshipped, but she could not bear to leave her grandfather's church where she was highly active and embedded in social networks. She felt a deep attachment to the church building, which had a long and proud history of being one of the first black churches in the area. She described singing on Sundays, and constant daily prayer protected her "core" as increased acrimony threatened her "sanity." Alice became more and more resolute about claiming her worship space. The climax of her story was an emotional release during worship. It was an event that she said demonstrated the unpredictable and serious nature of her anger and resentment; at the same time, it was a valiant performance of defending sacred space. The following description is from my interview notes, as she requested I not tape the interview:

> Alice "lost it" during one Sunday morning service, something she said she should not have done. Her husband kept coming to church each week with the woman whom Alice had suspected he was having an affair with for many years while they were still married. Alice was sitting in the choir, singing, facing the congregation, and the anger kept building up inside her. During the part of the service where visitors were introduced and people greeted each other and "mingled," with organ music playing in the background, Alice went down from the choir and "right over" to the woman and told her that she was a "whore" and that she "had nerve coming to this church." Alice then went back and sat with the choir. Her ex-husband stormed into the vestibule and told the men gathered that Alice should be "arrested or kept away from the church."

Alice made clear to me that this was not her ex-husband's family church, and that he had become a member of the church more recently. Alice's father and grandfather were both very active in the church and she had worshipped alongside her sister and her mother in these pews since she had been a small child. It was her church; even though she soon heard that some people wanted her removed from working with committees because of what happened, she remained in this church, sitting in her pew every Sunday and singing in the choir. Alice said the outburst was wrong, but served as an example of the dangerous potential of her emotions that she was actively trying to manage through services and a Christian counselor and her support group.

Natalie, Jeff, and Alice demonstrate how individual divorce work was accomplished in black church religious space through community ritual, despite the respondents' feeling that others were disapproving of their actions or life choices. Their engagement in collective worship was a performance that assuaged embarrassment. Although level and type of social shame was different in more liberal congregations, similar dynamics of accomplishing solitary divorce work through group worship surfaced. Many of my Jewish respondents described synagogue services as providing a critical space for navigation of sacred passage.

Rebirthing

Karen was a white Jewish woman in her forties who worked in a professional position with a nonprofit organization. Her marriage of fifteen years had recently ended. She described the divorce experience as death and brokenness: "It is totally a death and it takes a grieving process and it takes support and it affects you like a death. . . . People really need to be treated during the divorce like it's a death. It's a very hard time. . . . You are broken." As her marriage came apart and her college-age child lost interest in attending services at synagogue, Karen left the Conservative synagogue where her son had had his bar mitzvah and joined a Jewish Renewal synagogue that she described as spiritual, with "great music."

Synagogue services, musical from start to finish, resonated in memory for most of my Jewish respondents. Jeffrey Summit (2000, 25–26) describes the central Jewish worship experience: "Jewish prayer is sacred text performed. . . . At times the leader solos, at times the congregation sings a melody along with the leader, at times all the participants are 'doing their own thing.'; . . . the whole congregation is an orchestra, praising and petitioning God." The music "lifts the worshipper out of the ordinary world, transforming both the individual and the community" (102). My Jewish respondents offered vivid stories of participating in this virtual orchestra so as to calm emotion, repair self, and connect to Jewish community and ancestors. Karen described music and meditation in services that represented private yet communal ritual: "Songs, music, chanting, bringing the community together. We sing out loud, really loud and spirited. And it shifts me from being caught in the pettiness in my brain, of going around and around, to just resonating inside my body. And then I shift and then we do a mediation of the certain prayer, the *Amidah,* and I just go into the

Amidah and I do my own private words." Karen made clear that she did not talk with people at her new temple about the separation; still, the congregation's musical spirit gave her energy to return to parenting a teenager and handling a demanding full-time job.

Saturday morning services routinely served as an emotional tool to make sense of feelings as her marriage ended: "I found the weekly portion of the Torah was unbelievably parallel to what I was going through. Whatever the Torah portion was at the time, I could identify, whether it was in Egypt and you are going through narrow straits, or whatever the weekly portion. . . . It was mind-boggling how much I could just read into that and say, oh, my God, look at this." Her new synagogue became a critical space for her to embrace her Jewish identity and do the work of self reflection: "I found myself in this safe haven of nurturance that was not alien or alienating. . . . How did I get through it [the divorce]? . . . Knowing every single Saturday I had a place. And this was over a long period of time, because when my marriage was failing I had to get out of my house. . . . [*She is on the edge of tears.*] My husband is a very decent man. . . . I wasn't angry. . . . I mean, some people paint or write poetry, or some people go hiking. For me, Saturday morning was going to shul and just having that whole, being surrounded in that spiritual environment."

She described the rabbi at this Jewish Renewal synagogue provoking feelings through guided meditation during services: "The Rosh Hashanah before I decided to talk [with my husband] about leaving, my rabbi did a meditation. He had us strip ourselves of all our clothes and step into water, and then the message from God that he said is 'You are loved.' And I broke down and I could not stop crying and that was when I decided to get the divorce." In her story, Jewish themes of death and rebirth came together in services to bring emotional resolution: "So it was a big deal; it came from being in the synagogue. And I knew, I knew that was the turning point. It was on Yom Kippur of that year, it was just all about rebirthing—a really big deal. At that time, I needed to forgive myself."

Karen's approach to ending was a creative mixture of Jewish renewal synagogue worship, traditional Jewish ritual and practice, and feminist ritual approaches. After receiving the *get*, Karen made an appointment at Mayyim Hayyim, described on its webpage (http://www.mayyimhayyim.org/) as a mikvah and family education center where "the spiritually diverse needs of 21st century Jews are met by reclaiming the ancient tradition of immersing in the mikv[a]h." Mikvah immersion is traditionally used for conversion and female ritual cleansing after menstruation or childbirth, but some contemporary mikvot have been refashioned to fit individual spiritual pursuits and community marking of passages. Ceremonies can be private, with the assistance of a mikvah guide, or with friends and family. Karen created her own community mikvah ritual. She described her experience with the "living waters:"

> I just had one very powerful experience, and that was getting prepared. You really have to do everything, and I looked in the mirror, and I either heard a voice that said [*her voice gets very soft*] either "You are loved" or "You are beautiful," one of those two things, and it was really incredible.
>
> But the actual immersion in the water, I don't know if I was nervous or uncomfortable . . . or if the guide. . . . I just didn't connect with her. . . . I was nervous. I mean, I remember the day, I remember everything very clearly, but I remember feeling strange going into the mikvah, into the water. It was just a strange feeling. It felt cold. It wasn't. . . . I didn't feel warm and fuzzy. I got my warm and fuzzy from my friends and the community, after. You know, doing that alone is pretty intense.

In Karen's story, the ritual immersion was not as powerful as her own creative assembling of a spiritual community of women that helped her feel she was truly transitioning: "It was really intense. . . . I walked in and the Rabbi [from her job] was here and when I saw her I felt taken care of. . . . The actual dunking and that experience, I didn't really feel anything; it was afterward, when we sat around, we were all together and we sat outside and we were singing some prayers and singing some songs and we went out to lunch afterward. . . . I just felt so supported and loved by my coworkers. It was great. It was great." Karen, now single with her child moving to college, gathered her own community of Jewish women from her workplace to witness her transition.

Karen described her mikvah ritual as a birth or passage to new life: "I just felt like I had a new beginning, . . . a new beginning for me. It was the end of history, of baggage that I was carrying, and now it was time for me to start emerging as a different person, which is an ongoing process." It was a "birthing process. I emerged having worked through, never completely, but having worked through my coming out [of marriage], my birthing, my going through the mitzraim." She stopped, and then sighed with relief: "Oh, I really need to say that, I'm so glad I said that." Her story reflects the individual emotion work found in larger cultural divorce-work scripts accomplished through Jewish community. "I'm beginning a new life," she told me, "I really deserve to be loved in the way that I deserve to be loved."

Karen was one of several Jewish respondents who described finding deep connections through community rituals and synagogue services.

An Anchor

Jill was a forty-five-year-old white Jewish woman who lived in a middle-to-upper-middle-class suburb outside a major city in the Northeast. Jill had been separated for a significant time, but was still in the process of legal divorce proceedings. Even though her husband had moved out about a year earlier, she was still very much "stuck," as she put it, in the "early stages" of grieving: "I am really grieving. I can't believe how I'm grieving. . . . It's ridiculous—it's too many months—but I'm sure I'll heal." She lamented the loss of her children's presence on a daily basis: "Divorce is very painful, and I don't know if it ever really goes away. Very painful. You expect to have your children for eighteen years and then they go to college, that's the expectation. Now that time has been cut and shortened. . . . It's really the price you pay."

Jill's loss was that of a dream of forever-after that began early in life: "I met him when I was eighteen. We were together since 1981, so it was my expectation that we would be together forever." She talked about being deeply ashamed during the first year as she separated, of speaking to only a select group of friends and family about the divorce. She was perplexed: if divorce was so accepted, why did she feel shame? Like many of my respondents, she spoke with sociological reflection, acknowledging the pressure to emulate a normative family and yet recognizing widespread acceptance of singlehood and divorce, and embracing the idea that she was on some type of journey that would lead to a fulfilling life. Jill decided that shame was her problem and thus something she could work on and rise above for herself and her children.

Given the weight of her emotions, I wondered if her husband had requested the divorce, but she explained, "He moved out. He had had enough. It was a dead marriage. In hindsight, it was dead, done, finished, unhappy, dead. He just had the courage to do it. I would have stayed in the dead marriage for the sake of my children. Because I do believe children want their mom and dad under one roof. It is their greatest wish. I do believe that." Jill's description speaks to the limitations of researchers who use analytical categories in studies of divorce, such as "initiator," "leaver," "left," or describe endings as simply "mutual."[6] What she describes is both mutual and an individual decision to end.

A core thread in her story of Jewish services as an emotional tool for coping with loss and assessing what went wrong in her marriage was the physical death of two family members:

> My husband lost his sister. One year later, I lost my dad. When he lost his sister, he became angry at God, rejected religion, stopped saying Kaddish [*mourner's prayer*] after a very short time. . . . Then I lost my dad suddenly, and then I did Kaddish for eleven months. . . . It made me connect to my dad and it made me heal. My husband was resentful and admits this now, almost jealous that I found something that comforted me, and it was religion. I didn't go off the deep end, I wasn't any more religious or observant, but I went almost every Saturday for eleven months alone, which. . . . I would have liked a spouse with me during that time.

Jill continued to appeal to Jewish tools for facing extreme loss. Friday night Shabbat service was an important practice for her, but it was hard for her to articulate why. She said, "I'm not a hundred percent sure I believe in God. . . . I feel that there is something spiritual above us and I'm very connected to the traditions, very, and to prayer." I asked her if she prayed outside of services, and she responded, "On occasion, rarely." She connected spiritually through routine singing of the psalms and liturgical prayer in services, but when I asked exactly how prayer had helped, the living room grew still. I gave her space to find the words, but the silence grew past bearing and her eyes filled with tears. She said, "I'm O.K.," in a way that told me not to push. Later in the interview, she told me that she got most of her "religious stuff" during services. I decided then to gently probe again about what Shabbat services meant to her: "Do you remember any powerful moments sitting in services?" She became quiet again; her eyes again filled with tears. She looked up to the ceiling. I felt intrusive and changed the subject. Still later, I found one more opening that made probing about Jewish music and prayer possible, but I was cautious in phrasing my question. Jill had been talking to me about how the rabbi in the support group suggested that they use the Passover story to think about their own divorce as a journey from bondage to freedom. I asked her if there were any other ways that Judaism had helped. "That's a hard question," she answered. "I don't know if you can put that into words. It's an anchor." She paused, and then, "It's . . . an anchor, it's something to go back to, to go home to." Again she found it hard to speak, and indicated that she really did not want to go where my questions were taking her. I changed the subject again, but later reintroduced: "What do you appreciate most about services?" She answered: "Some of the prayers that I remember from childhood. I have a strong Hebrew background, and the rabbi's words always move me, hardly ever fail to move me. He is so moving. He is incredible, very special." Singing prayers and psalms in services, that is, connected her to her ethnic religious identity and provided a way, through traditional Hebrew prayers and tunes, to feel grounded.

The power of Jewish liturgical music combined with a deep connection to tradition produced highly meaningful worship for many Jewish respondents. Lynn Davidman (1991, 93–94) writes about women who were attracted to a modern Orthodox synagogue and who spoke of "missing a 'core,' a sense of being rooted in some firm, stable, and clearly defined way of being"; Davidman argues that "what they found so moving and attractive about the service was the singing, the songs. . . . There was a feeling of partaking of something rich and enduring." Through music, they were "put in touch with the Jewish people, past and present." Jeffrey A. Summit (2000) notes of Jewish worship, "The tune, separate from the words, serves as a portal to the past, a connection with ancestors, real and imagined" (33). Jill talked about feeling this deep ancestral and ethnic familial connection while surrounded by people who knew almost nothing about her family situation, and in a synagogue where it was mostly two-parent families with children who attended Shabbat services.

Respondents from other traditions talked about music and prayer in congregations as group practices that helped them do grief work. Martha, a white Catholic woman who was a cantor and an active member of a parish choir described singing as her "refuge" from divorce, as "not an escape" but, rather, where she knew she was "in touch" with herself: "I was most connected to who I was—the core of who I was." Respondents from the UU spoke of a similar use of music to aid in divorce work; my respondent

Sandy found the song *"Spirit of Life"* summoned Unitarian connectedness to a "web of being" that helped her cope with loss. Elaine, a professional musician and member of Sandy's UU church, closed her eyes and took deep breaths before telling me that singing had given her the strength to leave an enervating marriage, and had sustained her as she built a new life. She described singing in the choir and outside of church as "swimming around in God." The old church piano and the acoustics in the historic chapel had emotional resonance for her; music continually connected her to the congregation, where few actually spoke with her about the divorce.

Finally, like Laurie and Sue, many of my respondents found small groups and conferences for the divorced effective emotion workspace.

SMALL GROUPS AND ALONE WORK

BENEFITS OF A SUPPORT GROUP

- A person can discover "I am not alone."
- Feelings are validated.
- Coping skills are learned.
- Meetings can provide structure.
- A better understanding of the universality of grief is provided.
- Each person is allowed to "just be" wherever s/he is at.
- [The group] helps develop personal growth during this phase of life's journey.
- Time and space to tell one's story are available.
- One's giftedness is reaffirmed.
- Deepening [occurs] of an awareness of the "God-in-me." (CDM support group brochure, 2007)

Small groups are capable of producing intense levels of emotional energy and are a widespread religious tool in contemporary U.S. society for emotional labor.[7] Small groups provide friendship, close kin-like networks, community identity, mentorship, and ritualized space for emotional labor. In these spaces, therapeutic and religious beliefs regarding emotion work are made real through religious rituals of telling individual narratives, of song, and of prayer.[8] In small groups, expression of suffering brings a level of energy and excitement. Such groups are exceptionally able to reproduce collective emotional energy as individuals share their stories; religious tools like prayer and music through collective energy turn telling one's story into moral pursuit and a shaping of a moral self.[9]

I found small divorce groups in some form in all traditions, although many of my respondents were not aware of such groups and a handful of Catholics and Jews said they did not have such opportunities in their area. Most groups met during the week, sometimes in homes or local community buildings outside the congregation. As the excerpt I have quoted here from a support group brochure indicates, individual emotion work, growth, and the search for divine energy within were promoted as to be cultivated with others in a similar situation. A 1990 press release advertising a CDM support group in a local paper states that, in the group, "through mutual support, individuals rediscover their inner resources and are able to go on with their lives as whole persons." Laurie's account in chapter 2 well demonstrates investment in the creation of one's narrative of divorce work, and how the telling of that story in the group can give life to individual narratives of moral self. Some of my respondents also found community and new friendships through participation in these groups, but their stories were centered more squarely on the emotion work and relative skill building these collective spaces facilitated.

Jill, for example, talked about being "extremely private" about her divorce for a long period of time, but finding "an incredible support system," a network of close friends from a Jewish healing divorce-support group, as well as family members, with whom she could express her feelings. Jill participated in two Jewish healing groups. She described the first as a place where she did the initial "stages of grieving," crying and talking about the ending of what she had thought was a relationship for life. She credited the woman rabbi and social worker facilitating the group with having orchestrated just the right blend of Jewish song, meditation, and psychology.

She said the rabbi was open to working with people no matter where they were on their "path" to healing, letting them experience and nurture their emotions: "She validated the anger so beautifully." The rabbi began meetings "with a song or a poem or a prayer and closed with one," and sometimes would orchestrate a meditation that would "hit a nerve" and make Jill cry. One meditation stood out in Jill's memory; it was "about resting on someone's shoulders" and it was the Hebrew that, she said, got to her: "Don't know why, but I guess it was just the language and . . . [the rabbi's] input in terms of connecting Judaism to having a divorce and a *get* and maybe a mik-vah thrown in, and the whole cleansing thing." Embraced in this emotional energy, group participants were urged to talk about their own experiences, to tell stories that revealed feelings. The rabbi, Jill stressed, was very good at getting to the "feelings of divorce." She recalled group rituals during the early months of transition as powerful: "In the last session she held each of us and blessed us to heal, which was nice and extremely emotional. . . . Maybe we did [a ritual] holding hands. I don't remember. I was in bad shape then. It was a blur, I was in very bad shape; . . . nine months since I had separated, I wasn't in great shape." The social worker "balanced the rabbi's religious approach," providing therapeutic expertise and knowledge regard-ing emotions: "She explained things, why they were happening, why we were feeling a certain way, why stuff was happening psychologically. It was very interesting and very helpful. Great combination." The support group then gave Jill scripts to name the dynamic nature of her divorce grief: "I've worked hard on this. It's not a death. I have experienced death, my dad and another younger close relative. This is not a death. Those people are gone forever. . . . My ex-husband is still on this earth, very much alive, thank God. I don't wish him illness, and he's not gone from this earth. I can still see him and hear him, and sometimes I don't want to. . . . I am griev-ing some death of a relationship and a marriage and a dream, but not of a human being."

Support groups were also spaces where respondents were able to tell stories of selves engaged in co-parenting, working on ethical approaches to relationships with ex-spouses, and/or finding direction and strategies for sustaining relationships with in-laws and stepchildren. Parenting post-divorce brought frequent interaction with ex-spouses, as well as unfamiliar and nascent cultural expectations. Jill, for example, talked with me about expecting to do the work of negotiating a happy day for her son's bar mitz-vah and figuring out her relationship to her ex-spouse's biological family. Frustrated by the persistent sting of sadness, loss, and worry about her children, she followed the advice of the rabbi and social worker closely and joined for a second series in their Jewish healing support group. Grief, she told me, as she wiped tears from her cheek, needs time: "It's ridiculous. It's too many months . . . but I'm sure I'll heal." The group was a therapeutic and spiritual space where she could accomplish the individual emotional labor for self, children, and family.

In her story, the support group grew mystical: "I will tell you something that is pretty intense. . . . The two other people in the support group had the same names as my close relatives who had died. . . . It didn't hit me till weeks later. . . . Rabbi said it's *besherit*—two people to catch me." The Hebrew word *besherit* translates as "meant to be"; thus her use of the concept seemed to endow the people and the support group with mystical force. Jill had formed what she thought would be enduring friendships, connections that could push her to what she saw as an advanced stage of healing: "We've formed our own mini support group on our own; . . . we do have fun and laughs. . . . I don't want to go back to a place where I'm talking about all that sad stuff, I don't want to be there talking about this . . . for ever and ever; let's hope I won't. It will be a piece of me, an experience, but I hope to not make this my focus, my project. That's the goal; I'm not there yet." The group was helping her to work on the task at hand: to complete grief and marriage work and then move forward.

Jewish support groups in community settings like Jewish social services were careful about the level of religious practice they incorporated; still, they introduced religious tools to collective practice. One rabbi who ran such a group talked about trying to "bring Jewish wisdom, but making [the group] open to all Jews by being a bit generic." Generic for her meant providing optional resources—for example, providing participants with a list of Psalms that they could engage or not. She asked them to look at the list and see if there was one that spoke to them that evening. She then invited them to "share" why they picked a verse. In this way, she could "bring up a lot of spiritual questions and issues at work, in a nonthreatening way." She saw the exercise as a "process of bringing them to the spiritual," inviting the group together to approach the Psalms as poetry. In this way, explicit religious language was transformed into a more secular creative practice.

Jamie, a black Baptist pastor, held a grief Bible study class that united divine energy, prayer, and therapeutic discourse. He used David A. Seamands's (1981) book and workbook, *Healing for Damaged Emotions*. Seamands, a United Methodist pastor who taught at Ashbury Theological Seminary, stresses that being born again or "filled with the Spirit" will not "automatically" take care of "emotional hang-ups": accepting Jesus "is not a shortcut to emotional health" (12). Jamie drew from Seamonds's discourse, crafting a space where people could do the "hard work" that brought emotional health alongside Jesus's healing. He gave an example of a minister from another congregation who was having difficult financial times, had lost an appeal for joint custody of his baby, and then lost his job as pastor and thus his reputation in the community because of the divorce. Through the grief class, together with others who shared similar types of social shame, Jamie said, this man "reach[ed] a place of wholeness." Jamie stressed the importance of letting people talk about their experiences in the group, and then the key to healing, his therapeutic method, was "soaking this [expression of experience] in prayer."

DivorceCare's video and support group method encouraged individuals to tell their stories after prayer, and viewing the session video. The DivorceCare group I attended took place on the second floor of a large United Methodist church, in a Sunday school classroom. We began each meeting with standing in a circle holding hands in prayer, and then sat in chairs in a semicircle to watch the thirty-minute video session. During one group I attended, a woman cried quietly during an entire session. Crying as sacred expressive practice was felt by all attending, but we were also aware that self work in the group was controlled and monitored. DivorceCare, like secular support groups, had rules about expression of feelings: no "spouse-bashing," profanity, or blaming one's ex for the ending. The video messages also modeled this type of moral storytelling. During one session, a woman in her early twenties was harsh when speaking about her ex-husband. Disapproval from group members was unspoken, but palpable, and she did not return.

In most of the support groups, members were advised not to date other members. This was made very clear in a DivorceCare video series that stressed that serious individual emotion work necessitated avoiding distractions. Small groups were places where people could name and express their individual brokenness among others, but too much intimacy was discouraged. This taboo was reflected in the moral stories they told. Still, several respondents, across traditions, reported dating group members, and at the end of a DivorceCare focus group I conducted, two people who had gone through the program admitted to me that they were now married. The three people who told me stories of falling in love with a member of their support group did so in guarded ways and almost always at the end of interviews. One woman revealed this by accident in an interview, saying "Oh, I can't believe I just said that," and indicated that I should not tell anyone.

Todd saw a piece I had published online featuring early analysis and divorce resources. He had been through a DivorceCare group and other small group ministry programs in evangelical churches. At the time, he was struggling to establish a support group for people who were in the later stages of dealing with divorce, a phase he saw as essential for working on individual issues that might keep them from succeeding in future relationships. He wanted to know if I had knowledge of potential grants for his project. I had little in the way of funding ideas, but he agreed to meet with me and tell me his story. He was white, middle class, in his late forties, and from a small New England city. He was raised in the Christian Eastern Orthodox tradition, but converted to Catholicism to be married in the church with his (by this point ex-) wife. They were together for fifteen years, and their divorce was finalized five years before our interview.

Todd said he never embraced Catholicism and felt utterly alone in his parish when he divorced. Parishioners did not talk to him, and the priest never recommended the Catholic support groups that met within an hour's drive of his home. Divorce hit him hard because he had been raised without a father: "It was a horrendous experience because I took the traditional vows, to be married for life, in good times and bad, in sickness and health, until death do you part. I always took that very seriously, especially growing up without a father, because I wanted to be a father, and I wanted to have a wife, and I wanted to do things that my mother wasn't able to do." Catholicism failed to offer him a religious path for this performance of marriage and fatherhood post-divorce, and so, as his marriage came apart, he left the church, engaging initially in what he described as dubious religious pursuits in search of God and meaningful community worship.

In a heightened emotional state, with a "strong desire for God" and a need to understand what happened in his marriage, he joined what he named dangerous "cults." He called this his "crazy emotional period." He described the first encounter: "They gave me a book of how to know God, by Deepak Chopra. . . . I got scared after reading that book and I found out that he really was a cultist and did a lot of brainwashing and really did not honor the word of God." His second pursuit, with Christian Scientists, was equally disappointing: "I'm going to people and saying, can you help me understand the Bible? Help me understand God. Help me learn more about me and myself and this marriage, and nothing was working." Finally, he found a nondenominational evangelical church through a Christian Singles group that featured a DivorceCare support group. He went through the program twice and described finding energy through connection with others: "We were all sharing our experiences, men and women, young and old, and saying 'Wow!' we are all going through this together, and 'Wow!' God really does love us, and 'Wow!' God really does hate divorce and there is also a light at the end of the tunnel." He marveled, "They held my bleeding heart."

Still, Todd considered much of the work introduced in DivorceCare to be private, ongoing self work that would prepare him to form a lasting sacred life partnership. He read, kept a journal, and prayed throughout the day as he continued to work on forgiveness: "I haven't forgiven myself totally, because I'm still a new child of God. I have only been a Christian for five years. . . . I thought I knew God. I thought I knew the church. I thought I knew love and marriage. But I was so ignorant. It has been a good, painful process, but I have more to do." Todd reinforced assessment of the marriage, and the seriousness and time involved in recovery: "Most people really don't do the work. DivorceCare is a bandaid. . . . It gives you a lot of information. Virtually nobody . . . can practice those skills like forgiveness or reconciliation or furthering their life with Christ. . . . All you are doing is trying to get through day by day because of the emotional pain. . . . True recovery takes from one to five years." One has to, he added, put the time in to learn the "skills to go through the process of healing" and to learn how to forgive.

DIVORCE EVENTS AND ALONE WORK

Conferences and larger group events for the divorced also facilitated individual divorce work in collective ritual. Conferences, in title and structure, reflected educational space and practice. Most took place in educational centers or large congregations and used technology like PowerPoint, resembling business or educational models of learning; individuals attended classes or seminars. In these conferences and other large group events for the divorced, religious architects used emotion-filled practices like singing and prayer to endow learning space with sacred sensations.

The regional CDM conferences I attended were held in a newly built university space with media-ready classrooms, with approximately 150 to 200 people (about 10 percent of them men) in attendance. Most appeared between the ages of forty and fifty and were white; approximately fifteen were black; and there was a handful of Spanish-speaking women, who sat together. In the opening minutes, through singing and recitation, the space was marked by leaders as one where we would learn, grow, and acquire the religious and therapeutic tools to change together: "Our Loving Father, thank you for giving this day to us. Let us use it to grow more in your ways and to reach out to others along their journey." We answered, "This day is one of hope. A day to take a major step on the journey leading to the fullness of life.... There is discovery after loss, joy after sadness, and peace after chaos." We sang together, "I am strength for all the despairing, healing for the ones who dwell in shame." Each conference had a book table filled with titles on divorce and loss, as well as brochures, music CDs, and flyers and newsletters from service organizations, self-help programs, and singles groups in the region. CDM introduced reading—not only of sacred texts but also of self-help religious texts—as sacred practice, and provided numerous suggestions.

Separating learners into levels reinforced the idea that grief and marriage work takes place through predetermined stages. At the CDM conferences I attended, workshops on building communication were routinely offered, with participants separated into workshops for the "newly hurting," "beyond the newly hurting," and "all levels." Workshops included: Anger—Is It a Blessed Energy; A Healing Process—Annulments; Enhance Our Relationships with Better Communication; Intimacy and Sex; Are Men's Issues Really That Different Than a Woman's; Celebrating Being Single; Forget the Drama . . . Try a Healthy Relationship; and Exploring Remarriage. One CDM conference offered a labyrinth as a medieval Christian practice, "akin to taking a journey to the Holy City of Jerusalem," for "modern pilgrims," a "spiritual tool" to remind one of a "journey to the heart of God." Ushered in through prayer and spiritual songs, these workshops provided space for Catholics to change through acquisition of communication tools for managing individual and family emotions.

Baptist Singles conferences also emerged as rituals of learning where the divorced came together with other singles to complete their sacred divorce work. The National Baptist Convention, USA, Inc. (NBC, USA) is the largest Black church organization in the United States, and the divorced have become a focal concern of the organization's formal Singles Ministries. In 2006, these congregants held their Inaugural National Baptist Singles

Conference in Richmond, Virginia; the conference became the ground for a subsequent book, *Singles: Strengthened, Secured, and Spirit-Filled*, published by the National Baptist Congress of Christian Education. Conferences offered courses for participants, like "Single, Saved, and Satisfied" and "Life after the Funeral (for Widows and Widowers)." The expectation that participants would be determined students, ready to learn how to do the work of divorce, was well symbolized in the 2011 conference invitation that included emphasis on "Interactive Dialogue" and encouraged members to "Bring Your Laptops, PDAs, or Mobile Phones to Email or Text Your Questions and Receive a Biblical Answer throughout the Conference from a Selected Panel."

Speakers at these Baptist conferences constructed a community narrative that cast the divorced as vibrant Christians and an essential part of congregations—as *sacred singles*. In the text published from the first singles conference, Drew Marshall encourages singles that they "are a composite of gifts, personalities, energies. . . . We are single because of the death of a spouse. Also, we are single and never married, and we are single because we like it like that" (2007, 13). Including the divorced with other singles legitimates their position as a vital part of the church. Holmes writes that all singles are "unique, whole, and complete" (i). In fact, Marshall argues, as we see with CDM religious leaders, that single Christians "are the Church" (13). They teach Sunday school, they lead youth ministries, they work in the church office; "singles pay their tithes, give to the building fund, [are] energetic, enthusiastic, and bold witnesses of Jesus Christ for the kingdom of God," and they are "awesome, fearfully and wonderfully made." Marshall offers scriptural legitimation, for this statement, Psalm 139:14. Brought together through religious emotion, in this learning space, participants were introduced to a strong sacred singles script, where singles' most important role was to serve others.

One of my interviewees attended a smaller conference-like event sponsored by Women of Hope, a local ministry founded in 2009 by three black female pastors in a southern city. When I interviewed Kayla, a founder and "associate pastor" in a church her husband pastored, she told me that she had been disturbed by the "low self-esteem" of the largely poor or working-class women in her Baptist congregation, and so she had reached out to two other female pastors and founded Women of Hope. They worked together to provide an "inspirational event" that could speak to women from a variety of life positions, especially those who were struggling with relation-ships that drained their energy and resources and who were not in "healthy" marriages, or who had left their partners. Women of Hope reinforced the idea that women should not "settle for less," and even while encouraging married women to work on relationships, they made it clear that women did not need a relationship to be whole, and that some men were "baggage" dragging them down. The core message at their events was that Jesus was all they needed to find the strength to improve their lives.

Women of Hope held a conference in 2009 and again in 2011, hosting a range of women—single, married, separated, widowed, and divorced. Most of the women were black, 10 percent were Asian and/or white. The event was small and took place in a modest congregational space. Partici-pants were each given pen and paper with the day's schedule and a place for taking notes, as well as inspirational quotes and a package of Kleenex; the tissues represented an expectation that learning and worship would be accomplished through strong feeling or expression of emotion and was a familiar offering. During services I attended in black Baptist churches, ush-ers often walked through the aisles offering tissues.

During the 2011 Women of Hope conference, leaders staged a theatrical performance that built a high level of religious emotional energy. A young black woman sang gospel singer CeCe Wynan's popular song "Alabaster Box," aided by instrumental music played from a CD through the church's sound system, and accompanied by another woman who did an interpre-tive dance. "Alabaster Box" refers to an event represented in several books in the New Testament, in which a woman, named in Luke 7:36–50 as a sinner, washes Jesus's feet, bathing them with her tears, drying them with her hair, anointing them with oil from her alabaster box, and kissing them. Although some call her a sinner, Jesus tells her that her sins are forgiven, that her faith has saved her, and that she can go in peace. The lyrics are, in part: "She felt such pain, some spoke in anger, heard folks whisper, there's no place here for her kind. Still on she came through the shame that flushed her face, until at last she knelt before his feet. And, though she spoke no words, everything she said was heard. And she poured her love for the master from her box of alabaster." Brought alive through song and dance, this scripture depicted Jesus in close physical relationship with (his feet being washed with her tears, and she kissing them) a woman presumed deviant—an idea that worked to restore authentic Christian identity for attendees. My respondent who attended the event told me it had assured her that God was with her, "every step" she took, giving her the moral ground to tell me a story about how she planned to finally put an end to a physically and verbally abusive marriage.

ALONE/TOGETHER

My respondents were drawn to communal religious spaces to do solitary work. This contradiction reflects a historically specific dialectic: religious experience as highly therapeutic and private and deeply corporate. Religious pursuits in contemporary U.S. culture have become largely private and therapeutic endeavors, linked in intimate ways to the country's cultural emphasis on moral responsibility for cultivation of self, but a large and important body of literature reminds one of the persistent power and draw of collective worship and congregational identity.[10] Religious communities are uniquely fit for the largely private task of divorce work; collective practice through worship services, small groups, and special events produces heighted emotional and energetic space. In the words of classical theorist Emile Durkheim (1996 [1912]), a "collective effervescence" emerges where sacred beliefs gain force and people feel intense energy. The stories my respondents told of these experiences demonstrate a compelling "emotional energy"[11] or collective force that surged through these rituals, gathering the power of religious symbolic worlds to help mend or ward off social shame.

In my observations during services, individuals, across traditions, appeared aware that the people beside them might be experiencing devastating emotion—and might offer these persons a slight touch on the shoulder or an embrace, a look of acknowledgment of pain—but to bring oneself too much into another's emotional world seemed taboo. In some Pentecostal services, individual energy and emotion work did become the focus for collective worship, but this happened in well-orchestrated rhythms of worship where the person in need of healing took a position at the front of the sanctuary. Although I heard stories of divorced individuals coming forward to be healed in this type of ritual, none of my divorced COGIC respondents chose to do so. In their stories, the alone/together nature of divorce work in worship space reinforced the highly private and individual character of their strategies.

Private emotion work in congregations is a sacred moral performance with the power to affirm and repair religious and family identity. Respondents can, like Jill, affirm identity as, for instance, a mother and Jew surrounded by the congregation of a large synagogue whose members' knowledge of her family life is limited. In smaller church settings, such as those of Jeff, Natalie, and Sandy, solitary work takes on a particular kind of moral performance, in that members tend to know more about one another's relationships and losses. Doing sacred divorce work in the pews and in concert with others, in these cases, has a higher degree of potential shame and thus intentional performance. Natalie, for example, a COGIC first family member, stepped down from the choir and disconnected somewhat from others in the pews so that she could feel God and do the work she felt she must as a Christian and as a mother. Her actions were a valuable congregational performance, a performance of solitary work guided by the expectations of the religious community. Even Alice's emotional outburst during worship, although depicted in her story as "out of control," served as evidence to members (and to me) that she was working each week on serious feelings and that her attachment to the congregation was deep. Sandy's social shame was shaped in part by her congregation's efforts to promote LGBT marriage rights and her loss of the status associated with being a member of an "ideal lesbian family."

Size, structure, and character of congregations impacted how people experienced relationships with religious communities and thus impacted the character of their solitary work through collective ritual. Respondents across traditions spoke of congregational friendships severed and of people taking sides in the divorce, leading some even to move to another congregation. In one Catholic case, both spouses were active and well-known parish members, but the parish was large enough to absorb the relational shock— since they could attend different Masses. A few mainline Protestant women told of feeling immediately shunned from participating in the couple groups that they had been a part of, feeling that married women suddenly saw them as having a dangerous sexual energy. The smaller the congregation, the more likely congregational disruption and shame might occur, as happened in Alice's case and also at Shelby Chapel.[12] At Shelby, I interviewed a woman who had divorced a couple of years before she joined the congregation; she was previously in one of several couples composing a Wiccan coven, and when her husband had an affair, the small coven dissolved.

Regardless of the particular type of relationship to the congregation, size of religious community, or church doctrine, all respondents felt some degree of silence and potential for shame in their communities. Congregational silence and the heightened private nature of divorce shaped encounters with clergy. The rabbis, priests, and pastors that I interviewed emphasized the concealed nature of divorce in their congregations, and their feelings of being removed from the private relational lives of members. Still, a number of my respondents did turn to clergy at some time as they faced divorce, seeking religious strategies for managing their emotions or navigating family relationships, and wanting to protect spiritual status. In those interactions, clergy cautiously negotiated authority, assembling meaningful religious symbols and practices for members that validated marriage as sacred work and grief as painful spiritual passage.

4 ✳ CAUTIOUS CLERGY

Because what I'm finding out, being here a year, there are a lot of people who have been divorced but they won't tell you. And you are thinking that's been their wife all their lives.

—American Baptist minister

I know of about at least a half a dozen divorces that never came to me for religious divorce. And never contacted me. When do we find this out? We find out at the bar or bat mitzvah. That's when it comes to my knowledge, or when there is some other issue—life-cycle issue—that's when I find it.

—Conservative rabbi

One of the things in the African American community, most of the times the male does not attend church, so you don't know [about divorce].

—NBC, USA–affiliated pastor

All of the rabbis, priests, and pastors that I interviewed emphasized the concealed nature of divorce in their congregations. Because a number of congregants came from other parishes, churches, or synagogues, the clergy often remained in the dark about previous marriages; intimate family details lay hidden as people traveled from one congregation to another. Some clergy connected their lack of knowledge of divorce to high numbers of women attending services without their husbands; if no visible change occurred in presentation of self in the congregation, how would clergy learn of a relationship's end? In Catholic and Jewish cases, a member's desire for a legal religious divorce ceremony, an annulment or *get*, might bring a marriage's ending to a clergy member's attention. Still, as one rabbi of a large conservative synagogue in a southern city said, "Once I find out about divorce, it is a fait accompli and they just want a legal Jewish divorce [*get*] so they can get [re]married." In both large and small congregations, most felt removed from the private relational lives of members ending marriages. My divorced respondents confirmed their stories, indicating for the most part that their pastor, rabbi, or priest had been unaware of their divorces.

Clergy in the United States spend, in general, only a small fraction of their very busy schedules counseling members about family issues.[1] Still, about a quarter of my respondents did turn to clergy at some point during the years surrounding their divorce, and, when they did, it was primarily to reach out to acquire religious strategies for managing emotions or navigating family relationships, or to protect spiritual status. In these interactions, clergy carefully claimed authority, assembling meaningful religious symbols and practices that validated marriage as sacred work and grief as painful spiritual passage. Together, their stories demonstrate the limitations of construction of divorce practices in religious communities. Clergy adhered to a largely private therapeutic counseling model, and those who helped craft community divorce rituals did so, for the most part, cautiously. In one case, though, which I describe, a powerful group ritual broke boundaries—persuasive religious emotional energy lifted up marriage and divorce at the same time, bringing disturbing dissonance for some participants and legitimation of passage for others.

The story of my respondent Father Allen captures the essence of clergy's cautious approaches to the intimate labor of helping congregants affirm family and faith through endings: compassionate listening, careful sermons, and refitting existing practices for the divorced.

AN APPROACHABLE FATHER

Father Allen, a white Roman Catholic priest, had served a large parish in a southern city for over ten years. His parish was known for its informal acceptance of LGBT relationships, although the priests could not officially offer weddings for same-sex couples. Thus, he bemoaned, the parish had lost many of these Catholics to the local United Church of Christ, the "groovy Episcopal church," or the Metropolitan Community Church, where same-sex religious marriage ceremonies were publicly embraced. Feeling removed from parishioners' private family lives was a familiar experience for Father Allen. Unless married people sit in the same pew together and are known by others as a couple, "relationships end in quiet—it's not named, or if it is named it is named to a very select group of folks." In his experience, embarrassing encounters inevitably resulted: "I've said to someone, 'Oh, I haven't seen so-and-so for a while,' and they've said, 'We haven't been together for thirteen months!'"

Although Father Allen felt disconnected from the intimate details of some of the people sitting in the pews, some regular parishioners who were familiar with his approach came to him as they separated: "Somebody that is active in my parish and who hears me preach regularly, they are already going to have a sense to how I'm going to respond. If I'm a fire-and-brimstone preacher who is regularly announcing judgment from the pulpit, they may say, I'm not going to him. . . . The people who come to me are already in the pews and have an instinctive sense that 'This is somebody that I would talk to about whatever painful situation is going on in my life.'" The people who are "tangentially attached to church," and so "don't know what to expect and, when you throw in layers of 'Catholics [who] don't believe in divorce anyway and [think] priests are all mean,' they might look for help and listening in other places."

Father Allen's sermons, his implicit welcoming of gay couples, and his connection with LGBT Catholic groups like Dignity USA made him seem approachable to parishioners whose intimate life choices ran contrary to formal Catholic doctrine. He described the gay men he counseled as "already living with certain cognitive tensions between knowing that they are not quite living up to the ideal that the church preaches." Still, they suffered threats of religious and parental social shame similar to heterosexual couples when their relationships ended, and they had fewer legal resources to help resolve disputes. Like the rabbi of a LGBT synagogue I interviewed, Father Allen knew the religious space he created might be the only institutional path of mediation available to same-sex couples in his area.

Father Allen saw his sermons as a major religious tool for creating a welcoming parish. It was a challenging effort given that he did not pick the

Sunday readings: "There are consistent gospel readings that come up in the calendar that talk about marriage, and there are the few Bible passages in which Jesus talks about the divorced, and those are often hard to hear in context because they are two thousand years old and the language can sound harsh." He offered an example of his approach in a sermon: "This is tough to hear today, and I'm aware that many of you have had an experience of divorce in your family, and I have in my own family—my sister has been divorced twice." Acknowledging divorce in his family was a "way of saying, I understand that it's hard to hear this; now let's explore. What's the good news in the middle of it?" Another method he used was bringing up the topic of divorce in a sermon alongside other difficult experiences. He gave an example: "You just lost your job, your spouse just told you that they have fallen in love with somebody else. You are a single mom trying to raise three kids, and child support has been yanked." He tried to name realities based on what he knew of people without "calling them out individually." He offered another example of creating a space where departure from some ideal family could be normalized:

On Father's Day I told them that I won the parent lottery because my parents were just amazing, so I had an experience of my father that helped to illustrate the gospel passage for that day. But at the end of the homily I talked about— it's the gospel passage of Jesus calming the storm on the sea—I said, now I know earlier I said how my dad helped to calm my storm, but some of you may be sitting there saying, my dad didn't calm the storms, my dad created storms. At every Mass, people laughed, acknowledging. I said sometimes fathers reflect Jesus's love and sometimes fathers cause us great pain. I try to name pain in family relationships, without driving a truck through it, and give people permission to connect to the scripture on whatever level they are [at ease with]. With divorce, being a single parent, or being gay and lesbian and Catholic, if I can name that, if I can list other things, then nobody has to say, that's me, but they might be able to say, oh, that is me, and this is for me.

Father Allen also worked to alleviate the potential for Catholic shame by likening the divorced to biblical figures whose lives demonstrated some breach of moral/religious expectations and whose spiritual status was strong. He invited several women to reflect on and take on the symbolic position of "the woman caught in adultery everyone wants to stone." He stresses, "Jesus gets down with her on the ground and says, 'Let the one without sin cast the first stone.'" Father Allen then asks them to keep praying and reflecting on the dialogue: "There is no one left to condemn you; then neither do I. Go, and don't do this sin anymore." He told one woman to put herself "in there and ask, is there anybody to condemn you?" Then, "Jesus doesn't want you to feel condemned."

Given Father Allen's affirmation of muliple kinds of family structure, and his efforts to affirm Catholic identity through divorce experience, it is not surprising that some members and couples reached out to him for pastoral counseling. Several heterosexual and gay individuals had come to him over the years with issues related to making a decision to leave a relationship. People also came to him to seek guidance for parenting post-divorce, most especially, how they "should talk to their children about the reality of divorce." He was currently working with a woman whose ex-husband had been abusive. She had been "venting her anger at her husband in the presence of her children," and came to him to "seek guidance on how best to change that dynamic, as she sensed it wasn't good for the kids or her." Father Allen was working with her on "examining her moral responsibility to tell the truth, while at the same time dealing with her moral responsibility to 'do the most loving thing' toward her children and her ex-husband." It was a conversation he had had many times; divorced people want to know how their "faith can/should/might dictate and shape behavior toward children and ex-spouses."

In answering such questions, Father Allen worked to clarify forgiveness and reconciliation as religious tools for sacred emotion work. He noted an example: "I am working with someone right now who knows that we are supposed to forgive even our enemies, and right now her ex-husband is the enemy, and she asks, 'Does God really want me to forgive him?'" He added that forgiveness "is a process" that if rushed could do "violence to the person, just as with grieving. You can't tell somebody to get over it. That is going to happen in [the person's] own time!" Reconciliation through confession, he stressed, represents a different stage in the process: "Most people, at the end of a relationship, eventually come to the point where they say, 'Even if my spouse was an S.O.B., I was not the perfect spouse either, and can I confess that and bring closure.' Sacramentally, going to confession is one of the ways that we would do that." Still, he cautioned that people need to take their own time with rituals of reconciliation, "Don't rush confession";

he identified its value for the person for learning what he or she had done wrong in a relationship. The more people talked with Father Allen, the more, he felt, they would "realize the underlying issues," although "it might take a lot of digging." Reconciliation processes were like "AA or any of the twelve-step programs. First step is to name what has happened and what is hurting, and then we can move on."

Father Allen saw guilt and feelings of failure as emotions that led many parishioners to him in "looking for permission" to divorce. "In terms of Catholicism," he noted, they were focused on "the permanence of marriage." People had grown up with "sacramental language for marriage," and so felt that "Catholics just don't do this, even though the numbers are, yes we do." He sometimes felt manipulated by individuals and couples who might "say they want counseling for the marriage, but pretty quickly what you sniff is that they are looking for permission to end." He sensed them asking "Is God going to hate me if I do this?" or "Does God think I have failed, too?" Ultimately, most were "looking for where is God in the midst of all this." He would take them gently to a core theological position that affirmed their religious and spiritual potential and worth: the promise of new life after sin and grief.

Rebirth and concentration on the Paschal Mystery[2] is at the center of Father Allen's message of repairing Catholic identity. Thus, he invokes a religious concept that resonates with the heart of therapeutic culture and divorce work: pain/death as purpose, and illness as road to recovery. As in DivorceCare and in Jeff's narrative of the restorative power of collective music, brokenness is seen as effective liminal identity. The Paschal Mystery, representing the salvation in Jesus's death and the notion that suffering leads to new life and renewal, is a powerful religious emotional tool. Easter, like Passover for many Jews, is associated with family cultural practices and formal religious rituals. If people are at an appropriate place in "grieving and pain process," Father Allen sends them back to the Easter story: "At the end of Good Friday, everything seems lost and everything is broken and He's in the tomb and nothing good is ever going to happen again. And then two days later, in our tradition, the answer is—oh, new life can always happen. New hope can always happen." He brings the parishioners to the "heart of the gospels, the dying and the rising. They have all heard those stories since they were kids." It is different though, he insists, when people "read them as adults, through the lens of this very painful ending," to "believe that some new life can come out of this death"; the mystery of death-to-life takes on new significance.

Father Allen also works to refit existing rituals into instruments for sacred divorce work. For example, he, like several other Catholic priests and leaders with whom I spoke, sees annulment as a "spiritual" and "therapeutic" ritual. The annulment process is, he feels, an exceptional time to mine the past, to assess, to retool, to do serious self work through extensive reflective writing about the relationship in preparation for the annulment: "At some stage in the annulment process, after they have done what they can do, pulled the paperwork together, written what they are going to write, and have talked to me several times, then they are ready. But they have laid a lot of groundwork for that." Dissecting what went wrong in a marriage is crucial, in his view, to claiming new life, especially if one desires remarriage.

Ultimately, though, Father Allen understands the Eucharist as the most effective Catholic ritual for sacred grief work: "I tell them, just look around the church and know that, [for] everybody else sitting there, there is something broken in their life. There is some aspect of their life that is also not in complete agreement with what is in the catechism of the Catholic Church." Thus, he stresses, divorced persons are the essence of the Catholic Church: "I tell them the church is not a ship for saints but a lifeboat for sinners. We are all in this together—from the guy saying the Mass to the usher in the back and the homeless guy sleeping on the steps." Father Allen believes the energy of religious emotion is strong during this ritual: "Something very significant happens in Mass as they hear the scriptures and then celebrate the Eucharist." This participation activates the Paschal Mystery and fortifies a congregational bond around brokenness: "There is a point where the Eucharist gets broken and I often, in teaching, will talk about how that's a crucial moment in the Mass, not only symbolic of how we believe that Jesus was broken in his crucifixion, but . . . also where his brokenness touches ours. So I say, whatever brokenness you bring, put it right up and know that it is connected to what Jesus experienced in his brokenness. I try to get them connecting that moment to what is going on in their lives and what is happening ritually." Through this ritual, food that is symbolic of body and blood is put into one's physical self; the juice and bread representing divine symbolic energy fill the body. This is a routine Christian body practice for my respondents across Christian traditions, one with persuasive emotional powers; Catholics had daily access to this ritual.

Above all, Father Allen told me, he tries to provide a space where he can be a "compassionate listener and listen to their pain." He knows he cannot change the church, that it is always going to "uphold what it understands to be the ideal in every situation and, for marriage, [this ideal] is forever": despite the very "elaborate annulment process, we are going to uphold the ideal that heterosexual marriage is where the expression of physical sexuality finds its ultimate moral end." But, he stressed, "Divorce is human reality" and "What the priest does is say, 'What are the cards you have been dealt and what is the most Christ-like thing you can do?' So the couple with eight children says, 'Father, we know the Church teaches against artificial contraception, but what can we do?' I can't stand in the pulpit on Sunday and say condoms are fine—my small salary would be cut." Instead, he deals with individuals and asks them to "consider their particular divorce circumstances, and pray about it" to find their path. Thus he upholds contemporary understandings of Catholic identity, affirming divorced parishioners' religious bonds in their creation of religious self. As Jerome Baggett (2009, 5) suggests, the "pejoratively intended moniker 'cafeteria Catholic'" can be understood as a source of agency in constructing a strong religious identity that resonates with one's lived experiences, rather than as a sign of religious weakness.

Like Father Allen, each clergy member with whom I spoke understood divorce as a human reality that demanded individualized spiritual work. Each saw divorce as similar to other types of family experiences that brought deep emotions and called for both therapeutic and religious tools. Like Father Allen, these clergy knew that their professional knowledge and access to religious tools, and the status they held as religious leaders, gave them some measure of moral authority in the eyes of most congregants; however, all balanced their desire to assemble strategies for members with an unspoken caution and respect for the boundaries of family privacy and autonomy in contemporary U.S. society. Thus they carefully negotiated breaking silences around divorce in their congregational worlds as they provided sacred paths for transitions in identity and for balancing the contradictions of marriage and divorce culture.

GENTLE PRACTICES, CAREFUL SERMONS

I attended services at the UU Chapel when Jerry's church was dealing with the aftermath of multiple separations, and so I was in the congregation on the Sunday morning when he gave his sermon on ending relationships.

Its theme was that most endeavors—relationships, jobs, life itself—naturally end, but that in US culture a person becomes caught up in feeling like a failure if a significant relationship or enterprise ends. It was a difficult sermon for him to write, in part because he had just finalized a break-up with a long-term girlfriend, an emotional experience he decided to address in his message from the pulpit that Sunday morning: "Writing the sermon was challenging personally. . . . I knew that it was a touchy issue with the congregation, and it was nothing I'd preached on before, and it was really important, so I really wanted to handle it with care, so I spent more time on that sermon." He was nervous about addressing this issue from the pulpit, as he felt an unspoken taboo regarding conversation about the number of recent break-ups in the congregation.

I asked him what he wanted to accomplish with the sermon. He responded: "I think the goal every Sunday, for me, regardless of the topic, is to bring people closer to what I call God." The way that Jerry imagined God differed from the way that black Baptists did who envisioned sacred singles in intimate relationship with a supernatural God, but its end was similar—to bring the numinous into therapeutic emotional strategy: "There are all these books on how to divorce; . . . there is 'the art of divorcing well,' all these practical steps . . . a lot of self-help stuff on divorce." But he wanted to reach the goal of "just being closer to God—to rise above feelings of anger, . . . to rise above your reactions and . . . to accept a lot of this mystery." To ease the silence and any social shame at work in his congregation, he drew from his own experience:

> Somebody just went from being crazy about me to dumping me in a short period of time and I wanted to know why. One friend finally said, nobody knows why, she didn't have to give an explanation. . . . It was very helpful and so I wanted to pass that bit of advice on in the sermon. In a way, the end of relationships, . . . you can take one of two ways. You can become more entrenched in your position—entrenched in your victimhood—or you can move toward forgiveness and understanding, or at least just say, "It's all a mystery." To say I don't know and all I can do is accept this and move on and be the best person I can. And I think that's deeply spiritual. Our first response is to, you know, fortify a defensive position, and I think that [not doing so is to be] moving closer to God and health and wholeness, all wrapped up together.

Jerry's approach affirmed divorce work tenets as spiritual pursuits—rejecting victimhood and demanding forgiveness and self work—but also challenged divorce-work scripts that insisted on assessment and discovery of reasons for why the relationship ended. Most things, he insisted, did end, and the divine was part of that process. He saw the sermon as a success, and when I asked several members about the sermon, they felt it had been appropriate, well received, and needed.

About half of the clergy I interviewed said they had never addressed the experience of divorce in a sermon. The other half told stories of cautious ventures, identifying two major concerns that inhibited attempts to preach about the subject: congregants' strong dislike for depressing topics, and fear of contributing to shame for divorced congregants. One Reform rabbi noted: "I've talked about divorce. But I've never made it the center. I did death once, on the High Holidays, and sent a few people screaming from the room, so I'm very reluctant to address those kinds of issues." This was a significant statement, given that death is a central theme during Yom Kippur. One Conservative rabbi noted that, with the size of his congregation, he was likely to have bat or bar mitzvahs most weekends, making divorce not an appropriate weekend topic. When clergy did address divorce, they did so in a veiled manner. Jerry was the only clergy member who talked of crafting an entire sermon around the subject. Most messages about divorce were marginal, in talks and, like those employed in Father Allen's strategy, were delivered embedded in lists of other life woes. One black Baptist minister said he would "add divorce in, but it's not the focus of the message; it is just a little nugget." For example: "I did preach a sermon entitled 'Responding to life's pain with Sampson.' Sampson goes to visit his father-in-law and he says, 'I want to see my wife.' His father-in-law responds, 'You can't see her, because she is in the room with your friend.' His friend had his wife, so he is in pain, and I talked about responding to life's pain. Sampson responds negatively; he goes down the street and he falls prey to Delila. He gives up everything that was invested in him because he's responding to life's pain, 'I want to see my wife and I can't see her.' You could see the response on people's faces all over the church, because so many people are broken." In other words, he was telling me, "If you really deal with divorce in a sermon it will push people away." Instead of explicit mention of divorce and the temptations he understood as accompanying divorce's emotions, he often turned to naming "brokenness" in a broad way, and used various examples of painful conditions to demonstrate the need for close relationship with God to heal from broken conditions.

Clergy used existing religious ceremonies and rituals in a similarly judicious manner.

Refitting Existing Practice

As demonstrated above, clergy engaged in active interpretation that involved refitting religious symbols to resonate with divorce experiences and threats of social shame. Jerome Baggett (2009, 220) articulates the process precisely in his study of contemporary Catholic identity: "Reframing is the process of using evocative symbols, unmoored from their traditional meanings, to essentially create religious truths rather than looking on them as signifying some objective religious truth." These symbols have power and "spiritual value"—"reinterpreted *as symbols*, which opens up new possibilities for conceptualizing and connecting to the sacred." I found that clergy's refitting, or reframing of religious practices, for the divorced were of two types: interpretation of familiar routine symbolic ritual, and the reframing of more formal ceremonies and religious divorce documents.

Annulments in the Catholic tradition, and *gets* (divorce documents) in the Jewish tradition were routinely adapted by religious officials to match contemporary family and marriage circumstances. Interpretations by priests and rabbis from varied movements produced multiple methods and avenues of obtaining these official religious documents to mark the end of a sacred union. Gets have been the subject of much controversy in Jewish communities as the traditional, patriarchal version interprets a husband as giving his wife a get; women whose husbands will not grant a get (*augunot*) are in a disadvantaged position with regard to marrying again in the Jewish faith—a position of most consequence for those adhering to Orthodoxy. Rabbi Alan Lew (2000, 8), in his pamphlet *Looking Back on Divorce and Letting Go*, affirms the power of marriage as he interprets the *get*: "Love is as strong as death. When we marry, we become one flesh; an indissoluble bond adheres. . . . Our marriages never leave us. They cling to us in our dreams. . . . But the ritual of divorce covers them over with a fresh act of will" (6–7). As with Catholic annulments, individuals appeal to religious officials through formal proceedings and receive some written affirmation of dissolution of the marriage bond; unlike an annulment, the get affirms the sacredness of the union that existed, and at the same time legitimates the ending. In more contemporary versions of the get, the practice also makes the divorce meaningful.

The rabbis with whom I spoke, from Conservative, Reform, and Reconstructionist traditions, talked with me about the importance of remodeling the Jewish divorce to fit contemporary marriage relationships and to fashion the practice around an individual's particular emotional needs. For example, one Conservative rabbi of a large temple in a southern city argued: "In many cases, it is just perfunctory. They want the divorce, they need the divorce to get remarried, and it was so long ago that it really is just a religious legal document." But in cases when the experience is "raw" or "near," he "cannot treat the get lightly." In these cases, he "gears the ceremony to fit the emotional needs. If it is raw, then you need to talk with them about the pain and how they can make this a final step to leave the marriage behind and start anew." In such an instance, the get is "a ritual symbolizing accomplishment."

Another rabbi, from a Reform Jewish temple, encouraged people to talk with him about an "appropriate" ritual: "There is an assumption that a wedding has to take place under Jewish auspices, but they don't think of ending the marriage in the same way. . . . Ritually it doesn't bother me that they are not thinking [of] it, but emotionally it is a problem. I think there is a great sense of closure and healing when you end a marriage not in a courtroom, but with a ceremony; one of the things that religion does really well is rites of passage, life's major liminal moments in your life." He explained how the Reform movement's version of a traditional get, called a Document of Separation, had been shaped to reflect contemporary marriage: "It is usually done with both the wife and husband present, but can also be done with just one person if necessary. The document has three parts; the wife and husband each leave with their torn section and the rabbi keeps one section for the records"—more egalitarian than the husband "giving the wife the get," as in the Orthodox ceremony. This rabbi makes clear to those who want to do this ceremony that it is not the document itself that is emotionally and spiritually fulfilling, but rather the emotion that surfaces during the ritual: "Standing on the bema here in your own sanctuary, in your own synagogue which has held both positive and negative lifecycle moments— you might have [been to] a funeral here, as well, or a bar mitzvah—and standing here and having your rabbi read you through a ceremony of acknowledging the beauty and power of your relationship up until now and [recognizing] that you are moving on to other places—that is a very powerful moment that you ought to have." He recalled that in such familiar religious space powerful emotions surfaced as paper ripped, symbolizing the tearing apart of a sacred union.

The potential for such religious emotion likely depends on what level of meaning and attachment an individual finds in the synagogue space, and the particular circumstances of the marriage. One Reform rabbi from a large synagogue in the Northeast saw the ritual as a tool for parents to help children accomplish crucial emotion work: "I think there is something healing and powerful for the kids, even though they cry and they are upset. You know, children always secretly fantasize their parents will get back together, and this helps them to understand that it is not happening."

I interviewed Rabbi Netter via phone about his divorce and the process of writing his 2002 book, *Divorce Is a Mitzvah*. He told me a story about his efforts to make divorce sacred. In the Conservative temple where he worked, there was a display case with a book written by a rabbi with a long tenure. The book was standing straight up and centered in the case; Netter's book was to the side and had fallen over. He found symbolic meaning in this positioning. During one encounter outside the community, a Jewish man had asked him, "Why don't you write a book called 'Murder Is a Mitzvah?'" Netter works hard in his book to remove the threat of social shame in the Jewish community, and, like many of the rabbis in my study, he tries to soften the potential for social shame by casting ending as a process that demands ethical pursuit through familiar rituals like the get. The "central question governing divorce, as it is the ultimate question of every aspect of personal life," is how one is to "seek the holy and the sacred" (5). Netter uses a powerful Jewish tool by naming divorce a mitzvah, as eleventh-century French biblical commentator Rabbi Shlomo Yitzhaki (the famous Rashi) had. Netter stresses, "A mitzvah is a response to the voice of God commanding us to behave in a particular way." Divorce, in Netter's view, is very much like other challenging life experiences, those occasions when Jews seek familiar rituals to navigate life changes. "While all other life cycle events are public, divorce is intensely private; . . . in most divorces, none of these trappings of religion is present. God is conspicuously absent—exiled, as it were, from the shards of shattered dreams" (2002, 118). Netter describes the value of bringing the sacred to the process through the get: "The love of my youth died on the altar of divorce the moment I handed her the *get* and said the words of the divorce formula. Like Isaac before me, I ascended that altar to die to my past . . . to bury that part of my identity that no longer defined me, only to emerge from the altar to begin the transition to my new life. . . . It was one of the most painful experiences of my life, but in the final analysis it was a gift, and it was a blessing" (130). Rabbi Alan Lew articulates (2000, 1–2) the potential for such a religious ritual to reconcile cultural contradictions that hold marriage as sacred, even as divorce becomes sacred process:

> Paradox is the language of the soul. . . . The ritual of Jewish divorce also rests on a paradox. When a Jewish marriage fails, divorce is absolutely necessary. The very powerful spiritual act we performed under the *chuppah* (the marriage canopy)— that profound alteration of the universe—simply must be undone. Yet at the same time, it actually can't be undone. Love is as strong as death, and marriage, if it contains even the slightest hint of love, lasts forever; its consequences reverberate until the end of time. So when a marriage fails, we must divorce, in order to undo that which cannot possibly be undone.

Karen pursued a formal get in a Conservative synagogue and then followed it with another traditional ritual reshaped to fit divorce experience: immersion in the ritual bath at the mikvah center outside of Boston. Her get was not the mutual ending ceremony that Rabbi Netter described in his book, or the egalitarian one on http://www.ritualwell.org/, but for her it produced a feeling of deep connection to an ethnic tradition: "I was at the synagogue looking at these beautiful trees, and I sat there . . . The rabbi follows a script and it is very traditional and I felt that I was in presence of hundreds and hundreds of years of ancestors that were in the room, because we were following a very structured procedure where he would document things and write things and you would get an actual document, and it was, for me, very important. I didn't really talk to my husband at all."

Priests talked about annulments as emotional tools, shaping what could be an empty appeal for church validation to a process representing an emotional journey. Father Allen, for example, said of the annulment process: "I don't know what value the document has for the person who is in front of me, other than it gives them freedom to marry again in the church." But, he felt, if he and the person seeking an annulment put serious time and therapeutic effort into the process, it could have value as a sacred practice:

> So I always try to explain it and work it with them on a much more pastoral level. Some people hand them forms and say write an autobiography, but if

someone comes to me I will meet with them at least three times to simply listen. I want them to tell me the story of their relationship. It is more time-consuming for me and for them, but I would say that, at least 50 percent of the time, at some point in the conversation they will stop and say, "I've never told anybody this" as they are telling the story of their relationship. And, to me, those are the important moments, because they are finally able to name that.

Father Allen believes the petitioners are then ready to "put pen to paper for somebody else to read," that "it is the human interchange, the listening, and then [their] finally feeling free to name something that happened that is still hurtful on some level, or that they remember and said, 'I never told anybody that.'" I asked him what happens if the person's story "does not match the requirements for annulment," and he responded in a way that indicated willingness to shape the practice to fit individual circumstances: "In my experience, when I sit down and listen to somebody, 90 percent of the time I think it is possible to find something in how they described it that fits within the church's definitions of how to grant the annulment." If they tell the story, and he doesn't hear anything that indicates an annulment, he asks them to come back: "There is just something that I haven't asked right or they haven't told me on the first bounce. Or I ask them to see another priest or advocate who might be able to deal with them in a different way that I think might get us there." If all else fails, a person can resolve the issue in their heart alone with God: "We have this elaborate annulment process, but if that fails for someone, the 'internal forum' is like confession and a way to find the best thing to do that is going to be good for all involved." Father Allen's appeal to the "internal forum" represents a controversial post–Vatican II approach that takes authority for annulment out of the hands of formal marriage tribunals and into the hearts of Catholics in their private relationship with God.[3] For example, CDM founder James Young writes that the divorced "alone can decide whether there is any barrier that keeps them from receiving the Eucharist in faith and love" (1984, 72). The internal forum matches contemporary Catholics' claiming of narrative authority and discernment of what makes a good Catholic.

During one CDM conference, a priest, from a mid-Atlantic state, worked to counter complaints that the tribunal gives out too many annulments and that the rich can buy an annulment, noting that the fee is only a quarter of the cost and that, further, the tribunal "works with people" who do not have the funds. He talked at length with participants about how Jesus responded in Matthew 10:6 and Matthew 5:31–32 to Jewish divorce law, disturbed that men could simply decide to divorce their wives. Women, he said, "were important to Jesus, Jesus first appeared to women in the Bible. Jesus's concern for women and how he saw women being treated in Jewish law is why divorce is forbidden." But the annulment process today, he explained, was more of a "healing process," where a woman giving her "deposition" is "telling her story."

For both of these priests, unraveling the threads of the marriage—the marriage work of divorce work—was doing primary divorce-emotion work, and they helped to facilitate this. Those seeking an annulment were asked to dissect the relationship through a series of questions that shaped their narratives of emotional endings: Was there a misunderstanding of *fidelity* on the part of a spouse as they entered the marriage? Had one of them married in "fraud or error"? He explained, "If you marry someone and you are thinking to yourself that, if you don't like something, . . . if they get fat or if they do this or that, then I'm leaving, [then] that's grounds for annulment. . . . You have to enter the marriage without entertaining the possibility that you may get a divorce or you have invalidly contracted the marriage." He gave examples of the kinds of questions posed in depositions:

Describe any unresolved differences, quarrels, break-ups, etc.

Discuss your family of origin—education, whether they were broken or dysfunctional in any way. What was your relationship with your parents?

What were the reasons you decided to marry your former spouse?

Did you have any doubts before you got married? Did you discuss these doubts with anyone?

How important was it to you that the marriage produce children?

Did you use birth control, and, if so, for how long?

Did it seem to you that you and your spouse were like partners?

Discuss any decline in communication.

Did you have any problems with intimacy or sex? Was there anything about your sexual relationship that made you feel uncomfortable?

Did you have fidelity problems? Was an apology made?

What was the reaction by the faithful party?

What was the cause of the final break-up?

Sometimes priests saw cases move beyond their therapeutic expertise, and assigned a psychologist to assess individuals' stories for signs of fraud or error. Although annulments may seem legalistic and a mere rehashing, the annulment can be, as a CDM priest argued during one conference seminar, "very cathartic—a final time for people to get out the issues—and then receiving the final decree tells them it is finally over and to go on." Annulments, refit into contemporary therapeutic form, provided a safe and familiar process through which priests could facilitate sacred divorce work, and provided a concrete religio-therapeutic role for the divorced.

Religious leaders also reached outside formal divorce practices to find routine symbolic ritual practices that would speak to the emotional needs of those facing divorce transition and social shame. For example, Catholic clergy, like CDM architects of sacred divorce work, stressed working to disabuse notions of exclusion from the sacraments. Several of my Catholic divorced respondents who had not talked with a religious leader assumed their formal access to the Eucharist was in question because they were divorced. Priests clarified for the divorced that remarriage without an annulment was the official condition for which individuals would lose formal access, but offered the internal forum as justification for access to the Eucharist even in these cases. Daily engagement with this sacrament was a powerful religious tool for maintaining Catholic identity through divorce, and priests and other Catholic religious leaders were inclined to reinforce its practice. Father Allen had well described its potency in religious emotion: "Something very significant happens in Mass as they hear the scriptures and then celebrate the Eucharist," activating the Paschal Mystery and fortifying a congregational bond around brokenness.

Father Allen and another priest with whom I spoke had also adapted the "sacrament of anointing the sick" to help the divorced: "I may play with the sacramental anointing a bit, with exactly what the church's rules are on that, but when I talk about anointing, especially if you do it publicly, which is most powerful, you get whole groups of people together that want to pray for healing." Both were careful, in their interpretation, to use a discourse of healing and avoid calling the individuals deviant or sick: "I phrase it, 'Anybody in need of healing in body, mind, or spirit.' And I have folks who have experienced divorce who come up front to receive it. That is one of the ways they seek healing—they come and they want to be anointed. They may be standing next to a cancer patient, but on a deeper level they know that everybody is in pain here."

Most rabbis recognized a silence, in their religious communities, surrounding divorce and the need for divorce rituals beyond the get. Rabbi Hollander writes: "Unlike mourners of a physical death, one who mourns the end of a marriage digs no grave, and has no *shivah* (formal period of mourning). No one brings food, stays to offer comfort, nor holds one's hand" (1994, 202). She suggests refitting Jewish rituals related to grief, loss, and mourning for people in the midst of divorce. Not surprisingly, she turns to Yom Kippur, the Jewish Day of Atonement, during which Jews remember those dear to them who have died. Death, atonement, and rebirth are core religious themes during Yom Kippur. She offers readers a ritual (202) of "Passage: A mini-Yom Kippur (Day of Atonement)":

> The time before the wedding is as *Yom Kippur*, a time to come before God, to review one's life, to fast, to do *teshuvah* (to repent or return), to be reborn.
>
> The evening before the divorce, I began my fast. In the morning, wrapped in my *tallit* (prayer shawl), I recited the *Viddui* (confessional, said before one's marriage, on *Yom Kippur*, and on one's death bed), acknowledging my part in the undoing of the marriage.
>
> As on *Yom Kippur*, I wore no jewelry, no make-up. I dressed in white, the color of the *kittel*, the garment that traditionally shrouds Jewish men on their wedding day, on various Jewish holidays, and at their burial.
>
> Divorce and *Yom Kippur*. Loss. Death. Straying from the path. Rebirth. Freedom.

In the same volume, Nina Beth Cardin (1994, 206), an advisor to students at the Rabbinical School of the Jewish Theological Seminary, refits several symbolic rituals to produce a visceral image of breaking social and religious bonds: The ritual was "designed to be performed by a woman surrounded and supported by her friends and family. The setting should be familiar and comfortable. . . . Particularly appropriate would be the Saturday night after the actual separation, following *Havdalah* (ritual that separates Sabbath or a holiday from the weekdays). Both marital separation and *Havdalah* mark the crossing of a threshold from one state and time into another." She combines this routine weekly practice with other symbolic rituals and sacred objects: "Through the use of a cloth—specifically a portion of a pillowcase or sheet—and its act of tearing, this separation ceremony is meant to evoke images of marriage and divorce. In addition to the image of sexual intimacy, the cloth and its tearing also allude to the cloth of the chuppah (wedding canopy) and the cutting of the get (bill of divorce) when divorce is final. The act of tearing summons associations with keri'ah (rending a garment in mourning)." Cardin's refitting of practice combines rituals of mourning with sacred marriage imagery and weekly sacred time–the end of Shabbat and the move to the new week.

Several of the rabbis with whom I spoke turned to the Passover story as symbolic material for individual divorce work. They understood the power of the ritual as reflected in that part of Karen's story where she described her combination of divorce practices as "having worked through" her "coming out," her "birthing"—going through "the mitzraim" (narrow straits). Netter ends his book with a reference to the Passover story and the reading of the Haggadah (the Passover liturgy): "In the middle of the Haggadah, just before the meal is to be eaten, there is a powerful little prayer. The prayer speaks to all of us who have been in a personal mitzrayim, . . . who have ever felt bound and constrained by life's traumas, who have ever suffered a personal crisis." The prayer, he says, is about being thankful to God, "who took us out from slavery to freedom, from sorrow to joy, from mourning to festivity, from darkness to great light, and from bondage to redemption" (186). Netter (2002, 112–113) legitimates the creation of rituals for divorce as divine action: "To make order out of chaos is a highly religious act. It is what God did in the beginning. . . . All creation is painful. All creation is unpredictable . . . but . . . all creation is Godlike, . . . creating order out of the chaos is mirroring the Divine. It is what God did at the beginning of the universe. It is what you do now."

Catholic and Jewish clergy had access to traditions rich with daily and life cycle ritual practices, but clergy in other traditions also worked to reframe symbolic practice and ceremony for the divorced. Mainline, evangelical, black church, and UU clergy did not have longstanding individual divorce practices like annulments or gets to refashion, but they did suggest to members who were ending a marriage that routine practices like attending weekly worship services, daily prayer or meditation, journaling, or reading the Bible were rituals that could accomplish divorce work, and they routinely turned to their symbolic worlds (see chapter 2) to interpret such practices in ways that brought connection to the sacred and affirmed religious and family identity. For example, UU ministers suggested that divorced people might light a candle or "say something" (no matter how vague) during the "joys and concerns" part of the weekly service to acknowledge through religious ceremony that they were experiencing transition. In the black church tradition, some clergy used the practice of Bible study groups and developed groups with themes of grief and loss. And of course, in all traditions, clergy supported and sometimes participated in the small group/support group format, bringing their religious toolkits full of familiar and evocative symbols and practices and using them to cast the divorce experience as sacred journey and/or relationship with divine healing energy.

Most of such routine rituals were individual-feeling-work strategies that took place through private communal worship. Promoting such alone-together ritual was, like refitting existing divorce practices, a nonthreatening intimate labor strategy through which clergy could suggest practices, but in which individuals remained in control of the course of their emotions. Still, some clergy did attempt to help members shape more explicit and participatory group divorce rituals in congregations. Such public invitation for congregants to join in reclamation of religious identity through divorce inevitably crossed into dangerous ritual territory.

Attempting Innovative Community Divorce Rituals

The clergy I interviewed from more conservative religious traditions did not speak about working to shape larger congregational rituals to mark divorce; they promoted individual and private small-group practices. It goes without saying that, for clergy to introduce new community rituals marking divorce, they needed the full support and input of the individual or couple ending a relationship, as well as congregational support for participation in such a ritual. Even in congregations that may be considered more liberal in their support of multiple types of family structures, clergy identified resistance, lack of participation, and disapproval of more public divorce rituals. These factors made such innovation rare and perishable.

Most stories of community divorce ritual where participants gathered as witnesses represented amicable endings of relationships, and took place in essentially private space. For example, Margaret, a UU minister, described her involvement in a ritual of separation for a lesbian couple who had been members of a congregation for about twenty years. The ritual took place in their home and with their closest friends, their kids who were grown, and the former husband of one. She described the ritual: "They had taken words from their commitment ceremony, marriage, or civil union, and they interpreted how they had honored those and yet the time had come to release one another. Everybody was gathered around in a circle, and I read their statement of release, and they released each other with a hug. They drank from a bottle of wine . . . a lovely bottle of wine that they had purchased together while married. They opened it and they drank from the same glass, and so it was sort of like the reverse of the Jewish sharing of wine, and they vowed to keep their family, their 'chosen family' their friends, intact." This was a communal ritual with select congregational members present, but it was also a space removed from the UU church building. The friends, family, and members of the congregation who were invited knew what the ceremony would entail, they knew each other, and they knew the couple. The level of negative feelings associated with the ending was not high. Those present acknowledged participation in the ritual through gathering in a circle and holding hands—signaling cooperation in the religious emotion at hand.

Sandy and Elaine's minister, Jerry, tried to offer his congregants a chance to bring a public ritual of divorce to the congregation. His motivation came in part from the fact that several core couples were ending relationships and he wanted to break the silence around divorce in his congregation. He attempted to work with Elaine and her husband to develop such a divorce ritual, but the couple were not "enthusiastic" about it, as Elaine and her exhusband confirmed in interviews. Jerry had pointed them to Carl Seaberg's book, where he knew there was a rite of divorce, but instead they took control of their own "coming out divorce ritual." They came up with their own brief public marking of the ending and their transition from an "ideal church couple" to divorced members of the congregation. Jerry described this: "During a church musical, they performed a skit where the ex-wife made her 'exhusband' the subject of a joke." After the final dress rehearsal, Jerry recalled advising the ex-wife: "You have to show his permission because otherwise they are not going to laugh at a thing you say. They'll be saying, 'Oh my God, did she just refer to her divorce, and did he know she was going to do that?'" Jerry worked with the couple to make clear that both were involved in performing the "joke." Still he found the skit a little uncomfortable: "I think it distracted people, but it was a way, publicly, of acknowledging the divorce. A couple of people laughed a little bit. It was almost taboo."

The fleeting nature of the ritual that Elaine and her husband created, and Margaret's example of a controlled and largely private communal ritual, demonstrate the social boundaries of public divorce ceremonies; detailed and prolonged sacred divorce ceremony demanded cooperation from all, and private space. Amy's example, which follows, illustrates the repercussions of performing more public community divorce ceremonies. Her story also speaks to the troubling dissonance that ritual participants may feel when both marriage and divorce are marked as sacred through collective ritual in familiar public congregational space. In her case, the emotional religious energy was intense and highly effective in marking the ending, but shocking and emotionally taxing for some who attended and did not expect to get swept away in a collective effervescence.[4] The ritual accomplished its end, which Amy, a sixty-year-old white Jewish woman, named as the marking of a "violent passage."

Amy, like Jill, was deeply drawn to Hebrew language and prayer. She described her divorce as mutual but painful, based on the realization that she and her husband had different goals for life as their children left for college. She said that, once they had made the decision to "release each other," and Amy had decided to move to pursue a new path in life, "people in the congregation wanted to say good-bye" and planned a party for her. Her ex-husband told her, "You know, we don't need a party, we need a ritual." He had been participating in a New Age spiritual group and so went to his spiritual guide, and she talked to her rabbi. The religious leaders spoke, and then they all worked together to develop a ritual, which took place in Amy's synagogue on a Shabbat afternoon. About fifty family and friends from the local community and congregation attended. Amy described the ritual in detail: "We walked in together with a cord that his spiritual leader had given him. It was a beautiful, burgundy cord, like you would use for fancy trims. We had tied it together around our waists and walked in together to symbolize that we were coming in together, but that we each would leave separately. We each had someone speak to the community for us about what was happening." Per the suggestion of her rabbi, they each "prepared something to say to each other that acknowledged the goodness, why we were making this choice, and what was missing." They heard each other's words for the first time during the ceremony:

> I talked to my husband about how he had allowed me to put down roots and feel secure, and that in doing that I discovered more of who I was. . . . I

understood that my new path was something that he couldn't do with me. . . . He didn't say anything in his about why we needed to separate; his words were just full of love and how much he loved me. The rabbi wanted us to eat something that had to do with the sweetness of our relationship, and also something that had to do with sadness. . . . Figs are symbolic in Judaism. Figs were the first fruit, the one Adam and Eve ate. They are sweet; I picked the figs from a tree I had passed often on my way to work, to represent the sweetness of what we had had together. And then we drank salt water for the tears, like we do on Passover. Near the ending of the ritual, my husband took a special ritual hand-flaked stone knife that his friend had made for him, and cut the cord connecting us. The rabbi had told us: "I want you to break something." And my ex-husband said, "Why? That is so violent." And the rabbi said, "What you are doing is violent, and you have to acknowledge that, you can't make believe this is all just sweet and we are friends." So, at the end of the ceremony the community sang some blessings for us, and then we had a plate wrapped in a napkin and we held it together and smacked it against the table. Then my husband took a corner of the cloth and pulled and all the broken shards tumbled to the floor. I just screamed—I'm telling you— you could hear a collective gasp from the whole crowd. My husband's friends ushered him out to a place they had planned, and two of my closest friends, as preplanned, took me into the rabbi's office and sat with me while I sobbed and sobbed and sobbed. One of them, who was a therapist, asked me, "Do you wish that you hadn't done this?" I stopped crying immediately and said no. It was very sad, but I was very clear. . . . But people were really worried. . . . The rabbi said we really shouldn't have done this on Shabbat. It was a very good ritual, but it was very, very sad.

KAY: A good ritual because—?

AMY: Because it was so real and so deep and it helped us articulate and make the paths that we needed to make. . . . At afternoon prayers, about an hour later, which I participated in alone with my congregation, I took out the Torah and walked around while everyone touched it. We looked deeply at each other . . . to assure them that I was okay. I felt more centered than ever before.

Amy's experience demonstrates the intensity of religious emotion that can surface when divorce work is accomplished in congregational space, and the troubling dissonance that ritual participants can feel when both marriage and divorce are marked as sacred through a large ritual ceremony. The gathering of individuals in large groups adds collective energy to the religious emotion at work. A private get, for example, may be filled with religious energy, but add children, other relatives, friends, and invite the wider congregation to participate, and the potential for the emotion to grow is strong. Imagine one hundred people witnessing, as Rabbi Netter describes, the love of his "youth dying on the altar of divorce." Amy's ritual demanded serious emotion work from congregants, friends, and family as they experienced the power of religious emotion ushering her through a painful transition. Even more, they were asked to participate in a ritual marking "true love" as terminable. Amy commented: "It was very hard on the family members. You know, you go to a wedding and refresh your vows. Well, what happened here [was] I heard people come and say, Oh my God, my wife is going to leave me. It was a terrifying thing, showing through ritual how you can be married for thirty years and how you can come apart. [Our children were there.]" "We spoke to the children in the rabbi's office before we went out. . . . People shy away from people who are divorcing, and it gave the community a way to support us, [but] I think it was very hard to do and after we did it, we knew why people don't do this. It's hard; it's worse than a funeral, in some ways."

I later interviewed the rabbi who led this ceremony, and he confirmed the heightened emotions and what he saw in retrospect as the inappropriate nature of the ritual: "I told Amy, when I told her I would talk to you, that I'll never do that kind of ceremony again. It was absolutely like out of a movie." He reflected: "The whole sanctuary was full, and I'm looking around the room and see the anguish in peoples' faces, like 'Why the hell am I here?' I remember this one guy came up to me afterward and said, 'Who decided to do this!' He didn't want to be there in the middle of that painful ceremony." The rabbi took some blame for underestimating the emotional power of such a ritual: "I really should have had the common sense to say that it was ill advised for several reasons. Number one— because if one assumes that it was good for her, I'm not so sure it was. It really foreclosed the full exploration of the feelings of her for her partner. It exposed him to the public." The rabbi also named the lack of clearly defined ritual roles for others present: "Number two and more importantly, the two grown kids were there, and it totally threw them into it, and it made them feel vulnerable in ways that they couldn't discuss. They weren't part of the ceremony; they weren't discussing. It wasn't right or fair for them. Also, it was not fair to the community. They received an invitation to come to an ending ceremony. They didn't really know all that would happen, they were not prepared. It wasn't fair." If someone were to think about conducting such a ritual, he made it clear, they should think "about what is the role of the community before the ritual. Are they voyeurs? It is uncomfortable to feel like a voyeur."

In the end, he doubted the religious and emotional value of any public ceremony: "I'm convinced that you shouldn't do it publicly. Even if so, I should have given the community time to prepare. This kind of ending is not fit for public modality. . . . It could [work with] a few people." He described what he thought would be appropriate: "Years ago I read in [the Jewish feminist magazine] *Lilith* [that] a Reform rabbi in Seattle advised that both partners should have grown escorts with them—so you go in separate directions with the friends after the ceremony and lead that passage into the world." In the end, he preferred doing this type of intimate labor as a highly private ritual: "When divorce ceremonies are done, I've found it is best with one person. I've done about ten such ceremonies over the years. I've never really liked the get and having both spouses there."

Each of these ritual attempts illustrates the power of religious space and symbol to mark transitions, and the dangerously sacred nature of divorce, calling attention to such endings and the sacred power that emerges through carefully constructed collective ritual. Elaine and her husband recognized this, marking their divorce only briefly and disguised in humor. Margaret and the two women ending their marriage understood the social force through their combination of symbolic gestures and crafted ceremony in home space with a small community of family and friends. Amy and her husband understood the impact that their ceremony would have for the community in marking their ending as mutual and recognizing Amy's departure from the community. These were cases where congregants sought clergy assistance to help reshape and create religious meaning to make sense of divorce transitions and affirm their identity as religious selves and good parents and family members. In most cases, clergy were not aware of endings as they happened, and, when they did work to refit and interpret religious symbols and practices for congregants, they used guarded approaches.

GUARDED EMOTIONAL LABOR

It took me eleven months to tell my rabbi that I was separated. I'm now separated sixteen months. It was something I felt uncomfortable about, ashamed
about. He is a very approachable young man who is not much older than we
are. It was a conflict of mine. . . . I told him on e-mail. And he wrote a beautiful
e-mail back saying that [his] door is open. I asked him to stick to e-mail, and
then I saw him a few days later, and he was great, he was great. . . . He greeted
me at synagogue, "my correspondent." He praised me, how I seemed to have
been strong through this, because he had no clue. . . . I showed up on Shabbat; my husband was never with me anyway. . . . So, he had no clue. He was
shocked, actually, as was the rest of the world.

Most clergy were cautious in providing divorce-work direction and lending
a sympathetic ear, waiting for members, like Jill above, to reach out and lay
the ground rules. One rabbi of a 650-member Conservative synagogue in a
mid-Atlantic state said: "My posture in life is, you call me, I don't call you.
Basically, I don't feel the right to be intrusive into people's lives. They might
feel like they can't say no to the rabbi." Besides, he stressed: "I'm busy doing
so many other things. I do thirty funerals a year and I teach four classes
a week!" Time constraints, fear of crossing intimate kin boundaries, an
emphasis on marriage ceremonies, and jobs dependent on routine congregational assessment came together to shape clergy's guarded approaches.

Clergy preferred adopting the compassionate listener stance and were
cautious about claiming professional expertise in counseling. Father Allen
told me that most priests lack professional degrees that would qualify them
as counselors. Still, like other clergy, he sometimes engaged in limited counseling: "People who are connected to the church will want to come to us
for some kind of marriage counseling, or, if the husband or wife has left,
some come to say, How do I get through this. This is maybe 20 percent of
my work." Some clergy qualified their expertise, noting they were trained as
a counselor but only engaged in crisis counseling and were careful to refer
members to a "professional therapist" when they thought extended therapy was needed. One rabbi in a large Reform synagogue in a northeastern
city noted that, at Hebrew Union College in the mid-1990s, the students
"had counseling classes, but we didn't have training in serious marital or
divorce counseling. The goal of the rabbinic program, at least at the time,
was to give us enough information to not do any harm and know when

to refer. . . . There was never an assumption that we could hold ourselves out as counselors or therapists." A black Baptist minister in a southern city noted: "I believe in referral because I realize as a pastor I can only take you so far, and there are other agencies and so forth that can handle other stuff." Another black Baptist minister of an urban southern church noted: "If someone came to me I would refer to a counselor, one that I know around here who is a pastoral care counselor. Someone outside of the church who knows the nuts and bolts."

Clergy felt more comfortable claiming therapeutic authority when it came to pre-marriage and marriage counseling. In black churches, especially, where a larger discourse about lower marriage and higher divorce rates in black communities was a topic, clergy stressed putting their efforts into pre-marriage counseling and helping marriages last. One African Methodist Episcopal pastor lamented: "People are not getting married anymore. More and more people are having children out of wedlock, and in the black community this is a huge problem. It is a tragedy." Marriage is not happening in the first place, he said, and this is "an area where the African American community is bleeding and in great need of help. Pastors are scared of this. They don't have models to work with, so it doesn't get addressed."

Several clergy members, from both conservative and liberal congregations, wanted to talk about their efforts trying to save marriages, refocusing our conversation even as I stressed my research interest in people's experiences of endings. An example from a black Baptist minister:

KAY: What do you say to someone who has left a marriage?
(*Silence*)
KAY: Did they not come to you?
MINISTER: No, they didn't. One of the things that we have here that I think is a blessing is a marriage ministry, a couples' ministry. Couples get together, talk; they do a retreat. Where we get away and . . . have sessions on how to hold on in rough times and how to understand. The key to the marriage, I tell people—I raise the question—[is] do you talk? Do you communicate? That is something that most people don't do.

That many clergy across traditions wanted to tell me stories about keeping marriages together, even though my core interview questions were about how they engaged those who were divorced or ending a marriage, is not surprising. Clergy were comfortable in these scripted roles they performed more frequently through premarital counseling and marriage ceremonies.

My interviews suggest that, although all clergy stressed the importance of marriage work for couples considering ending, their approaches regarding reconciliation once a person had made a clear decision to end varied. Two of my respondents in conservative Protestant churches who had been in physically abusive marriages chose to stay away from their minister and from lay counselors in their congregation to avoid what they saw as a blind emphasis on reconciliation.

Like Father Allen, several clergy felt that people who were having marital difficulties "used" them—seeking them out under the pretense of receiving religious counseling for marriages, but really wanting religious permission to end the marriage. The pastoral counselors I interviewed confirmed this dynamic; for example, one Methodist counselor noted that most are divorced in reality if not yet in law; "before they enter my office, even though they are trying to work on the marriage, one person has already made the decision." Lilly is an example of someone turning to clergy after a decision has been made, guiding her pastor to validate her own interpretative authority. She was a fifty-six-year-old African American woman who left her husband of thirty years, with whom she had had two children. Lilly claimed individual authority through a sacred singles script: "I prayed and I waited and I listened to hear God speak to me that it was time because I'd done all I could do to try and make it work." She waited until she had moved out, and then told her best friend. Weeks later, she went to talk with her pastor: "He listened to me and asked, 'What do you mean you moved out?' I said, 'I moved out. I packed up and found me a house and I moved out.' He said, 'Have you been back?' I said, 'No.' And he said, 'You moved out?' And again I said, 'Yes, I moved out.' It wasn't easy. I'd been in this relationship for over thirty years. Starting a whole new life was, he said, 'courageous.' I told him, 'It takes faith and courage, and right now I'm kind of shaky, but I'm determined because I believe this is what I'm supposed to do." Throughout her telling of her story, her pastor listened and legitimated her actions, affirming her sense of having followed God's word and the religious meaning she placed on her emotional ending of the relationship. He questioned her, but only briefly, and, she said, ultimately affirmed her sacred path. In the COGIC case, several respondents also brought their decisions about marriage directly to God through prayer, rather than decide through meeting with their pastor.

Clergy tread lightly in claiming moral ground, or in using core religious beliefs to get members to at least talk with them. Margaret, a white Unitarian minister, described learning of a couple's breakup through another member and then reaching out to the couple: "I knew that it was a difficult situation. I asked them to come in and visit with me after the divorce was final and they did." The former husband at first resisted, but Margaret carefully approached him, drawing from core UU beliefs, "Look, I can understand you don't want to do this. But shouldn't we, in honor of human beings and what faith teaches us about the inherent worth and dignity of every person—wouldn't it be good if we could—just have something that brought more peace and closure in a way that makes human sense, as opposed to legal sense?" A difficult meeting followed, but one she saw as accomplishing marriage work and emotional reconciliation: "I had them talk about what good things they could take away from it all. What they learned." Margaret felt strongly that the husband needed to work on communication issues that might get in the way of building another life partnership, but her approach was nonthreatening as she emphasized marriage work for both of them. At the end of the meeting, "They were hugging and saying good-bye and letting one another go." They each told her that, "if they had left it the way it was when they left the lawyers, they would have had a wholly different perspective on the ending." Margaret described the process as "beautiful," and "sacramental to watch." She called the couple to the table with the limited authority she had, and interpreted religious ideals to fit divorce work: "They did it. I just set up the frame by which they did it." Margaret thus affirmed UU principles of individual authority in crafting spiritual emotion work.

Unlike the physical death of a family member, where clergy roles are well rehearsed and mutually understood, family disruptions like divorce or dealing with addictions lacked practiced social performances. For example, one Protestant pastor from a New England congregation stressed it was difficult to know when clergy are wanted: "Some people come and think, Oh my gosh, I'm going through this hard time and my minister didn't call, how horrible! And other people are like, What are you doing here?" Several clergy members talked about feeling vulnerable and out of place in the middle of couples who are ending their marriage. One COGIC pastor told me that he kept a "safe distance" after "learning his lesson" when one couple called him to their home during a domestic violence dispute where he felt helpless and out of place. Clergy felt multiple factors at work in trying to decipher if, when, and how to approach congregants as they were struggling with and ending marriages. Adopting the position of compassionate listener helped clergy manage the equivocal nature of this intimate labor.

In Sandy and Elaine's small UU church, Jerry held the only official pastoral position, and he said his goal was to be an understanding listener. He was careful about intruding in members' health and family issues and generally waited until members came to him. Several members who had relationships end as members of his congregation told me they had gone to talk with him. When they did come to him, he created a therapeutic space in his office. Sandy recalls her first visit with him as just a time for her to "weep in his office." The next visit, Jerry invited her to start writing down her feelings: "He was like, just make these quick little things, a picture or a little written paragraph. He has a way about him, you know to anchor and reflect, but not in a forceful way—[not a] 'Now you should be doing this!' He will sometimes reflect personally on things that happened to him, but it never turns into being about him, which I appreciate."

My respondents expected that their ministers, rabbis, and priests should listen attentively to their feelings. If clergy could not do this labor themselves, given the size of a congregation, some had pastoral assistance from lay or professional church staff, or constructed small group spaces where members could find compassionate listeners. Margaret's church, for example, like many other UU congregations, had an organized group of "lay pastoral care associates," people who would, she said, "mostly listen" and let people "speak without judgment." They would also inform her of members who might need help. In two of the largest churches in which I conducted field studies (one mainline, the other evangelical nondenominational, and both over 250 households), the congregation had an official pastoral counselor on staff, someone whose primary job was to listen to church members and offer advice if desired.

Jamie, a black Baptist minister in a southern city, had a master's degree in pastoral care and counseling. He was new to his congregation and, so, careful not to ask too many questions about individuals and families he was just getting to know. When divorced members came to him for individual counseling sessions, he gave them space to "walk through the pain of their lives."

He described patient listening: "I only spoke when there was the opportunity to speak. . . . I just let them run on. . . . You just let them talk and then, when they get to the point where they want to hear from you, you speak. Or they will break down, and you will talk." Drawing from classes he had taken in seminary, and later through the National Baptist Congress, he had created a "grief Bible study" that ran for six sessions, another expressive space where people could "pour out what they were feeling." In his most recent class, seven out of the thirteen members were divorced.

Clergy who did delicately reach out to members they suspected were in the midst of separation and divorce waited for subtle clues. In the black church case, ministers gingerly approached couples; for example, two ministers noted that they would throw out "nuggets" if they learned of a couple having difficulty or an individual dealing with a breakup. Daniel, a pastor in a large urban Baptist church, said: "If I'm led to it by another member or gossip, I would throw out some nuggets, as a good pastor. I would say, 'We need to talk now?'" Also, he would notice if couples who attended church together stopped coming or sat in separate pews: "Eventually you would see one fading off; as time would go on they would bring someone they were dating to church. So that left you, as a preacher, in an awkward position." I asked Daniel why he thought most people did not come to him: "Shame, pride, hurt, disgust, so many reasons. Mostly pride. Because most couples paint marriage as though it is the best thing in the world, and then, when it collapses, it brings a sense of shame and guilt." I pressed: "So they don't come to you?" He replied, "Very few people, until it's final." He said some women in abusive situations would seek help and advice, but "So many people wrestle with divorce alone. . . . The thought of people knowing their business, the shame" kept even some abused women away. They felt, he said, "a sense of defeat . . . , as though they are lost, they didn't accomplish the American Dream, living with a family, a husband, the one you love."

How much clergy knew about congregants' partnerships, and the authority these clergy had to break silences through guarded practice, was related to clergy credibility, which surfaced in two primary ways: when one spouse saw clergy as being too close to their soon-to-be-ex-spouse, or when clergy experienced their own marital disruptions. Most of my respondents in more liberal religious traditions did not put much weight on whether or not their religious leader had been divorced, and in fact some, like Jill, found such a status reassuring. But in more conservative churches, a minister's divorce often became a concern to members.

One COGIC minister of a small southern rural congregation, who had not been divorced, told me, "Some members can't handle their pastors being divorced." Two of the black Baptist ministers I interviewed in cities in the South saw divorced pastors as a pervasive problem. One said: "The ratio in the clergy is high, and I think all except one, out of ten of my friends—one or two, maybe, have *not* been divorced, and they are under forty-three. Maybe two out of ten—so it's high among the clergy!" Five of my respondents told stories about divorced pastors who did not meet their expectations of a "Man of God." Two pastors in my sample from conservative churches (one a white evangelical Southern Baptist and the other a COGIC minister) had been asked to leave the ministry because they became divorced while serving their congregations. Daniel reflected: "It was interesting; one of the things that I noticed in interviewing for this job was they wanted a preacher who had never been divorced, but they have been divorced. Some of the people who set up the criteria, they have been divorced themselves! I think that is just crazy."

Divorce is a more of a disruption for clergy, given the demands and public nature of their jobs.[5] While a divorce prior to becoming a minister can lie hidden, experiencing divorce is hard to hide, especially when a pastor's wife or husband probably has some role, formal or informal, in congregational life. When clergy divorce, expectations of sacred divorce work bear down, and members of a congregation may judge them. For example, one black Baptist woman made a point of telling me that she was not close with her pastor, because she felt he had not managed his separation well or demonstrated to the congregation that he was doing the necessary marriage work: "Some people left the church because of it. . . . This was wife number three. . . . I told him, I said, 'What is going on?' You know. And he finally said that they were in counseling. And I said, 'You are about to lose your church if you don't say something.' So he got up and he said to the congregation that he and his wife were having some problems and were in counseling, trying to work it out, and people were supportive of that. I was even supportive of that, because I think a lot of us had been in the same boat at one point or another. . . . I think everybody was of the mindset of 'Hey, you can't condemn him for getting a divorce, everybody is supposed to be happy.'" She said that talking to the congregation and going to counseling as the marriage ended helped repair some damage, but she was also clear that she would never reach out to him to talk about her divorce. Essentially, in her story, she held the authority, counseling him regarding affirmation of his religious position through divorce experience.

CAUTIOUS ENCOUNTERS

Important patterns emerge in the stories of the twenty-five professional clergy I interviewed, in clergy texts, and in respondents' narratives of interactions with priests, pastors, and rabbis. First, the limitedness of the authority that clergy had over congregants' relational lives was vivid and shaped cautious approaches. Most important, the sermons, rituals, groups and individual counseling sessions the clergy constructed generally respected the private nature of divorce, thus adhering to divorce-work principles and maintaining the sacred character of marriage and life partnership. Constructing highly sacred symbolic ritual for divorce work in collective religious space made the delicate nature of balancing marriage and divorce culture almost too visible—and thus too threatening to life partnership as sacred.

Clergy owned religious emotion through their relationship to religious tools. As they communicated intimate care strategies for repairing social bonds, they were keenly aware of the emotional power that their bodies, language, and voices had, and of the command that their symbolic worlds had for helping members fend off family and religious shame and propel sacred passage. Emotional sway came from their voices that delivered weekly sacred messages, their hands that touched sacred bread and wine. Their influence was also garnered through the authority to perform marriages, baptisms, and religious conversions. Still, any authority that came from this religious emotion could be undermined by their own performance of family, and depended in some part on their tenure, relationship, and history with the congregation.

My respondents' stories indicate that the creation of routine structured divorce work through more open congregational religious ceremony is doubtful. Some UU members attempted public congregational moments of recognition: Sandy lit a candle for ending her relationship, during Sunday service, and Elaine and her husband created their own brief comic performance of the ending; still, these were brief and fleeting practices. The ritual Margaret facilitated implied a congregational presence, but the ceremony took place in the nonthreatening private space of the couple's home.

Amy's story was the only one that demonstrated a more public congregational ritual that used religious symbol and emotion to frame divorce as sacred experience, but her assessment and the reflections of the rabbi who conducted the ceremony indicate that such a ritual was too uncomfortable and, for the time being, will remain rare. Specifically, some seemed emotionally disturbed by the theatrical and highly emotional ritual performance, which magnified the precarious nature of marriage and life partnership and, even more, the sacred nature of divorce culture. Two people who loved each other deeply and had been together for many years were making a well-thought-out decision to end their relationship on the basis that they were moving as individuals in separate directions—this was a difficult narrative, for individuals invested in life partnership as sacred, to hear through profound collective ritual. Perhaps even more unsettling to some, the ritual could be seen as validating serial monogamy through persuasive collective religious emotion.

In the end, clergy were there to engage in intimate labor for members, to provide religious tools and effective scripts for emotion management, but they were not there to impose these, and had limited authority.[6] Emotion work and spiritual identity remained largely in the hands of individuals. As Stephen Hilgartner (2000, 5) noted regarding the social performance of expert guidance, "The ability to offer authoritative advice is obviously not an entitlement, automatically bestowed on any group that seeks it, but something that advisors must actively assert, cultivate, and guard." This is exceptionally so in therapeutic culture, where individuals are understood as actively seeking remedy and meaning across institutional contexts.

Clergy learned to negotiate authority through individual relationships in congregations. Several respondents talked about engaging in such intimate labor with divorced members as "on-the-job training." Father Allen noted that there "is an assumption that a lot of this kind of learning will be done as either seminarians or junior clergy, where you are sitting at the table with a pastor that is hopefully older and smarter. . . . What I'm sharing with you is sixteen years of either asking smarter people or making huge mistakes . . . and learning the lessons."

A private, personalized approach by clergy is likely to be pervasive across the majority of religious traditions in North America. Julie MacFarlane (2012), for example, found a similar refitting of traditional Islamic law and principles to individual circumstances. In interviewing imams in the United States and Canada, she discovered that they routinely adapted religious divorce decrees to fit personal circumstances, and that some of the divorced individuals she interviewed would shop around for an imam who would give a desired response.

Although many respondents were drawn to particular congregations because of family and individual religious history, a person could still leave a congregation. Clergy were well aware of this dynamic; and thus even conservative clergy knew that they had to actively interpret and uphold marriage doctrine in ways that allowed for sacred divorce practices.

The individual and private nature of respondents' search for therapeutic and religious strategies highlights the multiple forces at work in the creation of religious identity through divorce transitions. Some respondents appealed to clergy, but they more often assembled their own religio-therapeutic repertoires, activating the emotional sway of religious symbol, language, and sacred space outside of congregations. Thus clergy represent one religious tool in the lives of my respondents who, born of a therapeutic culture invested in individualism, recognized that they had the moral authority to construct their own versions of sacred divorce work.

5 ✳ RICH LIVED PRACTICE

Nancy Ammerman (2007, 2014) and Meredith McGuire (2008) call attention to the significance of a lived religious lens that captures the subjective and bodily experiences of religion and spirituality as they occur in everyday life. My respondents took collective meanings outside of their congregations and into their everyday lives as they managed divorce. Their religious tools held efficient emotional force: "*Spirit of Life*" accompanied Sandy as she sang alone at her potter's wheel, and the love ballads that Jeff first felt in the pews of his home church were stored inside, stirring a closeness with divine energy as he rode in his car listening to familiar words and music.[1]

Fairly secure in middle-class positions, most of my respondents had the time, money, and transportation to attend functions in multiple spaces and to access media resources. Their stories show a strong emphasis on the individualism that drives religious and therapeutic culture, as they narrate efforts to work hard, take control of their lives, and move forward. An analysis of how my respondents assembled religious practices from varied sources in day-to-day life brings to light dynamic constructions of religious identity, family, and approaches to divorce work shaped by economic position. Distinct and multiple religious approaches surfaced in their stories of lived practice as they managed emotions associated with transitions to new family, changed religious roles, and, for some, serious physical challenges.

"YOU WILL RECEIVE A ROSE"

Sue's religious practice was full and varied. She attended Protestant services, a DivorceCare group, and Catholic mass, prayed in the hospital chapel where she worked, joined CDM support groups, went through an annulment process, and engaged in continued conversation and prayer with her "friends" (as she termed the saints she felt a closeness to), especially Saint Therese the Little Flower. She had stayed in an unhappy marriage for years because she felt it was what she needed to do to be a "good Catholic"; as she left her husband, constant prayer in everyday life helped her affirm her religious status.

Although drawn to mass for emotional nourishment and connection, Sue also described feeling alienated by homilies that continually reinforced normative family ideals. To avoid the shame such worship experiences brought, she often prayed in the Catholic hospital chapel where she worked: "So I would go to church Monday through Friday at the chapel because I would not be hearing a homily. . . . I wouldn't be with families, and I wouldn't see husbands and wives. You protect yourself. But you don't want to walk away from God." She fought to claim a strong, individual Catholic identity: "I don't want to really be singled out. . . . I just want to be a Catholic woman. Yeah, I'm a Catholic woman who happens to be divorced, but I'm a Catholic woman first."

Given that she worked in a Catholic institution, she had more than her desk or a break room for prayer; she had access to a physical space with visual reminders of religious emotion—pews, stained glass, images of crosses. In her work life, she had sacred space at her fingertips; in the hospital chapel and other everyday spaces, she initiated contact with God and her saints. Sue's private devotional prayers to certain saints represented essential lifelong relationships that had the power to manage painful emotions and to bring tangible results. The teachings of the Catholic Church, were "very important" to her, and her relationship with holy figures was a part of her and a vital force in her lived religious life: "They are my friends. Saint Therese Little Flower—I've had a devotion to her for a long time. Tradition is that, when she hears your prayer, you will receive a flower, you will receive a rose. You either smell it, see it, or receive it, and I cannot tell you how many roses have come my way. Saint Jude, Saint Joseph, Mary, you know; I cannot—they are my friends, and you can't turn your back on your friends. You know, you can't say, 'You don't exist any longer.' So I can't; they are my friends. They got me through all that I needed to get through in these last thirteen to fourteen years."

In Sue's narrative, Saint Therese the Little Flower is a major character and an instigator of good fortune. She answered Sue's prayers during the final difficult years of marriage, as Sue left her husband and managed her son's resentment; the saint helped her construct life as a single woman. Sue talked about her relationship with the saint as giving her the material needs that allowed her to take control of her own life—to be a single Catholic woman with sacred purpose. First, the saint sent her a colleague at the hospital who had a condominium for her to rent, and then brought another employee who prayed in the chapel beside her and became a therapeutic confidant. Such material and nonmaterial gifts were "roses" from Saint Therese, a sign of the saint's everlasting presence in Sue's life as a companion and guide when difficult personal and family problems or transitions arose.

As Robert Orsi (2005) makes clear, such Catholic devotionalism represents complex networks of relationships between individual bodies, holy figures, and human connections that surge through everyday lives. In Sue's story, holy figures and therapeutic counseling served as emergency intervention when life-threatening divorce emotions presented: "The day that I contemplated suicide, God, my guardian angel, guided me to my therapist's office, and God was with me the whole time and he held my hand through it all." Without God and her friends the saints: "I would not be here today. I would not have what I have and every step of the way opportunities, doors of opportunities have opened for me to have a better job at work, to work in administration, to increase my pay, to have this condo." She credited her health, her relationship with her adult son, and even her children's and grandchildren's health to her holy friends and God's active hand in her life: "None of this could be possible without God, none of it. Absolutely none."

Prayer and her relationship with the saints, as well as other religious practices inside and outside of formal religious spaces, gave her the emotional, physical, and material tools to become what she understood as a better and stronger self, to do the divorce work necessary to move forward. Her efforts in multiple spaces and spiritual relationships made divorce a sacred path: "I do believe that God takes you out of bad situations because you are dying. I was dying in the marriage, and God doesn't want that for any of us. So I believe that He takes you out of the situation, gives you the opportunity, because we all have free will." In her story, a performance of free will is center stage: she takes responsibility for her growth, and plays a highly active part, becoming a better self for her son, herself, and those God meant her to serve in grief ministries in her new life as a single woman.

Prayer in musical, written, or spoken form is a religious tool to bring order and meaning as well as the power to cope with difficult life circumstances.

Prayer is essentially a religious practice aimed to produce emotional connection with a force larger than the self. That force can be an ethnic-religious people, such as Jill's Jewish ancestors, with whom she bonded in synagogue services. It can be imagined as spirit or energy, as in the understanding by Elaine, a Unitarian Universalist, of singing as "swimming around in God." It can be seen as a collective energy or a life force, such as Sandy's "web of being." Prayer can be inward focused, meaning it emphasizes examining or transforming individual bodies and emotion; outward focused, meaning it emphasizes linking together with other people; and/or upward focused, concerned with a divine-human connection.[2] Prayer practice takes many forms and is an accessible religious tool regardless of economic position.[3] In my respondents' stories, there is a largely *meditative prayer* function—people experiencing connection to a force larger than themselves, a link that facilitates a calming of emotion and a sensation of physical healing.

Sue credits divine connection to keeping her alive, healing her body and mind from depression, and giving her a place to live and work. Elaine sings throughout the day, working to replace the energy that fighting with her husband drained from her body. Martha, a Catholic who suffered multiple physical traumas and abuses in her life, described singing as taking her "down to the molecular, the subatomic level," a place where she was reminded that she was a "creation of God's love" (God's love as "literally part of the atoms and molecules" in her "cellular structure"). Adopting a lived religious perspective leads to a focus on the application of such religious emotion in body-healing processes. Meredith McGuire (2007) calls attention to the embodied and practical nature of religious practice, noting, "If we want to understand the full range of religion as practiced and experienced by ordinary people in the context of their everyday lives, we need to be aware of how people's religious and spiritual expressions engage their material bodies and address their material concerns" (187). She adds, "Human bodies matter, because those practices—even interior ones, such as contemplation—involve people's bodies as well as their minds and spirits."

My respondents' narratives generally demonstrate multiple approaches to sacred divorce work as they sought to heal bodies and minds and affirm family and religious social bonds. These respondents' stories of lived religion demonstrate that they may have been fixed in distinct traditions and congregations, but they had exceptional ability to acquire strategies from religious and secular sources to craft individual repertoires of divorce-work strategy. In additional examples, Janet seeks out small-group spaces and positions visual images of the psalms in everyday space as she deals with the end of her life partnership, the death of her son, and the death of his father. Emma and Brenda tell stories of numerous individualized religious practices that come together to give strength of body and mind, practices they describe as making them better able to care for self and children and forgive ex-spouses. Walter and John tell of sacred divorce work that crossed multiple spaces while they managed feelings in ways that legitimated their roles as custodial fathers and strengthened their spiritual position; their approach to lived practice complemented the fluid and open nature of contemporary family structure and changing form.

"MUSIC WAS MY ESCAPE"

Walter was employed full-time as a music ministry leader in his small family COGIC congregation. "Pentecostal, Church of God in Christ," he said "is all I know." The church was his life's work and his spiritual and family home. His father was the minister, and thus Walter had congregational status as a "first family" member. There had been times when he wanted to go to another church but, as a "loyal person," stayed because his father "needed" him. He did not leave when he divorced; rather, he kept to himself: "One thing I've learned about the church, and that I've especially learned about going through this divorce, is that a lot of people speculate about . . . fault . . . , so I had to protect my son and my daughter [by keeping] people out of my business. I didn't even tell my mother or my parents until it was necessary." In his story, protecting his son and daughter was not easy; he described the years around his divorce as a trying period.

Walter talked about having to fight dangerous emotions capable of destroying family relationships: "I really had to keep myself in check, as hard as it was. It was tough. I really wanted to put my hands around her [ex-wife's] neck." He knew the anger was "natural," but also that he had to work to control it. As he talked of the hardship, his eyes became teary: "I really had to be extra careful how I carried myself. There were times that I would be riding down the street and would burst out crying. I would be like I don't know why I am crying. Hurt and anger. I went from two incomes to one income. My son and daughter were living with me. Everything was falling on me. Sometimes the pressure was like crazy."

The major thread in Walter's narrative was of taking control of his emotions for his children's sake. He talked about how he turned his passionate anger into what he later described as a deep forgiveness and loving lifelong dedication to his ex-wife: "I didn't see a counselor. What kept me sane and kept me from going off was going to church, the word of God, and reading my Bible. That is when I really started searching scriptures, as far as dealing with marriage and relationships." God, he said, spoke to him: "Where it says in the Bible that 'we wrestle not against flesh and blood'—well, what He showed in that was that the battle was not between me and her—it was between the forces of good and evil." Walter became able to separate the forces of evil from the person of his ex-wife.

Reading the Bible was not the only religious practice that Walter activated in his everyday world. Listening to music outside of services, along with writing, performing, and recording music outside of the congregation, were essential in his efforts to calm his anger. "There was a song I used to sit and listen to, over and over. 'Do Not Pass Me By.' I used to listen to it over and over and over, then start crying." His pursuit of hearing and making music outside the congregation provided emotion work in a safe space where he could express feelings that he did not want his children to hear: "Music! Music was my escape. Me and my partner had a production company. I found myself writing songs about marriage, divorce, and love. We even wrote this one song that said 'What God has put together let no man put asunder.' It was an awesome song. . . . I was in a zone, then; music was like helping me heal. I was getting it out on paper, instead of holding it in and wanting to kill someone." Walter shared a CD with a song whose slow and steady beat accompanied lyrics that expressed his anger, his position on his ex-wife's behavior, and an effort to reach out to others. The chorus was "What God has joined together let no man put asunder." The verses included lyrics with these words: "You made a vow before God and man. Now you want to go and change the master plan. . . . You have a home. You have kids, what you thinking about, in a room in another's arms with the lights out. You say it's love, it's love, but it's not the same because your marriage license is in another name. . . . So you go home to your husband and you go home to your wife. . . . Don't you defy that marriage, . . . Go back to your wife. Go back to your husband." Music was Walter's job, his emotional release, and his life's work—an easily accessible tool for conjuring religious emotion. He hoped the song would save marriages, but, even more, he understood writing, performing, and recording this song as his way of taking care of his children by gaining control of his emotions.

As Tia DeNora notes (2000, 53), music can help people "shift mood or energy level, as perceived situations dictate, or as part of the 'care of the self.'" Music can be a vehicle people use to move from stress or fatigue; its "specific properties—its rhythms, gestures, harmonies, styles, and so on— are used as referents or representations of where they wish to be or go, emotionally, physically." Music was at the fingertips of most of my respondents; they were not all composers, musicians, or loyal choir members, but they could at least sing softly to themselves, and had the resources to listen to music on electronic devices like IPods and smart phones. Almost all respondents talked about the emotional power they felt when singing or listening to familiar hymns and religious music or liturgy. Those who identified as musicians and performers talked about the creation of music as efficient expressive practice for managing painful or volatile emotions and their physical manifestations.

Composing music was creative emotion work for Walter and other respondents, who offered me copies of their recordings. Aaron, for example, a thirty-year-old white nondenominational evangelical Christian, had married immediately out of college, but divorced five years later, at age twenty-seven. We talked for an hour on the phone, one morning three years after his divorce. He felt guilty about his "addiction to pornography," which he saw as responsible for his divorce, and said he was still in love with his ex-wife. He had struggled with feeling out of place and had been severely depressed: "I just wished I wouldn't wake up. I never planned to commit suicide or anything like that. But life lost its thunder for me, and I didn't want to keep going." In addition to attending a new church, reading the Bible, and praying throughout the day, doing music was, he felt, his most efficient practice: "It's hard to understand how important music is in my life. I am in a worship band at church, and they are great, but I also have my own band that I play with here, and I've written a lot of original music, probably like fifty or more songs. A lot of them stem in things surrounding the divorce and heartbreak and things like that. That's kind of how I've coped with things; instead of checking out or doing something destructive, I'll write a song about it. You know, thinking about it and seeing something positive from a negative experience has been good. You have a chance to share it with people." Aaron sent me a sound file of one of his songs that talked about being the wreckage of something that used to be whole, and of how God surrounds his body and lifts him up again. His story followed a script of free will/individualism, taking control of his life, and moving forward. With music, prayer, and finding a new congregation, he was able to find new purpose, work again in youth ministries, and concentrate on building the relationship skills to succeed in marriage.

Walter's concern and efforts regarding his children's health were front and center in his story, and he too presented himself as moving forward. He saw himself as a new kind of father, caring for his kids full-time and protecting them after divorce: "A lot of people can't believe that she let me keep the kids. I am, like, 'Yeah, because she didn't want a fight on her hands.' One thing that I understood is that my children did not ask to be here. At the time, we . . . agreed that it would be a better situation if they stayed with me." In his narrative, he also worked hard on his relationship with his ex-wife, doing the intimate labor of divorce necessary for his children to feel secure in their relationships with both parents. In addition to working on music, he often turned to the scriptures in his everyday life to help cope with emotions and manage his new relationship with his ex-wife: "'If your brother falls, you who are able restore him back'—Galatians the sixth chapter, I am paraphrasing . . . also in that same chapter, 'Be not deceived, God is not mocked, whatsoever a man soweth, that shall he also reap.' So I had to watch how I treated her. That's what kept me treating her like that. Never missing a birthday, never missed a Christmas, never missed a Mother's Day, because I wanted my kids to know: 'Despite what your mother did, this is what you are supposed to do. This is how you are supposed to treat her. I don't care what is going on, let's go and get a gift.'" He saw constant connection to the scriptures as helping his future relationship with his children: "She could never say that I didn't show my kids how they are supposed to treat her." Lived practice helped Walter manage fatherhood as his family changed structure.

Like others in the black church case, Walter also had a desire, hope, and belief that God could send him a new love: "Divorce is not the end. Sometimes you don't think that you would ever find happiness or love again. . . . I will tell you that it does happen again, and God can send you somebody that you can trust again. You can be happy again and really enjoy what marriage is supposed to be." Through his daily religious practice, he felt secure that he had done the necessary marriage work to succeed when God sent him someone: "It [the divorce] gave me a chance to sit back and examine mistakes that I've made, and I vowed that, okay, I will not make these same mistakes again. One thing guys got to know, and even women—you can't take your mate for granted. You can't assume that they know that you love them. You can't assume that she knows she looks good. You've got to tell her; if you don't, someone else is going to compliment her hair. If you don't see that she has changed her hair color, someone else is noticing. If you don't, there is somebody in the world waiting. They are waiting."

Many of my respondents talked about reading as effective religious practice. Reading the Bible helped Walter reflect and assess what went wrong in his marriage, but he also was able to search outside of his Pentecostal subculture for emotion-work strategies in other texts. He talked about reading secular and religious books, "anything that is dealing with marriage and the mind." The mind, he believes, is where the "whole process is taking place. That is why so many people go crazy and kill, because it's such a battle in your mind." Reading self-help books about relationships, combined with Walter's explicit Pentecostal strategies of "spiritual warfare,"[4] helped him calm the anger that raged through his body during those first months and years: "My blood pressure went up and I couldn't sleep. I'm thinking about this, how I'm going to do that, and then I'm arguing with her about this and that. Then you still have the emotional attachment. It's really crazy, at times."

Religious books, CDs, television, spiritual self-help, and online media venues were essential parts of many of my respondents' lived practices. Several women noted watching *Oprah* or similar talk shows as frequent practice for managing emotions and learning spiritual practices. Engaging print and/or online text and preaching was also a safe private strategy for acquiring what some respondents saw as expert religious and therapeutic advice. Popular self-help books like *Crazy Time* and the novel *Eat Pray Love*, a popular post-divorce travel and spiritual log published in 2006 by Elizabeth Gilbert (and which is a book that begins with a sobbing and broken self, a "madwoman" on the bathroom floor), were mentioned by respondents, across traditions. Several persons, mostly those from upper-middle-class backgrounds, noted sociologist Diane Vaughan's book *Uncoupling* as a "hot" read; one respondent even described it as a "spiritual read," and Jill called it "the Bible of the divorced." *Uncoupling*, they argued, captured the essence of what it was like to move through the transitions of ending an intimate relationship. This book was an important title in what one Jewish man named his "arsenal of books": "I've read many books. Some of them are quite secular; some of them are very spiritual or even religious. . . . The second [breakup] time around, I had my books ready to go and I bought a bunch more." Todd (see chapter 3) had amassed what he called his "love library" of "One hundred and twenty books . . . on God, love, and relationships." Reading these books made him grow and gave him insight and skills for marriage; he described them as not only "Christian" but "metaphysical" and "secular," as well. This library helped him communicate with his ex-wife and do the marriage work of divorce: "I physically sat down with her, and I said: 'I would like to ask your forgiveness, because in the past five years I really discovered that I made a lot of mistakes in our marriage. I had a lot of issues, ignorance, and pride, and I know that I hurt you and I hurt the kids.'"

In Walter's story, recording music with his Christian band, reading the Bible and secular and religious texts, and practicing daily prayer fostered his relationship with God, which he understood as helping him protect his children, nurture his relationship with his ex-wife, and learn how to establish a stronger marriage should God choose a woman for him. Even though, in this narrative, God was active in his efforts to calm body and mind, Walter's story was largely of a man taking charge, grasping familiar religious practices and beliefs to calm his emotions.

In addition to the composition of music and lyrics, daily practices of poetry, journaling, and other forms of religious writing were prominent in respondents' stories.

"THE AUTOBIOGRAPHY OF MY EMOTIONS"

I read a poem John contributed to a volume for divorced Catholics that I purchased at a CDM conference. The book was a text documenting his emotions throughout his marriage and divorce. I wrote John a letter asking him for an interview, and he responded. He was a white middle-class man in his late fifties and had been divorced more than fifteen years, and his storied emotional life of divorce felt complete and carefully fashioned. He talked in our interview about the difficulties and rewards of having full custody of his four children after his wife left him, and of the essential role that writing poetry played in his healing from his divorce.

John identified as a "very private guy" who did not open up to many people in his parish, which he described as "a huge church . . . not a small community where you know all the faces and names." When his wife left, he approached a nun who was active in his parish, and she led him to a CDM support group that he ended up attending for years. He later became a facilitator for CDM small groups and seminars. His position as a volunteer was a large part of his lived religious life, as was writing poetry, a life-long creative spiritual practice.

In a CDM newsletter, he writes: "Joining a support group following my marriage's demise was the single most important thing I did for myself to promote my self-healing. At the Family Life Office, . . . a wonderful and caring administrator for bereavement and divorced support group schedules her 'New Life' seminars twice a year—in the spring and fall. Hundreds of past and present members of those groups have 'God bless'-ed her for it."

During our interview, John stressed how important this eight- to nine-week "New Life" support group started by the sister was to him. He had full care of his children and was coping with feelings of anger and betrayal. CDM support groups and writing poetry helped him to father his children during this difficult emotional time. In the newsletter, he writes: "I restored my self-esteem, discovered . . . a person I had lost touch with over that awful time in my life, and began to understand a little bit better the will of our God and why things happen in our lives the way they do. I found a new confidence in my decision making, my parenting, and my fondness [for] writing."

Writing was a spiritual endeavor for John, an essential familiar practice ignited by his divorce experience and by finding community through CDM's small-group ministry. His involvement in the support group led him to write a poem that he dedicated to the group and to the members of every support group he facilitated after that. This poem, he said, represented a crucial stage in his growth:

THE ASSEMBLY OF CARE
They must have heard a calling, these who
Came together, not knowing each other's
Name, or how their spirits, stricken, came to
Be as they assembled with uncertainty. They
Came in need of life beyond their night of

Anguish endlessness. How common was
Their need to dry their eyes; to see a
Morning's light; to till their hearts; to plant
Another seed. Around the room they'd listen
And they'd share. I wonder if they have
Become aware how they were first for
Healing; how they are—simply by being
Here—the first to care for one another.
Nursed through their Night of Scars, they
Have become each Other's Morning Stars.
By need, they came. They leave to go on
Living. They came in need, but leave behind
Their giving.

John's ability to access this CDM support group—his knowledge of the group, the fact that his children were old enough to stay home alone while he attended, his car that enabled him to get to the meetings, and his job were key factors in how he came to activate his spiritual approach to divorce.

In his book of poetry, John documents his emotions through the marriage and divorce. Creative writing was an essential expressive practice that he carried throughout his everyday life, not a new activity: "Poetry began for me in my youth as a hobby, a conversation piece. Over the years, it became the vehicle of my fancy and the autobiography of my emotions. It was my company in times of loneliness, my haven from fear, my retreat into inner peace." His private lived practice became a resource for other divorced Catholics as he published his poems and taught seminars for CDM on poetry writing as a healing practice. His book, he writes, held his emotions in reserve for use by those suffering through endings: "They [readers] will . . . discover that their own terrible and shameful emotions kept hidden from everyone are here in print before them. It will feel as if someone has cut into the grave in which they have been buried alive, exposing them to new light and rescuing them from feeling alone . . . [and offering them] assurance, both emotionally and spiritually, of life beyond divorce. . . . Healing and growth really do happen. We find we overcome divorce not by being carried by others, but by realizing that God has given us the abilities to stand up again." John's poetry appeals to the strong individualism at the heart of religious and therapeutic discourse: in this view, individuals have

God-given powers to pull themselves out of extreme suffering and out from the violent feelings that accompany divorce especially when betrayal and rejection are involved. He used poetry to express his wrestling with suicidal thoughts as his marriage ended. One poem reads, in part: "One morning I set out from Woods Hole in yesterday's clothes and tacked right for the storm brewing off Nantucket. I went south that hour resolutely, unwavering, with the CB down, no food or drink or floatable remnants to reveal my grave decision, my grave's location, no compass necessary." It is a poem that ends with rebirth: "in the calm of the following morning—my eyes opened to a clean and crisp blue sky, Creation all over again." John takes feelings like loneliness and rejection and frames them in themes of death to life, pain to purpose; writing those words brought essential transformation, and he hopes they will inspire others. God, he writes, placed "something deep down inside of us. . . . It is his forgiving warmth reminding us over and over that we are worth leaving alive for two reasons: first, to discover in time how many other people have wanted to 'tear their mainsails to shreds'; . . . second, to allow us that infinite second chance of turning our turmoil into the triumph of self-recovery, to feel that wonderful sensation of being responsible—with God's coaching—for standing on our feet again."

John went to mass at his local parish while ending his marriage, but the community and practices most significant in his narrative of emotional life during this period were CDM's small-group ministry and his writing. He also purchased and read secular and religious books recommended by CDM.

Catholics like John, Sue, and Laurie, who were involved in Catholic divorce groups told stories of becoming, as the founder of CDM named such individuals, "gifts to the church." In assembling secular and religious practices for themselves and others, their narratives were not only of individuals who took control of their own emotional and spiritual lives, but also people who saw themselves as workers for God, encouraging others to accomplish sacred divorce work by producing inspiring texts, poetry, and small-group activities for others.

"I LIFT UP MY EYES TO THE HILLS"

Loss of individual health accompanying divorce brought its own character and threat of social shame to some respondents, calling for individual labor to address sickness of mind and body. Many of my respondents told stories of physical exhaustion and depression related to their divorce experience. In these cases, using numerous lived religious practices throughout the day became essential, in their stories, for healing. In a culture that emphasizes wellness and puts much weight on individual responsibility for health, fatigue and serious disease bring challenges to social status. For respondents who suffered from serious illnesses or physical injury, stories of turning to religion to make divorce meaningful entailed descriptions of self as engaged in grave processes of fighting potentially debilitating psychological and physical sensations.

Emma used multiple lived practices to recast divorce itself as willed by God and to reestablish her secure position as a single mother. She was a black Baptist woman in her mid-fifties who had been divorced for fourteen years. She worked as an administrative assistant in an office setting. She had one child from a brief marriage when she was in her twenties, and had lived comfortably for several years as a single mother before marrying her second husband. Emma's first diagnosis of breast cancer came just as she decided to end this second marriage. Cancer's social and physical challenges overpowered many of the other social emotions she felt at the end of a marriage that she described as abusive.

Emma's husband was in the military. He had been raised Pentecostal but no longer practiced any religion. One day while he was away for several months on ship, she was drawn to a Baptist church and became a member, along with her daughter. Her husband was not happy when he returned: "It was an area of contention, not because he didn't believe in God, but because he didn't like the idea of me going to church without him. I went by myself." He complained that she should have waited until his ship returned, to try out churches together. She responded, "I can't wait on you for my soul to be saved." His dislike of her decision ran deep and he constantly challenged her: "This is how blatant he was: . . . he bought a Koran. I said 'What in the world, you are not a Muslim!'" As he continued to question and oppose her religious practice, Emma began to feel justified in ending the marriage: "He was verbally abusive and we had a couple of physical altercations where I actually called the police and he was arrested and we had to do six months of anger management therapy, which does not work when it is court ordered!"

She prayed for God to change him, to "touch his heart," but in the end she saw God as not only supporting her desire to leave a marriage that was draining her emotionally and physically, but also ushering her to the door as well. She stressed not wanting to "break up a home," and mentioned having just bought a house and not wanting to disrupt her life again. But, as she continued the lived practice of reading the scriptures and praying constantly throughout the day, her leaving became inevitable and she saw the decision as endorsed by God. "What God had joined together," she said, "let no man put asunder. God has not joined everybody together." In Emma's story, the divorce itself became sacred, charged in its curative power.

Emma's central lived practices revolved around familiar hymns and psalms activated throughout the day, and an intimate prayer relationship with God. These were practices that she could easily access, and she understood them as saving her life. Reading the Bible, praying, recitation of familiar psalms, and singing of cherished religious songs helped relieve the depression and sickness that came with cancer treatments and helped her stay strong for herself and her daughter. Emma had embraced music as lived practice long ago: "I love music and I sang a lot when I was younger." Most important in her narrative, these practices helped her end her marriage, an ending that emerged as a sacred, life-saving action in her story.

Speaking from a conservative black church position, Emma understood that God had given her the courage to leave an abusive relationship and that she was "unequally yoked," meaning that her spouse was not a Christian. Having the strength to end a marriage that was not "meant to be" in the first place was what saved her life, she said, and gave her the space to become stronger and healthier.

Emma credited her lived religious practice and faith, then, for her life: "I'm a cancer survivor and, had I not had my faith, I think I would be dead right now. . . . I believe I'm a walking miracle." She received her cancer diagnosis two months after she and her husband had separated. She didn't tell people at her church about the cancer or the divorce; she didn't want to be in a "fishbowl" with everyone's "eyes on" her, although she did join a breast cancer support group, for two years, that helped her confront illness and divorce. "In the African American community," she said, "we resist support groups." She was the "only other African American there," and she was also the youngest, but over time this group too became an important spiritual link to others: "Cancer doesn't care what color you are. Cancer is cancer, and we all had the same experiences. . . . They used to just keep me laughing, they would just tell these stories and they would laugh, and that was what was good for me with that, because, in the group, we just felt like people."

Emma described her faith in God, the support group, active daily prayer, reading, and music inside and outside church as critical to her survival: "Everything was orchestrated by the Lord, because, if I had been in that marriage, I would not have survived. Because when I went to my doctor, when I told him what I was going through, he says: 'You need absolutely no stress in your life now, none.' And I went through chemo for six months and it was just me and my daughter. And I did it. I went to church every Sunday, and I sang in the choir, and I went out with my friends." She saw God as giving her the ability to continue driving, which allowed her to stay connected to her congregation and to the cancer support group.

Cancer brought unsettled life for several years. Recitation of the psalms during the day helped her manage the anxiety and fear that came with her new social position as divorced and a cancer patient, and to reject seeing herself as a victim: "I would read the psalm 'I lift up my eyes to the Hills from which cometh my help, my help comes from the Lord.' I mean, I had to almost recite it like a mantra, like constantly, have it just going through my head to keep me at peace, so I could sleep at night, so I could get up and go to work in the morning, so I didn't go, 'Oh God, why did this happen to me?' on a regular basis." She would also sing to herself hymns from her church choir that would help her calm her emotions. She repeated the lyrics to two of her favorite hymns that followed her during the day: "Every day is a day of Thanksgiving. God's been so good to me, every day he's blessing me," and, from the Twenty-third Psalm, "leading me to lie down beside still waters, he restores my soul."

Emma understood that people in her church thought God meant for married people to work through their problems, that the Bible said she should do everything she could to save the marriage. This strong belief likely shaped the character of the story she told, which begins with her asking God to help her save the marriage and with going to court-ordered counseling with her husband. But it was God's will, she also made clear, that she concentrate on caring for her own emotions and, for her daughter's sake, to get out of an abusive marriage with a "nonbeliever." Her teenage daughter was from a previous marriage and so had no obligation to maintain a relationship with her stepfather. She described a full and happy life with her daughter before the marriage and relief that they were by themselves again.

Emma's story was about personal resolve and finding peace and a sense of calm through song and prayer that affirmed God as her immanent provider and protector through serious illness and divorce. She presents herself as someone who has survived divorce and cancer and learned to manage the chaotic and disturbing emotions of both traumatic events. She insisted that, through the divorce, "I found myself. I got myself back." Like other respondents, she saw herself as returning to some true and thus stronger self through multiple religious practices inside and outside congregations.

"MY BLESSINGS"

Brenda, a white United Methodist woman, ended her third marriage because of her husband's infidelity. She went to services at the Methodist church she had attended most of her life, despite feeling the threat of social shame given the congregation's knowledge of her family history and previous marriages. In addition to her faithful attendance in her home church and her deep connection to Methodist prayer and liturgy, she read Buddhist texts, engaged in yoga practices, attended DivorceCare, painted, and felt an essential connection, through individualized prayer practice, to nature. These combined practices, fashioned over many years, helped her combat the physical fatigue she felt as she worked on forgiving her most recent ex-husband and caring for her adult child from her first marriage, who continued to live with her.

During our interview, sitting on her patio, she demonstrated a physical prayer she had constructed. She spoke the words with great care and seriousness, while moving her arms, hands, and head through what I recognized as yoga poses. Sitting outside, near the water in her backyard, she welcomed me into her sacred space to witness recitation of prayer and movement: "I believe that everybody is connected to God. . . . One of my prayers every day is 'Help me to be open to the love and healing.' In fact, I pray that for my son, and I still pray for [my ex-husband] every day. And in the morning I come out here and I call it my blessings, and I actually use some of my yoga positions to do them: 'Father, thank you for this day. I commit it to your will and way. Bless the part of me that longs to stay and let it be. Bless the part of me that rises to the challenge and let it go in strength and peace and may the peace of God go with me. Bless me and help me to be open to the love and joy and health and healing that you have for me and humbly lean on thee.' And I still say it. 'Help him to be open to the love and joy and health and healing. And bless [first ex-husband's name] and [second ex-husband's name], and bless the people that I have loved. Bless [son's name] and help him to be open to the love.' . . . I made it up to go with the yoga prayers, years ago, [to say it] every morning, and I pray for certain people if there is something special going on that day." Praying for her recent ex-husband helped her relieve the anger and pain of his deception, and helped her to forgive. Through these prayers, she worked to reconcile her feelings for her ex-husbands and to gain strength to help her troubled son. Forgiveness was at the center of Brenda's sacred divorce-work practice.

Brenda also talked about numerous practices that gave her physical stamina to make it through each day. Healing body exercises were important in her spiritual repertoire. She attended a yoga class once a week, as did several other Protestant and Catholic women I interviewed who incorporated a transcendent God from Christian and Jewish traditions with notions of mystical self, Eastern religious meditative practices, and a concept of universal connectedness. She identified as a visual artist, and saw her painting classes as spiritual pursuit. Her prayer practice contained multiple levels of focus and intention—inward to the body, outward, connection to the divine and to others, and appeals for health and wellness of family members. Prayer, for Brenda, had been a lifelong project of connectedness to what she termed divine energy, molding spiritual self and promoting growth. She distinguished her image of God from the vision of other Methodists she knew, who spoke of God using masculine and corporal descriptors: "God's presence has helped me with everything in life. . . . I do believe that he gives me strength, and it doesn't even have to be a 'he,' it can be a 'she' or a spirit. I don't see it as a person, exactly, but I believe that it is the spirit of the universe, the life force, when I am quiet, . . . , and I have a quiet time every morning. I need some time just to be quiet and be with nature. I can get in touch with the spirit that is within me." She worked to activate this power in multiple spaces throughout her daily life.

Brenda felt that change, made active through daily religious and spiritual practices, was the essence of life. She explained: "We are supposed to evolve, become wiser, at peace with ourselves, become more whole. . . . As long as we are in this world, it is supposed to be hard because life is a school." Brenda had worked with Elizabeth Kübler-Ross as a volunteer, in the mountains of Virginia, and her description and investment in emotion work reflected this important association: "We are supposed to evolve, become wiser, at peace with ourselves, become more whole. . . . Elizabeth Kübler-Ross says that, as long as we are in this world, it is supposed to be hard, because life is a school. It is supposed to be hard, so that we can learn more, and when we have learned and taught all that we need to teach, then we graduate." Life as a difficult school merged in her story with concepts of Christian salvation, the Bible, and Kübler-Ross's books as significant religious tools in her divorce-work repertoire.

I was surprised to learn that Brenda had also attended a few Divorce-Care support group sessions. Her friend invited her to go. Brenda thought the video she saw in the group helped her in understanding how much energy endings can drain from a body, thus validating her view of why she had been feeling so tired and depressed. The friend had also lent Brenda a bracelet that she wore, which read, "I can do all things through Christ who strengthens me" (Phillipians 4:13). Brenda wore the scripture to restore her tired and emotionally exhausted body. She said just glancing at the bracelet helped energize her throughout the day.

Brenda's strategies originated from primary socialization in religious worlds, the evangelical subculture, familiar religious figures, stories, verse, creative artistic endeavors, talents, and her time with Elizabeth Kübler-Ross. Although she called herself a Methodist and was grounded in her lifelong congregation, she used multiple sources to manage the physically draining emotions of her third divorce. Her lived practice helped her in caring for an adult child who was depressed, sustaining an ongoing positive relationship with his father, and finding forgiveness and thus a good relationship with her most recent ex-husband.

"THE LORD IS MY SHEPHERD"

Janet's story demonstrates a similar kind of concerted effort of highly active seeking to activate religious emotional power in everyday life to ease painful loss and manage relationships with children and ex-spouses. I include her story here as an example of heightened loss, grief, and social shame. As with Amy's story (chapter 4), focus on the extreme boundaries of performances makes social forces vivid. Janet had suffered extreme family loss and ongoing trauma, and, like Brenda and others I interviewed, she was able and skillful in assembling and activating lived practices, in imaging a path forward for herself and her elder son, telling a story of doing mothering in the wake of her younger son's suicide.

Janet was a white evangelical Christian who had been married for twenty years to a man who abused drugs. He had died recently, very shortly before their divorce was finalized, and several months after their teenage son committed suicide. Hanging above us on the wall as we sat at Janet's small kitchen table was a picture of Jesus as a shepherd and the words of the Twenty-third Psalm. As we ate the soup she had made for our lunch, she talked about how recitation of the Twenty-third Psalm activated familiar religious emotion. For her, the power of the psalm was a God-given tool for assurance of divine presence:

> I woke up one morning saying out loud the words of a scripture. . . . I had no idea what I was saying: "The Lord is my Shepherd. I shall not want. He makes me lie down in green pastures," and I thought, "What am I saying?" It [is not] a scripture I'm familiar with. . . . I reached next to my bed and I picked up my Bible and I said that's that shepherd psalm and I'm trying to find it . . . paging through my Bible . . . oh, it's Psalm 23. It was Sunday. I went to church. . . . The first words out of my pastor's mouth were, "Today I'd like to talk about the Twenty-third Psalm." It wasn't the type of church where you would ever display emotion, and I was just sitting there with tears running down my face. . . . I went up to the pastor that day and I said, "Can I have a copy of your sermon; I really believe the Holy Spirit was using you today." Years later, when my husband and I were going through everything, I was so angry with God and angry at my life journey, I wasn't happy; I saw myself, even, not putting my children first anymore. . . . And the phrase came through my mind, "the valley of the shadow of death," and all of those memories came flooding back to me, the morning that I woke up saying the Twenty-third Psalm. . . . I realized it was all that same thing happening again. . . . I just felt so clearly that the Lord was saying to me . . . "I am with you . . . I haven't left you alone . . . I've brought you full circle . . . here you are reaching for your Bible and . . . I'm showing you the same words." . . . It left such a life impression on me. . . . I went to an antique store and bought that picture. . . . [*She points to the picture on the wall above us*.].

We looked at the framed image, sharing a moment of silent recognition of the weight that this prayer had come to carry in her life.

Janet gave me a copy of an interview she had done for a local paper on her involvement in a bereaved parents support group. During our interview she talked of her son's "passing," but left the article the task of filling in the details. The kind of social shame she experienced over mothering through divorce was extreme, given that her son had become involved in drugs and committed suicide in the wake of family disruption.

Her story of slowly separating from her husband over the years included actions taken to care for the mental and spiritual health of her two sons as she tried to do intense marriage work with a spouse addicted to cocaine. She went to twelve-step groups to find strategies and made sure her sons had a community at the church. Still, her youngest started using drugs and became remote from both parents and his older brother. He grew more distant and eventually committed suicide. In that same year, a few months later, her soon-to-be-ex-husband died. Janet's pain was enormous. She described feeling as if she had died as well yet knowing she had to stay alive for her older son and be an emotional support and family for him: "I need to be the best that I can possibly be for him. How much can he take?" Although there still seemed to be a great weight of sadness about her, during our interview she conveyed a sense of peace as she described practices that allowed her to find strength for her older son and new purpose in life.

The Twenty-third Psalm represented a major strategy in her daily life. It was at her kitchen table as she sipped her morning coffee and when she returned home from her clerical job to heat up her dinner. It was there as she wrote in her journal each day. She showed me her bank checks; the first two lines of the psalm were inscribed on them, there with each check as she struggled to pay her bills. (Her husband had spent much of their money on drugs during the marriage. She described him as out of control during the worst times: "He would go away for a day and a night and then come in the middle of the night, wake up my children, and say 'give me all your money—don't wake up mom.'") The psalm served a profound emotional function throughout her day, instigating a strong connection to a divine presence that provided her with what she described as a stillness and peace from potentially debilitating relational and financial loss, and pushed her to find new purpose as a single woman.

Like many of my respondents, she had assembled religious practices from multiple sources throughout the years. She was grounded in an evangelical Christian subculture through her large church, and she attended services on Sunday and during the week. Journaling was another essential everyday practice: "I kept so many journals to get through those years. It helped to see things in black and white. It's such a testament of God's goodness, because at the time you just feel that it is all bad, and then when you read the journal you see that you made it through." Her bereavement support group and other small groups at her church were significant practices, as well. The bereavement group was a place where she could go with "any emotion . . . I could be angry [or sad or have other feelings, and] the group was my refuge."

More recently, she had started, and was hosting, a group at the church and in her home. The group was based on Presbyterian minister Richard Morgan's book *Remembering Your Story* (2002), which encourages making life transitions meaningful through explicit religious intent and the process of remembering and recording one's stories and connecting them to God's story. She described the process: "They give you all these ways for recording your life's journey: . . . a little bit of drawing with it, . . . childhood memories." She reflected: "I've always had some group, and things that I'm reading. Right now I just have a Bible study that includes a group of women, and there are opportunities for our stories to come out—help, I guess, supporting each other." Giving back to others became an important part of her lived practice.

Janet had also rejected some strategies that she felt were out of line with her belief system. For example, the grieving parents group, in an effort to be accepting of all faiths, wanted to support members who were turning to "mediums and spiritualists," those trying to reach beyond to find a message that their child is well. Janet described herself as accepting of different religions and "just about every kind of thing for healing," but "There is a point where I draw a line about certain things." Trying to speak to children who had died, Janet felt, was not about "moving forward" and so seemed wrong.

We looked through Janet's journal after lunch. The story documented in the journal and in her interview presented her efforts as efficient practices. Like those of other respondents, her narrative ended with resolution— evidence that she was moving forward to new life purpose and construction of a new kind of family with her remaining adult child. When we spoke, she had just made an important decision; she was finally going to finish her college education and work to pursue a degree in art therapy, a career path she understood as a spiritual endeavor because she could use her experience with painful emotions to help others. She told me a story about her young son that spoke to her efforts to make a new life after death: "I remember my youngest son saying, when we had to break it [first separation] to the boys—I just remember my youngest son in the backseat, and I remember. . . . We were on our way to a football game or something. He was probably about tenish, and his little voice. My husband was trying to explain, 'I know this sounds bad, and I'm going to have to go away,' and my son said, 'Well, they thought it was sad when Jesus was crucified, too; they thought that was a bad thing.' We all just turned around and looked at him. We were so shocked. It was amazing; I thought, 'What insight!'"

FIXED AND ABLE SEEKERS

When we think of religious ritual, we often imagine individuals practicing in formal religious settings where actions and beliefs have been passed from generation to generation. We visualize collective spaces—churches, synagogues, mosques, and temples—where people bring private concerns to collective meaning making. Tens of millions of Americans do gather for worship in local congregations each week, many seeking community and worship in times of grief and hardship. The majority of my interviewees were grounded in particular religious congregations and subcultures, but their narratives of emotion work indicate appeals to a variety of cultural sources, subjective experiences, and networks of relationship. Their stories demonstrate the practical coherence of multiple religious strategies for managing fluid individual and family identity in contemporary Western society. They suggest as well that economic position plays a critical role in choice and activation of religious tools.

My respondents chose self- and family-care rituals that eased, for them and their children, transition from one kin configuration to another. Walter and John used religious emotion to soften depression so that they could concentrate on full-time fatherhood and children's emotions, and day-to-day educational and physical needs. Brenda and Walter used religious emotion to forgive and care for ex-spouses. One woman described a private ritual that released anger toward her ex-husband and brought her closer to her daughter: she recited the Serenity Prayer as flames destroyed her marriage certificate in a pan on the kitchen table. My respondents' lived practices had *practical coherence* (McGuire 2008, 15); they validated and calmed emotions that threatened changing relationships with kin. These respondents talked about rituals as restoring body energy, "calming brains," and/or easing fear, anger, and anxiety. Their practices eased social shame and solidified religious and family bonds.

My respondents drew from multiple religious sources and sought spirituality in different spaces, but most strongly identified with a religious tradition and/or congregation. Instead of envisioning Catholics like Sue or Methodists like Brenda as seekers moving from one spiritual source to another, one may better understand them, as Baggett (2009, 67) envisions his respondents, as "'indwelt seekers'—quite active within and loyal to their institution but with the caveat that the faith they hold dear must resonate with their own experience and make sense to them on their own terms." Most of my respondents' narratives of assembling and practicing sacred divorce-work strategies were reflective of this type of secure or grounded seeking. Sue turned to various religious and spiritual resources and traditions, but in the end she told me, "I just want to be a Catholic woman; ... I'm a Catholic woman first." I interviewed one man who identified as a "spiritual Jewish atheist." Reading Buddhist texts and amassing a large library of spiritual and self-help books was central in his lived practice, but reciting the Mourner's Kaddish for the death of his relationship, attending Jewish services and healing groups where he sang Hebrew prayers, and searching for a synagogue home that was welcoming to singles was prominent in his story. Walter's job, family, and weekly worship were firmly established in the Pentecostal church, but his sacred divorce work drew from sources outside the congregation and COGIC tradition. Brenda strongly identified as a Methodist, but her practices also included painting, yoga, and DivorceCare.

My respondents described efficient emotion-work practices that were practiced and familiar, and that they had the means to activate. A few respondents struggled financially after divorce, but they still had the economic resources to purchase media and the ability to be active in congregations. Each had some economic and social resources with which to experiment, to seek therapeutic and religious sources from numerous points.

One way to put my respondents' abilities in perspective is to think of limitations other researchers have noted. Sociologist Susan Crawford Sullivan's (2011) work, for example, illustrates how women in poverty are often cut off from congregations and are thus limited in the ways they assemble lived religion; their resources can be limited to, for instance, individual prayer and reading the Bible. Sullivan's narratives suggest a qualitatively different lived religious approach. By contrast, my interviewees were rich in available sources; they could travel to and across congregations and small groups; they could purchase media (albeit at different levels); some assembled "love libraries" and "arsenals of books."

My respondents lived religious approaches also indicate levels of incorporation of particular therapeutic tools. For example, writing was almost always promoted in sacred divorce-work resources (as in therapeutic culture) as an effective emotion-work tool, but not all of my respondents embraced this practice, a few who attended divorce small groups begrudgingly did such emotion work. Several DivorceCare participants called journaling forced homework. Music was an active tool in many respondents' narratives, but there were a few who said music was not important, emphasizing other practices, like prayer, as most essential.

As they took care of their everyday emotional life, my respondents' individual collections of efficient practices allowed them to travel with ease across religious traditions and sacred space. Sociologists of religion have recently called attention to the pieced-together and portable character of religious worlds which allows people to live in an increasingly diverse society with the reassurance of religious explanations and identity.[5] Nancy Ammerman (2003, 224) argues that "individuals improvise religious narratives out of past experience and interaction." When people tell their stories, they "signal the presence of religious ideas, symbols, story lines, and sacred coparticipants within a wide range of social contexts . . . invoking religious narratives of widely varying scope and robustness." Theodore Sarbin (1995, 218–219) calls attention to this compound nature of moral stories, of people assembling tools "constructed from one's imaginings as influenced by cultural narratives." Ammerman (2010, 162) reminds us that many people "are connected to multiple religious organizations, each providing more and less complementary resources for engaging with the spiritual world." Religious groups, too, even those that "construct and maintain fairly tight boundaries," are likely "connected to a broader network of presumably like-minded organizations, from publishers to broadcasters to manufacturers of religious paraphernalia, each of which can introduce new religious elements into the system." In proposing a plurality of religious life across cultures and historical periods, she suggests that "religious petitioners rarely confine themselves to the official rites offered by people in power. . . . Patchwork quilts full of holes might better describe how sacred worlds function than sacred canopies" (156). Her metaphor is particularly apt for making sense of my respondents' attempts to construct sacred religious paths. Their quilts were sewn with customary traditional patterns and acquired motifs.

6 ✳ RELIGIOUS EMOTION AND MULTIPLE FAMILY FORMS

The majority of my respondents found emotional tools in congregational worlds. These local assemblies were essential spaces for tailoring their middle-class lived religious quilts that radiated the warmth of therapeutic principle and religious emotion. In their stories, the emotional energy activated in congregations worked to legitimate their choices related to family and divorce experience. Congregations were settings for individual performances of doing sacred divorce work, with props and costumes that signaled serious moral effort and connection to spiritual authority.[1] My respondents' persistence in engaging congregations, even though many felt uncomfortable silences and social shame, speaks to the precious emotional energy and social benefits they found in these collective spaces.

Congregations provide familiar and frequent emotionally significant practice. Made up of people who come together regularly, congregations foster connectedness in those who gather over time, offering stability in gathering place, and type of activity.[2] Thus, they hold great emotional sway when traumatic life events occur. Nancy Ammerman notes (2005, 2) that "when crisis strikes, even the most autonomous seeker is likely to look for the comforting presence of the gathered faithful; and when persons and families pass significant milestones, the witness of a community still seems important." Most of my respondents' stories demonstrate the seeking of sensual command in congregational spaces; they are narratives of moral energies rising from ritual practices and the feelings attached to body experience of sacred space and relationships.

People commit to congregational spaces where familiar music, objects, people, and rituals induce emotion.[3] Stephen Warner (2005, 153) describes congregations as places where "one's faculties and senses are mobilized to attend to the light streaming through stained glass (and a shadow across the soloist's face), the sound of the choir (and of a crying child), the grip of the greeter's hand (and the harness of the pews), the scent of the incense (and of someone's aftershave), and the taste of communion wine." The feel of the wooden pews that Alice, Jeff, and Brenda sat in as children held this kind of emotional energy, as did the touch and sound of choir robes worn by Natalie and Alice as they sang each week with the same group of people. The Hebrew songs that drew Jill and Karen to synagogue services had deep emotional body resonance. My Catholic respondents talked about the power of the Eucharist, a physically rich practice that they could engage in every day if they needed to, a familiar ritual where belief in divine presence, the taste of bread and wine, walking reverently in line with others to receive these, and the words spoken came together to direct emotions and revive religious identity.

Some of my respondents left familiar congregational spaces when they felt little connection, finding emotional energy through different rituals in new religious assemblies. Todd described feeling disconnected from the Catholic community to which he had converted when he got married. Lacking a lifelong connection with Catholic Eucharistic rituals, and disillusioned by what he understood as silence and lack of community concern for his divorce, he went searching in multiple religious communities for worship spirit and tools for managing shifting identity. He ultimately found power sitting together with DivorceCare group members during weekly services in the nondenominational evangelical church where the group took place. He sensed profound connection in these individuals, describing them as holding his "bleeding heart," as he engaged in private emotional labor. Their presence beside him in the pews brought sensual command, and through communal worship made DivorceCare's prescriptions more meaningful.

Many clergy had social power that could endow the therapeutic seeker and multiple family forms with sacred status. Clergy's authority lay primarily in emotional sway: the familiar voice that delivered weekly sacred messages, the association with sacred ceremonies like marriages, baptisms, and conversions. Priests, rabbis, and ministers offered a number of powerful routine religious rituals to members, and in some traditions adapted existing divorce practices (for instance, gets and annulments). Clergy and pastoral counseling practices thus provided spaces where peoples' choices about ending marriages and negotiating new family structures could be legitimated and social religious bonds affirmed.

My respondents' congregational engagement and lived religious practices were efforts to make sense of emotions and order lives post-divorce so that they could imagine themselves as good parents, religious practitioners, and for many, persons successful in new life partnerships. Religious worlds and the symbolic emotional energy they carried in rituals, texts, community roles, ideas, and sensual command thus were valuable therapeutic goods in the production of moral stories. Such social power through religious emotion holds the potential for both dangerous and beneficial processes and beliefs: dangerous in that religious emotion can promote deviant labeling, constructions of pathology, persistent marriage work in the face of family violence, rigid attachment to normative family forms, and reinforcement of excessive individualism; beneficial in that it has the power to encourage people to be active creators of communities of belonging and to care for others, and in that it can serve as a legitimating force for existing family forms that eat away at the privilege and myths of normative family. Scholars of religion and religious leaders would do well to explore more deeply the weight of social responsibility that comes with such sensual command in the face of changing family forms.

BALANCING CULTURAL CONTRADICTIONS

Congregations were particularly able to help individuals make sense of contradictory cultural beliefs and practices related to multiple family forms and beliefs about gender—a key function of therapeutic institutions in contemporary society. Clergy practices validated individual choice regarding marriage and family issues, even as they reinforced the sacred and ideal nature of life partnership and, in some cases, normative marriage. Local religious assemblies constructed distinct beliefs, practices, and religious identity for divorced congregants, but they often did so by upholding marriage and divorce as valuable individual pursuits.

Religious themes of death-to-life and sacred rebirth and passage combined in emotional practice with therapeutic discourse to balance dedication to life partnership alongside divorce and singlehood. Activating religious themes of injury, death, rebirth, and passage through hardship eased the balancing of cultural contradictions. For example, one way that evangelical Christian architects communicated heterosexual marriage as a God-designed institution was by framing the divorced as in a special position of "brokenness" that had the potential to bring them closer to God and Jesus as "physician." Jewish architects and respondents activated divorce as a sacred passage from death of a marriage to renewed life. Several respondents became absorbed in the sensual command of Yom Kippur tunes as they imagined themselves in the process of moving from sacred marriage to sacred singleness. The Jewish *get* facilitated the balancing of marriage and divorce as sacred through sensory acts: two of my respondents described the paper tearing as a profoundly moving sound that brought a visceral, physical response affirming the sacredness of the marriage and a release to construct new identity. In CDM and other Catholic efforts, religious leaders fortified sacred roles for the divorced, naming them the "most like Jesus," envisioning them as embodying the Paschal Mystery—that is, as people who felt the experience of death and new life in exceptional ways.

Congregations had convincing emotional tools, sacred actions, and collective identity that upheld the tragic and painful nature of death alongside its curative powers, thus reinforcing both marriage and divorce as sacred, and rendering multiple contemporary family structures meaningful. In the black Baptist case, the divorced were imagined by religious architects as like Jesus in their sacred singlehood (Singles 2007, 32): "Singles, we do not need to worry about any societal stigma associated with being single. We are in good company because Jesus Christ, who was single, was the greatest person—single or otherwise—to ever walk this earth." James Young, in a 1983 NASDC conference speech, told attendees: "Not that long ago it would have sounded quite strange to speak to one of divorced Catholics as a gift to the church, but certainly over this last decade that is what you have become." In the Jewish case, the process of divorce became a mitzvah for many respondents and rabbis. Divorce identity as someone caring for the emotional needs of self and family, bolstered by religious emotion, eased marriage/divorce contradictions.

Unitarian congregations and the media resources they recommended invited members to do their own balancing of contemporary family contradictions, a religious call for individual reflection and expression of feelings that merged seamlessly with therapeutic culture. UU ministers in my study, through their counseling role as gentle listeners, encouraged individuals to find what they thought had been good about their marriages and how they might better communicate in future relationships. Divorce resources recommended by UU leaders promoted individual reflection and creative assessment of marriage. *Let's Talk* asks readers to think: "What is your definition of marriage? How have your attitudes and beliefs about marriage changed over time? . . . What makes a long-term relationship work? What makes love endure?" Additional questions follow that invite reflection on same-sex marriage: "In what ways, if any, is holy union different from legal marriage? . . . Are long-term relationships between same-sex couples different from long-term heterosexual marriage?" (5).

Religious architects also eased contradictions by distinguishing healthy families post-divorce from unhealthy families. Families headed by single parents and blended families were valid as long as divorce work had been accomplished and people had command of their emotions. For example, in DivorceCare a "broken home" was determined by parental actions: "A single parent home is a family. A broken home is when there is a single parent home that is out of control. A family is when there is a single parent home that is in control." Blended families were legitimated with caution: "*Combusted* is the great word for the situation of a blended family. There is everything you need for an explosion." Individuals who did not take the time to do divorce work are at high risk of pathology and divorce a second time around: "Going too soon is the single biggest mistake of all; . . . to use a relationship as medication will be the first mistake." Across traditions, healthy blended families were seen as possible after sacred emotion work was accomplished.

Religious energy and strategies helped many of my respondents make sense of shifting ideas about gendered parenting. Men and women talked about taking care of their own emotions so that they could "be there" for their children as the primary custodian; these narratives were gendered stories of trying to be emotionally present for children. Walter and John saw themselves as breaking new ground as fathers. Each began his story of parenting articulating that he was part of a new generation of men who were taking full responsibility for the welfare of their children and doing a different kind of fathering post-divorce. Walter's story highlighted controlling anger through prayer and music so that he could assert primary caretaking. He argued: "Women are more liberated; . . . a lot of women are taking on some of the roles that some of the men would have. They are like, okay I am tired of this, you keep the kids and you have the house. It's crazy, because you didn't find women that would leave their kids. That is why a lot of people can't believe that she let me keep the kids. I am like, yeah, because she didn't want a fight on her hand."

The mothers and fathers in my study all felt pressure to be active in their children's lives. Contemporary mothers are expected to spend a great deal of time and energy nurturing children, and women continue to do the majority of caretaking in this society, but men are called to emotional task as well, and in many ways the experience of divorce magnifies awareness as men struggle to redefine and fulfill expectations of contemporary ideals of fatherhood (Townsend 2002; Gerson 2010). The mothers in my study, more often than the fathers, expressed a feeling of guilt that they were only partially present in their children's lives. Their performances of motherhood were shaped by larger ideals of mothers as being present for children throughout daily life (Garey 1999; Hayes 1996). Mothers whose children spent significant time with fathers told stories of filling empty space with religious practices, new community and/or therapeutic relationships, and work. In contrast, fathers with shared custody or visitation schedules seemed proud of this weekly time and talked about the things they would do for their children. The few parents (two women and two men) that I interviewed who had not seen their children for many months or years told stories of how they tried to reunite with their sons and daughters, and the ways they turned to religious emotion to help manage their feelings.

Ulrich Beck (1992) analyzes the changing circumstances of women in contemporary Western society in terms of *individualization*, a distinct process of social structuring that constrains modern persons to be responsible for crafting their own biographies. Women are under much pressure to consume self-help resources, services, and products, and feel heightened conflicts between work and family identity.[4] As a group, women may experience a higher degree of fractured identity, but many men experience demands to perform intimate labor alongside breadwinner-father and parenting ideals. Gendered identity can feel even more split for all as divorce bears down. Congregations are spaces where such fractured selves are met with therapeutic identities and religious purpose. In our contemporary Western world where religious and family identity is fluid and demands processes of self-realization, religious emotion can bring force to individual management of self and family position.

In the black church case, balancing marriage and divorce culture took place through the idea that God *could* send the right spouse at any moment and religious themes of God or Jesus as husband. Several women talked about God as filling a husband/provider role, easing the gendered social shame of single motherhood post-divorce. In the NBC text *Singles*, lawyer Carolyn Cummings writes: "As a single person and single parent for the past 10 years and the only breadwinner in my household, I have learned to lean and depend on Jesus. You have heard of 'ladies having sugar daddies' who pay the bills. . . . Jesus told me that he made the sugar and the daddy and He told me that He was my Sugar Daddy. He made me realize that He has been my Sugar Daddy for the past 10 years and for all of my existence" (35–36). The idea that God was in control of whom one should marry and that God/Jesus could serve as a husband figure was at work across conservative Christian traditions. Still, these themes and the extent to which they helped balance cultural contradictions seemed more pronounced in the black church cases. This finding could speak to larger social dynamics regarding blacks in U.S. society. As a group, blacks (especially women) are less likely to marry and more likely to divorce, and have higher rates of single-parent families than other racial groups.[5] These statistics are the focus of a "theological conservatism" that pushes black churches to be concerned about single mothers, absent fathers, and the dissolution of black families, thus promoting an image of heterosexual family that reflects "traditional Christian morality" (Wilcox et al. 2004). At the same time, rising numbers of black professionals in the United States are choosing to remain single, and as a racial group blacks tend to value extended kin structures outside legal marriage. Promoting divorce work that renders singles as highly sacred beings constantly contacting, leaning, waiting on, and learning from God reflected well-practiced balancing of multiple family forms and religious ideology in black church culture.[6]

Small groups emerged as an important religious mechanism for validating singlehood post-divorce. Performing familiar emotional labor for group members provided a religious role that embodied ideal qualities of mothers, fathers, and caretakers of kin. Such new identity as caretakers of multiple intimate others was appealing to my respondents as it countered threatening images of the divorced as selfish and disconnected from family responsibilities. In the DivorceCare support group I attended, some members talked about each other as fictive kin, and helped each other with home repairs and called on one another, between meetings, for emotional support. Building reciprocity and belonging through these informal networks of friendship and emotional support were common stories that eased social shame and cultural contradictions regarding marriage and divorce.

Congregations across traditions were communities where divorced parents could find fictive kin to help balance performances of being a single parent in a society that values normative family models. Divorced parents could feel as if they were doing parenthood and providing emotional care through a new identity as part of an extended church family. Several of my respondents talked about staying in congregations for the emotional health of their children. Tricia, a COGIC woman with a young daughter, told me: "I had a personal relationship with God and the Church was more of a support for my daughter because people really catered and loved her a lot, so a lot of people did a lot of things for her from the Church." Janet's teenage son committed suicide, but nevertheless in her story she presents the church as a positive emotional support, a place where youth ministers made her sons feel comfortable in expressing their feelings as they faced their parents' separation and their father's addictions. DivorceCare encouraged church community as a family for single divorced parents: "If you feel lonely, hurt, abandoned, then God has provided families for you to find a place of comfort. The church is the family of God." A divorced woman in the video states: "The church gave me a place now to take my children. . . . It is a healing place to go and I wanted them to have it." Clergy across traditions talked with me about their community as a constant emotional support for children whose parents had divorced. Margaret noted how in her UU congregation people made efforts to embrace children who sometimes felt shame for being there only on alternate weekends because of custody arrangements. Several other congregations sponsored therapeutic programs for children, some more explicitly religious than others—for instance, DivorceCare 4 Kids (http://www.dc4k.org/) and Rainbows (http://www.rainbows.org/mission.html).

The balancing of marriage and divorce culture through congregational mechanisms reflects a larger social structure that legitimizes difference and range in family form. Congregations are institutional mechanisms that support a U.S. society where individuals begin and end life partnerships at high rates. Religious architects in my study all legitimated our larger "plausibility structure" (Berger 1967, 45–47): in the Western case, a foundation that upholds life partnership as real and instrumental for self-betterment, divorce as respected individual opportunity, and therapeutic pursuits as moral paths. In 1967, Peter Berger suggested that congregations of the upper middle class have come to be more like one another in filling a *psychological function* for members: "All religious institutions oriented toward the upper-middle-class market in America will be under pressure to secularize and to psychologize their products—otherwise, the chances of these being 'bought' diminish drastically" (148). Congregations' engagement with psychology and their investment in therapeutic culture across the middling classes have only grown stronger. How they adapt and creatively engage contemporary family forms and therapeutic culture is not a choice; rather, it is enforced by an active religious marketplace.[7] If congregations want to thrive, religious leaders must offer therapeutic strategies for balancing cultural contradictions related to multiple types of family and kinship roles.

ESSENTIAL ADAPTATION

Sociologists have long called attention to how institutional worlds must balance cultural contradictions. If congregations want to keep members and attract new ones, they must preserve distinct identity *and* at the same time enable family paths that embrace various contemporary family structures. As I have demonstrated in this book, declaring "Catholics don't believe in divorce" or that liberal religious communities have no problem with divorce shame is erroneous. Congregations across a continuum of liberal to conservative have adapted to and welcomed nontraditional families, even as they carefully maintain structures and programming that put marriage and normative family center stage.[8] The religious emotion congregations stir is a powerful mechanism; their architects have access to sacred tools, space, and time that make them exceptionally able to mitigate threats of social shame that can arise from the cultural contradictions inherent in multiple contemporary family forms.

Congregations, as a distinctly American voluntary structure, are grounded in freedom of religious expression and choice; local assemblies are then primary spaces where more formal divorce doctrines can be challenged and creative adaptation can flourish. In the United States, religious people—for instance, Catholics, Muslims, Protestants, Hindus—create local communities where leaders and members can come and go volun-tarily. Thus, the local membership has much authority in shaping religious and political voice, and congregations, as Stephen Warner (2005) notes, can "chart their own religious course despite their denominational ties" (163). Such power suggests congregational authority to craft divorce-work strategies from therapeutic culture and local religious symbols, language, identity, beliefs, and practices—in essence, all discourses available. As they construct their distinct strategies, congregations recognize divorce as an outstanding evangelical opportunity.

Religious architects across traditions saw divorce as a time when peo-ple would search for meaning and understood their community as able to answer that need. DivorceCare's website notes that events like "divorce, loss of a loved one, substance abuse, addiction, financial crisis, and heath emer-gencies are often used by the Lord to open people to a relationship," and advise web visitors that "effective ministry by your church in such areas can serve as a gateway to those without a faith." The UU ministers I interviewed thought a great deal about how to make their congregations welcoming to all people who were going through major family transitions. The UU on-line resource *Let's Talk* suggests that "The experience of divorce or separa-tion can lead unchurched individuals to seek out a religious community such as ours for grief and healing, reflection and meaning making, social networking, acceptance, and belonging" (2). Jewish support groups, many of which were held in community spaces outside of synagogues, were open to non-Jews and made a point of trying to appeal to Jews from unaffiliated to Orthodox, imagining divorce as a critical time for turning to, or away, from tradition.

Informally, individual congregations have some freedom in how they adapt to contemporary social forces, and have the ability to construct their own oppositional narratives with the power of religious emotion.[9] CDM's early founders were invested in creating such a community narrative that spanned national Catholic communities. James Young's position as a Pau-list priest, the Paulists being an American-born group with a commitment to interfaith dialogue and bringing faith to contemporary conditions, along with the ideological force of Vatican II (1962–1965), gave him and other divorce ministry founders discursive space to envision the divorced as gifts to the church. From the margins, yet planted firmly in many dioceses through Family Life Offices and local parishes, innovators like Young and

Paula Ripple creatively engaged religious emotion and therapeutic tenets to build a group narrative that reinforced longstanding religious ideas about change as Christian identity. Using traditional rituals, symbolic story, and theology, CDM writers, event organizers, and speakers were among the first to reconcile marriage and divorce culture in contemporary Catholic style. They had much in common with Catholic groups like Dignity USA (an LGBT rights group), advocates of women's ordination, and the pro-choice groups that Michelle Dillon (1999) studied; all were people working within the religious tradition and using religious emotion and cultural tools to fight for institutional change.

CDM leaders continue to minister to the divorced, even though they have experienced a drop in membership and the closing of Family Life Offices where the ministry had much initial support.[10] In my interviews, some CDM leaders ascribed declining membership to loss of Catholic identity in the young and a shift to more marriage programming and counseling in dioceses. However, my analysis suggests that the decline may also be because, in the twenty-first century, divorce is more accepted in Catholic communities and CDM approaches have grown more common in a religious market where many congregations are adapting to multiple and changing family forms. David, whose marriage ended in 1988, told me a story of being removed from his position teaching Sunday school and feeling "like a leper" in his parish after his divorce, as if "divorce was something that people could catch." Although divorced Catholic respondents talked about more recently feeling alienated when priests introduced marriage as a sacrament during mass, they did not experience such explicit social sanctioning and stigma in parishes. Intimate family concerns like divorce and birth control have become increasingly more private and have less bearing on whether or not Americans identify as good Catholics.

There are clear limitations and boundaries regarding how congregations approach diversity in contemporary families. Most Catholic parishes and evangelical Christian congregations are bound by heteronormative visions of marriage and family, and institutional affiliations limit the extent to which they can formally adapt changing ideas about family in contemporary U.S. society. For example, an expectation that sacred life partnerships will be heterosexual is hardened through adherence to CDM language regarding marriage as a sacrament, a union attached to reproduction. Priests like Father Allen may have talked with me about ministering to gay and lesbian parishioners ending life partnerships, but their efforts were not overtly political like those of Dignity USA. As Father Allen noted, taking a formal stance on such issues could cost him his job. Conservative Christian clergy and most conservative resources adhered to heterosexual ideals for marriage and sometimes cast same-sex behavior as destroying marriages. Given growing support for LGBT marriage rights, more conservative denominations may soon be working to creatively engage religious emotion and therapeutic tenets to balance heterosexual marriage alongside same-sex marriage. How they approach this delicate cultural negotiation is an important question for sociologists of religion and family.

POTENTIAL FOR PATHOLOGY AND EXCLUSION

As religious architects work to balance multiple family forms drawing from creative use of religious emotion and therapeutic tenets, the potential for construction of pathology and exclusive sacred divorce-work practice lingers and deserves attention by both scholars and religious leaders. Historical lessons in how organizations have combined religious emotion as they creatively engage therapeutic discourse suggests a need for continued assessment of pathological constructions. The history of "ex-gay" Christian ministries, for example, whose goals are to "heal homosexuals," demonstrates dangerous engagement with problematic medical therapeutic discourse and practices.[11] Although use of shock therapy and other methods of ex-gay ministries may seem extreme, these manifestations serve as a reminder that religious creative engagement with therapeutic culture demands critical historical reflection on the part of both religious scholars and congregational leaders.

Religious architects and respondents sometimes presented divorced women and men as sexually needy, sexually predative, or sexually vulnerable. Such labeling represented gendered accounts of how people came to understand the particular distractions and dangerous departures regarding self work and family emotional labor. COGIC's McGrew writes: "The rejected one, most cases a woman, is left alone to grieve. . . . Open shame at having been left, and a feeling of unworthiness is the prevailing scene. . . . Those in such deep pain will want to show others that they are 'attractive to the opposite sex,' but know that it is not 'wise' to date right after the ending" (vii). DivorceCare experts warn women of a "decline in the moral character of our society" that includes a "proliferation of pornography," and stepchildren who are "often sexually abused." Women are presented as most vulnerable to this danger. DivorceCare's host warns, "We would like to help you from becoming a statistic by helping you understand how to know when you are ready for a new relationship and how to do it right if you are." Various religious divorce resources warned against the dangers of dating too soon and cautioned that powerful sexual needs need to be suppressed. Labeling the divorced sexually vulnerable or needy could have serious consequences in congregations where divorced individuals already felt excluded; two of my female respondents from mainline Protestant denominations described feeling that they became "dangerous" sexually in the eyes of married women in their congregations, and felt compelled to leave small groups composed of married couples and friends cultivated over years.

Gendered assumptions in small groups suggested serious obstacles and challenges for men who turned to religious spaces. Small groups were spaces where essentialist notions of women as more emotional or expressive than men surfaced. Some CDM leaders noted that Catholic men participated more frequently in conferences and workshops, which leaders interpreted as less threatening to men than the emotionally expressive support group environment. Men who cried or expressed emotion other than anger in groups were often set apart by other participants and leaders as exceptionally in touch with their feelings. I did not hear the same discourse regarding women; their tears and expression of emotion were expected, and in one case talked about by a male group member as excessive.

My male respondents' stories of selves in touch with their feelings and able to embrace religious emotion had a social weight that implies gender salience. Some literature suggests that men who identify with more traditional masculine gender roles may have a negative attitude about seeking help from therapeutic relationships that encourage expressivity and emotional vulnerability.[12] The religious men in my study were largely those who desired spaces for collective emotion work—taking on contemporary forms of masculinity that embraced expressivity and emotionality through religious/spiritual practices. As religious leaders work to provide integrated gendered spaces for the accomplishment of divorce work, they would do well to drop essentialist gendered understandings and embrace the complexity of individual approaches to emotion work.

Assumptions about how men and women approach expressivity and interact in therapeutic spaces can lead to explicit gender exclusion. In one case, a man told me he was confused and frustrated when the rabbi he had spent time with in a support group excluded him from the next group series, which she decided should only be for women: "I was hurt," he told me. "All women signed up for the follow-up session, and the rabbi and the counselor said that I should not go because they thought I wouldn't fit in with the group. I felt fine with it [that is, with being the lone man in the group] and the women told me they felt fine too, but for some reason [the rabbi and counselor said] don't come to the second one." Support group leaders, across traditions, talked about keeping an eye out for men who might want to use these groups to find dates. One Catholic support group made individuals come in for an assessment to determine their "stage" of recovery; they noted that one reason for this process was to weed out men divorced for a long time and who, they felt, were there to find vulnerable women. One rabbi approached understandings of gender difference by routinely holding separate groups for men and women. One of the priests I interviewed created a program only for women because, he said, "Women are particularly vulnerable to the financial and emotional stresses of divorce, and there are so many of them who need help." In fact, a few facilitators decided to allow only women because they saw women whose husbands had left them for younger women as deeply wounded and thought that the "last thing they want to see is a man."

Given that women participate nationwide in small groups and religious communities at a slightly higher rate than men, and given the dynamics noted here, it is not surprising that divorce may have "severe consequences" for the religious participation of men (Stolzenberg et al. 1995). Religious architects who wish to reach out to men need to find approaches to managing dynamics of gender in integrated and segregated small groups that invite male as well as female participation and commitment.

Sociologists of religion might pay more attention to research addressing women and men in poverty and their encounters with religious emotion as they face family challenges; such a focus would likely reveal mechanisms for pathology and exclusion. Historically, lack of access to social performances of a self as engaged in pursuit of therapeutic strength has led to deviant labeling for the working poor. Mothers who have not adhered to therapeutic standards have suffered heightened social shame and stigma as they faced therapeutic controls in welfare organizations. At the same time, the private nature of religious emotion in lived religious experience can be empowering to those without resources, offering avenues for construction of acceptable narratives of self and for contemporary family prayer and the reading of sacred texts (Sullivan 2011). Research regarding links among poverty, multiple family forms, therapeutic culture, and religious emotion is ripe for exploration.

It is important to remember that labels can offer avenues for lifting threats of social shame and empowering self. Labeling the divorced as potentially dangerous and filled with emotions that can harm self and others, and keep themselves from "healthy" new intimate relationships, constitutes valuable social power. Sociologists of medicine and deviance have long argued that internalizing medical therapeutic labels can offer individuals various types of social power, from moral performances of working on self to formal claims of disability rights.[13] In managing the label "alcoholic," for example, a person can acknowledge having an illness, alcoholism, and so can take on a repentant identity that opens possibilities for creating a new self in work and relationships.[14] The medicalization in divorce work achieves a similar end: the divorced are sacred in that they are full of charged, powerful, self-altering creative energy that they must manage appropriately. At the same time, the medicalization makes them more vulnerable and marginalized in congregations as a whole, and controls options for how they may activate therapeutic seeker roles. Emily Martin's work (2007) analyzes the complexities of medical/psychological labeling of bipolar individuals with irrational and exceptionally creative characteristics. The potential for added social shame in religious communities as a latent function of a divorce-work approach is a dynamic that many creators of sacred divorce work in congregational worlds have found disturbing. Those who recognized the potential for added shame sometimes directly countered it in their discourse. Rabbi Netter writes, "One day, . . . I trust, religious leaders will not view divorcees as being sick, they will see them as being divorced" (67). Young and other early founders of CDM made a point of talking about the divorced person as healthy but distressed, and local leaders told me about insisting that the ministry be named "with" rather than "to" or "for" the divorced. Complex dynamics of labeling places religious leaders who wish to empower the divorced in a challenging position that demands continued assessment of congregational culture and prepackaged programming.

Many questions remain to be answered by sociologists of religion and family regarding divorce work, religious emotion, and pathology. To what extent might individuals stay in physically or psychologically abusive relationships to avoid such labeling? How does the potential for pathology related to family dynamics and relationships get worked out in local congregations, not only in regard to divorce, but also to other kin disruptions, such as the addiction issues that Janet experienced with her husband and young son, and even the death of a spouse?

How divorce-work strategies and encounters with pathological constructions manifest in individual lives determines the character of social power. Women and men are not necessarily empowered as they activate divorce work discourse. For example, marriage work in divorce work, because it is difficult and intense labor, has the potential to keep abused individuals in physically and emotionally disturbing relationships. As Ingersoll's (2003, 107) work suggests, women invested in a particular religious worldview may frame stories about their relationships in a language of empowerment and mutuality, even if the reality of power dynamics in the marriage is more complex. Catholics going through separation processes could use "wrestling with God," COGIC respondents "spiritual warfare," and Unitarians "web of being" as religious tools to justify investing emotional labor in abusive marriage relationships.

INDIVIDUAL VARIATION

Activation of religious emotion and therapeutic principles takes on great complexity in individual lives. I found variation in respondents' stories regarding levels of adherence to dominant understandings of divorce work. Most men and women described endings marked by initial pain and grief, but some women talked about elation in the early stages of separation and divorce, where joy, happiness, and relief characterized endings. Kayla, a COGIC respondent, talked about how happy she was when the marriage was over, how she was not sad "one bit," but, understanding well the social performance expected in her congregation, she "pretended to be upset" in front of her pastor and church members. People don't accept religious doctrine and ideology, or therapeutic experts' advice wholeheartedly, without question, or in totality as they apply these to their everyday lives.

Most of my respondents, given their class position, had some choice regarding what to incorporate as practice and what merely to represent as active in their life story.

Alice provides an ideal narrative for thinking about distinct encounters with dominant knowledge, demonstrating distinct religious crafting and variation in incorporation of divorce work through religious emotion. She draws from a dominant script that embraces expressivity, but her story is of using "dangerous emotion" to protect her religious home. Although she feels she was a "basket case of emotions" and should not have called her husband's girlfriend a "whore" during the welcoming portion of the service, at the same time her story communicated a focused and successful effort to claim valuable congregational space. Dominant divorce-work scripts encourage the expression of emotion—but in controlled environments, with experts, through accepted religious rituals, or alone into a pillow behind closed doors. Alice's lifelong ties to her congregation, and her connection to religious emotion in that space, allowed her to shape and sustain this deviant episode. In her story, anger is aimed at another person during a familiar and emotion-rich moment of musical worship, and, in her narrative, the action ultimately reaffirms her religious bond and status in the congregation, an accomplishment of which she seems immensely proud.

Respondents, primarily white, who had spent months or years involved in religious divorce programs like DivorceCare, CDM events, or Jewish support groups, told stories that reflected a high level of incorporation of dominant therapeutic divorce-work scripts. Todd and Laurie, for example, who invested much time and effort in these programs, rarely veered from dominant divorce-work scripts. Direct and continued involvement in small groups gave these respondents explicit language and scripts. Laurie, for example, used the language of "hard work" and "vomiting up" emotions. She talked of "finding" herself in an effort to "glorify God" as difficult labor that could not be avoided. At several points in discussing sacred divorce work, she emphasized the individual nature of pain and self-reflexive inquiry; as noted earlier, she had described her parish group as not a support group, but rather one where members were expected to "stand on their own" and do the necessary emotional labor of grieving and figuring out why their marriage ended. Todd, who left Catholicism for a nondenominational church and found help in DivorceCare, also reflected a high investment in brokenness-and-recovery discourse; his comments detailed his journey through "crazy" early stages of divorce grief, searching, in what he described as dangerous "cults," for help and relationship with God. In his story, divorce work was a long, arduous, and potentially dangerous emotional process that involved learning to communicate well in intimate relationships and to forgive his ex-wife. Todd's and Laurie's stories clearly featured tenets of grief work and marriage work, especially in their emphasis on therapeutic forms of hard work in laboring through emotional stages.

Paying attention to variation in encounters with sacred divorce work leads us to consider individuals and groups that may be culturally removed from companionate marriage and Western therapeutic habits. For example, my initial intent was to increase diversity in my sample by interviewing recent immigrants and their religious leaders, but I had difficulty locating divorced respondents, and the religious leaders with whom I spoke defined different issues and dismissed the relevance of my research question for immigrant contexts. A Catholic Hispanic ministry leader in a New England city told me that divorce "was not necessarily a problem for the people that I deal with from El Salvador, because most of them aren't married. It's not an issue for Hispanics; they pretty much do what they want to do in terms of the state and the church." When I asked the priest of a largely Hispanic urban immigrant church in the Midwest about divorce programming, he said that divorce was not the issue; domestic violence and keeping women safe was his primary concern. I heard a similar concern over domestic violence from a rabbi, regarding recent Jewish immigrant groups from Argentina.

There is limited research exploring the relationship among religion, recent immigrants' experiences, and therapeutic culture.[15] Asking religious leaders about family dissolution may be more appropriate, given the way partners and families can be pulled apart by immigration enforcement and deportation. Focusing on narratives of such family disruption in cases where recent immigrants engage congregations deserves concentrated attention by sociologists of family, religion, and culture, and would provide a valuable window into variations in encounters with therapeutic scripts and religious emotion.

Variation in incorporation of religious tools and dominant therapeutic approaches suggests that probably there are religious people who largely reject divorce-work discourse, those who would say, "No, I am not grieving," or "No, I don't feel guilty." Some may say: "I am simply surviving. I don't want to express my feelings. They are just fine tucked away inside." It is likely that some of the many people who turned down my interview requests were those not heavily invested in therapeutic or religious scripts; they may also have felt that their ending was not pained or dramatic and so they did not have a story to tell, or they may not have been invested in expressing their feelings to a researcher. Radical departure from divorce-work scripts by those who identify as religious would be fascinating stories to hear—if a researcher could find a way to access these individuals. It would be interesting to know what are the competing cultural discourses that have the social power to fight expectations of self-realization narratives. Researchers might find out how these other discourses work to manage the dynamic and multiple characteristics of contemporary U.S. families.

CONGREGATIONS AS EFFICIENT CARRIERS

In contemporary Western society, religious assemblies are one setting among many that produce an increasing number of "construction kits" (Beck 1992, 135) through which the self can be reflexively made (Giddens 1991). Individuals with the means to purchase and travel can shop for thera-peutic and religious strategies as they weigh options. They can join online divorce groups, send their children to therapists or pastoral counselors, purchase books and movies, engage in online communities like Divorce Divas (http://www.divorcingdivas.com/), hire life coaches, send youth to the woods to find self—endless options to help manage work and family life. Individual moral narratives with scripts that reflect such consumption well represent the contemporary Western quest for self-fulfillment. One reason that the United States is so congregation-rich is that these spaces have adapted to provide distinct religious roles in this cultural environ-ment where what Eva Illouz (2007, 5) calls emotional capitalism shapes economic, relational, and gendered expectations of building selves through therapeutic goods. Congregations driven by the authority of religious emo-tion in a religious marketplace shaped by emotional capitalism can produce exceptional religious emotional energy for the dissemination and preserva-tion of therapeutic tenets.

Various congregational mechanisms assisted in sustaining therapeu-tic discourse. Reaching out to others through charity and good works, employing the golden rule, and other broad religious concepts, roles, and symbols reinforced the importance of therapeutic listening and caring for others. Weekly worship services were routine rituals where the solitary nature of self work was legitimated. Jeff sat quietly in the pews accepting his role as "broken," missing his children, and sensing the eyes of his mother and the congregation as he cried and sang. Natalie stepped down from the choir, taking her place in the pews to do the individual work of growing to a different "stage" of Christianity and finding a way to be a better mother to her children. Jill, like many of my respondents who had entered congregations as adults, kept details of her relational life private as the voices around her charged the space with emotional energy through music and prayer. In both large and small congregations, people described fading deeply into private space through sensual collective worship.

Use of media magnified the ability of congregations to transmit therapeutic principles and to balance marriage and divorce as sacred. Divorce media resources were efficient resources for congregations that wanted to offer small groups or grief classes for the divorced, providing predictable emotional approaches through technology. This was especially true in Christian traditions where today's media- and web-driven society advances numerous religious sources online and through print publishing.[16] I visited one Presbyterian, USA, congregation in California that had had a divorce ministry for decades. The congregation had a varied and rich history of media consumption for divorce programs, including sections of the evangelical DivorceCare program, an earlier therapeutic Divorce Recovery video series, and books and seminars by Henry Cloud (a popular evangelical author). Several mainline clergy and pastoral counselors told me that they were not inclined to use or recommend any religious divorce media (such as DivorceCare) as they saw it as coming from conservative presses; still, this did not stop them from tailoring conservative media products to meet their own needs.

The construction of divorce pathology in congregational spaces through media, collective prayer, and other religious tools was compelling. In addition to DivorceCare, popular evangelical media-enhanced programs like Celebrate Recovery, a Saddleback church (http://www.saddleback.com/) resource, were used in some of my respondents' congregations. In Celebrate Recovery, divorce is included alongside other "addictions," and divorced people among those in "broken" positions. A few of the DivorceCare leaders

I interviewed wanted to use Celebrate Recovery so as to include more people in their small-group gatherings. Media resources like DivorceCare and Celebrate Recovery traveled well across Christian congregations and were an efficient congregational means of transmitting therapeutic tenets and invoking religious emotion through fairly predictable group visual and audio performances.

Using technology like PowerPoint as part of worship services or as teaching tools also traveled with ease across congregational worlds, giving life to therapeutic discourse and bringing legitimacy to leaders' presentations of emotion management, in a culture where visual images gather authority and evoke an aura of proficiency.[17] For example, the divorced as harboring dangerous emotions was materialized visually through media in small groups and conferences. After everyone prayed together in a classroom space at a CDM conference, a priest presented a PowerPoint slide, "What does grief feel like?" Then he showed another slide to illustrate emotion, with the words: "exhausted, out of control, unable to sleep or sleep all the time, . . . workaholic, want to die." He continued stressing that "emotions well up inside" and that the body becomes a "battleground of conflicting emotions"; these emotions are seen as a ticking time bomb and can "explode" and cause great harm. Seated in a classroom, watching words and figures to describe emotions designed in sharp PowerPoint slides, worked to legitimate the knowledge of this religio-therapeutic expert. A similar dynamic was at work as DivorceCare participants watched persuasive visual charts in video form that quantified emotional fluids bubbling up, draining energy, and thus weakening moral reserves. Sound tracks in DivorceCare were especially powerful in complementing the visual depiction of dangerous divorce emotions, and were bolstered by scriptures that flashed across the screen.

When people join congregations, they expect access to particular therapeutic goods—a structure where individual psychological concerns can be addressed through worship, support or healing groups, and pastoral counseling. When my respondents met with clergy (see chapter 4), they did so in a guarded manner and with much individual power. Clergy provided confessional spaces that reinforced the private therapeutic nature of divorce work through one-on-one counseling efforts. Small groups are a common structural feature of congregations in the United States, and as demonstrated in Todd's case and those of a handful of other respondents in my study, they have the potential to encourage increased commitment to a faith tradition or congregation.[18] In my study, too, the divorce small-group and conference programs sponsored by congregations and larger denominations and ministries generally followed self-help and twelve-step model formats and so were important therapeutic spaces for the transmission of divorce-work strategies. Participants in small groups learned calculated means/ends approaches to divorce work. Grieving and learning took place through "stages"; expression of feelings in proper manner and place was presented in programs as efficient emotional labor, and reaching out to those with expert, specialized knowledge was encouraged. The use of prayer, music, reading and religious texts, and the construction of a new religious identity (e.g., divorced Catholics as The Church, the divorced as Sacred Singles), bolstered therapeutic tenets, reinforcing divorce work in congregations and ultimately helping members balance the idea that both marriage and divorce can bring sacred identity.

Divorce work made effective through religious emotion in congregations, fueled by small group culture, clergy counseling models, and media mechanisms, is a commanding force that can have global implications. Carla Freeman's work (2011) provides an interesting comparative case. Freeman articulates a heightened sense of entrepreneurship among middle-class women in Barbados who pursue "a new path of middle-class mobility that blends traditional values and practices with ones that are signalizing an emerging neoliberal spirit" (354). She finds that this spirit empowers women in business and marriage relationships, and that, even more, religion plays a role in encouraging "the desire for personalized care and individualized meaning" (262). Pentecostalism there, as in the United States, Latin America, and Africa, is on the rise, composing the second-largest religious group in Barbados, and is like the "megachurches in North America," and these local assemblies provide a "wide array of services, workshops, and groups," including marriage counseling (262). Freeman writes that "entrepreneurialism and the rise in therapeutic culture . . . is often filtered through religion, either institutionally (through a range of new churches and alternative congregations) or through practices that infuse subtle Christian messages and teachings." She argues that "religion itself is an important vehicle for propagating the entrepreneurial spirit, and marriage becomes a critical medium through which to experiment with a melding of new affective labors and desires" (360). In her work, congregations emerge as essential carriers of therapeutic rules and expectations for how emotional labor in marriage and families should be accomplished alongside individual efforts to improve self and succeed in economic pursuits. Freeman's argument is provocative. One can imagine DivorceCare traveling with technological ease through megachurch congregations in Barbados and beyond. Sociologists of religion would do well to investigate the impact of this therapeutic current fueled by religious emotion and ask how sacred divorce work programs might travel alongside marriage enrichment across the globe, further perpetuating assumptions about entrepreneurial spirit, self work, and acceptance of multiple types of family structure. Of interest would also be how divorce work assumptions encounter various cultural systems, and the gendered implications of such transmission.

Similarly, congregations as carriers of familiar emotional goods encouraged many of my respondents to travel across congregational settings, visiting small divorce groups and taking what they could from larger weekly services in other churches, parishes, and synagogues. Brenda, who identified as a liberal southern mainline Methodist, could activate her embodied prayer practice during an evangelical DivorceCare session; Sue felt accompanied by her Catholic saints as she attended services at a Presbyterian church; Natalie was "hit" by the Spirit in nondenominational services outside of her COGIC family church. Andrew J. Cherlin (2009, 110) makes the point that "some divorced individuals may react more positively to conservative Protestant churches' frank rhetoric that divorce is sinful and creates broken families than to the acceptance of divorce in many mainline churches," because they are drawn to the language of "recovery" in these churches. My analysis suggests that recovery discourse exists in all traditions to a certain degree, and so can attract various individuals for whom the concept of journeys from pain and brokenness to new life resonate. Most respondents were attracted to familiar religious symbols, and particular religious roles, but a core identity as therapeutic seeker often materialized through collective worship, music, and triggers of religious emotion in unfamiliar religious settings. Future ethnographic research might explore the processes at work when people travel through religious assemblies seeking strategies for managing self and contemporary family issues. Research could explore what boundaries are at play in crossing congregations in search of therapeutic encounters.

A COMMANDING "GIFT"

I hope that this book will push scholars and religious leaders to critically approach and further explore the essential links and authority born and wielded from the merging of religious and therapeutic worlds. Not all people who end marriages seek religious or therapeutic help, but those who do will find the assumptions and expectations of divorce work detailed throughout this book to be strong social forces. The symbolic form of divorce varies by religious tradition, but the threat of pathology and the call for emotion management in facilitating transition to a better self and managing feelings for self and family are noticeably similar. Breaking deep social bonds of parenthood and religious identity demands redefinition of self in a society that does not generally exile divorcees from congregations and community, but rather expects and offers multiple avenues for constructing new religious and family identity. The socially produced emotional spirit in congregations has given most of my respondents a confidence that their actions in ending relationships and transitioning to new family roles are morally sound, their identity as a therapeutic seeker convincing; congregations hold sensual command and therapeutic potential.[19] Use of this command has serious implications.

I only begin, in this book, to uncover the complexity and power of religious emotion in managing challenging family issues. There are likely many sorts of individuals who access the force of religious ritual and belief as they end marriages—those who identify as religious, and those who reject organized religious traditions. I limited my sample to people who identified as members of a religious tradition, but my analysis of lived religious life points to a research pursuit that I hope ethnographers will take up in working to make sense of the larger dynamics of divorce culture and the force of religious emotion. Researchers could explore the implicitly religious divorce-work practices (individual and group) that people who may not identify as religious employ, and in doing so work to uncover the full range of lived religious/spiritual ritualized divorce work. The various spaces for commercial therapeutic endeavors offer another topic of inquiry— for example, online communities like Divorce Divas (www.divorcingdivas.com), or the efforts of divorce party planners.[20] Sociologists of religion might ask to what extent religious beliefs and emotions are active, or not, in these efforts. Another important point of investigation would be the larger social power dynamics at work as race/ethnicity, class, gender, sexuality, and citizenship status shape accessibility to the activation of narratives of self-realization and engagement in emotional capitalism.

Religion, inside and outside of congregational walls, is a powerful social force that sociologists of the family might take more seriously. Strategies for turning divorce into, in the words of James J. Young, a "gift," are impressive social facts, empowering individuals and perpetuating the ubiquitous social power of therapeutic culture. People may reject dominant therapeutic approaches, but a moral imperative to be an entrepreneur of the self and to devote time and effort to feeling work in the maintenance and creation of kin relationships carries great social power in Western culture. Religious emotion is then a valuable individual and group mechanism for accomplishing this work, for balancing family and gender contradictions, and for ushering in changing family forms. Legal scholars and clinical practitioners in family courts should also push further in exploring religious implications and potential. These scholars and clinicians, too, might ask to what extent religious emotion holds moral energy for divorce processes that litigation and mediation does not. They might explore how religious approaches to divorce work may ease or magnify gendered dynamics in divorce processes. Religious traditions have recognized the need to provide alternatives to lawyers and secular mediators; still, researchers have not explored the extent to which these religious divorce mediation services uphold dominant discourses.[21]

The power of discourse surrounding emotions of endings as dangerous likely contributes to the "emotional divorce"[22] in courtrooms. Longstanding images of the angry, out-of-control, betrayed woman—from Medea to contemporary psychological gendered constructs of "alienation syndrome"[23]—indicate constructions of divorce-work pathology as influential. Scholars should consider how legal counsel and psychological "experts" might use divorce-work discourse in litigation and what the implications of this use may be.

Some may see religion as social force that holds onto sacred beliefs they see as traditional, more important, contemporary religion is a cultural institution particularly adept at balancing multiple family forms and ideology. Religious doctrine seems to play a rather small role in how people experience divorce in congregations. The Roman Catholic Church has a formal process for annulment, but how this takes shape in local assemblies, how a priest like Father Allen and the parishioners he counsels interpret its meaning and enact process, can be remarkably fluid. The same is true for DivorceCare; its evangelical family discourses are somewhat rigid, but as small groups of people gather together to watch its videos and engage in discussion and prayer, facilitators and members shape distinct encounters. There have been major changes in congregations and religious traditions over the last couple of decades, as they adapt to today's marriage/divorce culture and as more move to validate same-sex marriages. Social change does not occur in a single sweep of new ideas and strategies introduced by radical minds; rather, it happens over time and must work to some extent within existing structures of knowledge. Uncovering cultural strategies through an ethnographic perspective makes avenues for change at least visible.

APPENDIX ON METHODS

I began collecting data in 2005 with an interest in exploring how people who identify as religious experience divorce and how congregations and religious traditions may or may not provide resources and practices for ending life partnerships. I limited my focus to a fixed number of religious traditions and used several types of data collection to gain a more nuanced understanding of divorce experience. I also sought diversity in religious traditions, acknowledging some differences that may vary by race/ethnicity and class, and looked for those congregations and religious spaces where people were at work fashioning resources for those experiencing divorce.

I used a systematic coding process that demanded repeated review of data as well as ongoing engagement with existing empirical research. Such a process entails allowing themes to emerge from the data by maintaining a level of distance from existing research and theory, and at the same time engaging theory and empirical studies for comparison and theoretical consequence as the analysis emerges. My analysis took shape over several years of reading through my data multiple times, applying "open" coding techniques, and then more targeted and "axial" coding processes as dominant themes became saturated and links and relationships among these themes presented.[1]

I was tempted to continue collecting more data in the UU case and regarding other religious traditions (e.g., Orthodox Judaism and Islam), and to try additional paths for gaining entry into Dignity USA (LGBT Catholic organization) to gather narratives from gay men, but given time, resources, and, more important, the high level at which my themes were becoming saturated, I ceased data collection and concentrated on the task of articulating my emerging analysis. I hope that researchers will follow my work by giving serious attention to the traditions and populations whose voices are not in my sample. I trust that the concepts and social relationships I introduce in this book will resonate in new cases.

My divorced respondents were the core research participants in this study. The majority of the religious and secular resources I analyzed were those that they found significant. When possible, I conducted participant observation in respondents' congregations by attending services and Bible studies or other social functions, and interviewed the religious leaders my respondents encountered. Given that some told stories of divorce work spanning a number of years, many congregational settings, as these respondents had experienced them, were not accessible. Most of my divorced respondents were in their early thirties to mid-sixties and broadly middle class. I had more success locating lesbian respondents who were willing to talk with me than I had with gay men. I made sure to interview divorced individuals at various points from ending their relationships, to capture a range of experiences and types of narrative construction. The majority of people I interviewed considered their divorce to be a difficult life disruption that brought threatening social emotions, but several negative cases hold theoretical significance, as discussed in the final chapter.

In total I interviewed seventy-five divorced religious practitioners. For the most part, I have assigned pseudonyms to respondents. Most public figures and their writings and public speeches are real names. In cases where internal confidentiality is of significant concern for respondents, I have changed occupations and other key details, but I keep these descriptors in line with class, race, gender, and geographic location. One woman insisted that I use her real first name if I was going to interpret and write her story, and so I did. I gathered field notes in services, congregational social gatherings, and support groups, representing 125 hours of participant observation. I interviewed thirty-one clergy members, eleven other pastoral and lay leaders in congregations and divorce ministries, and three counselors who worked with Jewish support groups. I analyzed divorce resources online, and other media texts (twenty books plus hundreds of pages from websites and printed newsletters). I also analyzed historical documents and resources given to me by religious architects.

The media and divorce programs that I analyzed are by no means exhaustive of sacred divorce-work production. I chose them because they were significant for my respondents or represent significant points of innovation within traditions that clergy or lay leaders referenced. There are many others that could be considered. For example, a book written by a minister for a wide audience that has gone into second edition is J. Randall Nichols's *Ending Marriage, Keeping Faith: A New Guide Through the Spiritual Journey of Divorce* (the 1991 and 2002 editions), or Debbie Ford's (2001) *Divorce as a Catalyst for an Extraordinary Life: Spiritual Divorce*. There are also other video programs for the divorced in the Evangelical and mainline subculture, like the megachurch Saddleback's (http://www.saddleback.com/)

Celebrate Recovery. Although these texts are not part of the data I systematically coded, my review of their content suggests validation of the core themes and relationships covered in my analysis.

My ethnographic design reflects ongoing fluid and systematic analytic process. Questions, evolving analysis, and engagement with existing theory and empirical research determined sampling approaches that I detail briefly for each case. Such "theoretical sampling" (Strauss and Corbin 1990) drove data collection, and the social settings, types of individuals, and small-group encounters I sought were determined by emerging themes. Given the challenging nature of finding participants willing to talk about their experiences of religious practice and ending life partnerships, I utilized multiple strategies for gaining entry into religious communities and identifying respondents. I purposively gathered a relatively equal number of interview respondents who had been active in small groups and divorce ministries and those who had not. I describe below the ethnographic design that took shape in each case, and then address methodological challenges of interviewing individuals about life disruption and painful experiences.

EVANGELICAL AND MAINLINE CHRISTIAN CASES

I began my research in 2005 by spending several months conducting field studies in a medium-size evangelical nondenominational church in New England that was modeling its programming on the Saddleback church model. A friend led me to the congregation and then to a woman who had been divorced who was a lay leader in the religious community. The first woman I interviewed led me to two other divorced women in the church willing to tell their story. I went to several Sunday services, women's Bible studies, and women's breakfasts. The church had separate gatherings for men that I was not invited to attend. I interviewed three lay leaders, including a pastoral counselor, an associate minister who led a divorce small group, and a lay church singles ministry leader. Given that women make up the majority of participants in local religious assemblies, and my position as a woman, it is not surprising that the majority of the stories I collected in this case and in other traditions were from women. I tried to interview men in this first congregation who had been divorced, but the pastoral counselor did not think men would be willing to talk with me, and I suspect he did not even give the men he knew my contact information. I approached two divorced women during women's social gatherings that I had heard were in the middle of a divorce, and they abruptly told me that they did not want to talk with me.

This congregation had just started offering a DivorceCare group, my first encounter with the program. I interviewed the associate minister who led the congregation's first DivorceCare group. Given the seemingly widespread use of the DivorceCare program, I ordered the audio tapes from DivorceCare's website and transcribed the thirteen-week Divorce-Care video series. I also analyzed the accompanying workbook and the DivorceCare website. One can only order the video series if officially associated with a church, so later in my study I found a DivorceCare support group in a southern mainline Protestant United Methodist church and asked to attend. I was warmly invited and welcomed to attend a Divorce-Care group to view the video series. Given the highly emotional and sensitive nature of these meetings, I recorded general details of space and group practices and dynamics, but decided to leave the specifics of people's stories and feelings expressed out of my field notes. To supplement, I interviewed two members of this group privately and conducted a focus group with seven individuals who had attended a DivorceCare series at this particular United Methodist Church. I also interviewed five DivorceCare facilitators (two Mainline Methodist, three nondenominational evangelical), from different states across the country and different types of Protestant congregations, who offered the program.

In total, I identified and interviewed eighteen divorced evangelical and mainline Protestants (five men, thirteen women) from congregations that ranged in size and liberal/conservative orientation. I hesitate to put many of these respondents into denominational categories, as they crossed the boundaries of their congregational worlds in their multiple approaches to religious experience. Even more, some respondents belonged to mainline churches that, in my observations, had much in common in worship and belief with those that identified as evangelical. Some congregations that did not identify formally as evangelical had adopted media programming from nondenominational evangelical churches like Saddleback. I also interviewed the pastoral counselors of two respondents, one from a United Methodist church, and the other from a Presbyterian USA congregation. My respondents identified these congregations as liberal.

UNITARIAN UNIVERSALIST

The UU case is drawn more exclusively from one congregation (Shelby), where, over a year's time, I went to several services and church coffee hours and interviewed the minister, divorced members, and other church members. I was drawn to this congregation when a member heard of my research and suggested that I talk to people at her church because about 10 percent of their membership had experienced the ending of heterosexual and same-sex life partnerships over the course of one year. Sandy, her pastor, and other members of the congregation talked to me about the congregation being "in turmoil" over the break-ups.

I began fieldwork thinking I would interview the seven couples (fourteen members) who had significant relationships end at Shelby, but only five people who had experienced endings, the pastor, and two other members who felt affected by the break-ups were willing to be formally interviewed. The minister was happy that I was conducting field studies. As I noted in chapter 6, he was trying hard to address these endings and saw my coming to the church as a kind of healing process for the congregation. He understood that I would provide a confidential space for people to talk about their endings.

I also found the therapeutic and religious books that some research participants indicated they had read while ending. I called the UU Families Ministry and spoke with a woman in the offices about resources for the divorced in the UU tradition; she led me to the online resource *Let's Talk*. I interviewed an additional three UU respondents (two divorced women and one female clergy member) who belonged to larger UU congregations.

JEWISH CASE

My Jewish sample draws from Reform, Reconstructionist, and Conservative Jewish individuals and congregations. Identifying respondents took place largely through snowball sampling and by putting a call out on a Conservative rabbi listserve list. Some rabbis led me to congregants who they thought would be willing to be interviewed; divorced respondents also led me to their rabbis. I interviewed nineteen rabbis and twelve divorced Jewish religious practitioners. I also interviewed three counselors who worked with Jewish support groups; some of these support group leaders were more open than others in helping me find participants willing to be interviewed, and in one case, an organization that ran support groups refused to provide my name and contact information to its list of past participants because of perceived privacy issues. Given that rabbis and divorce respondents talked about the power of using the mikvah as a ritual for divorce, I visited a new mikvah center in New England and interviewed a volunteer, who then gave me a guided tour. She talked with me about her experiences helping people prepare for the mikvah, and gave me copies of prayers and other documents from the center.

Jewish architects of sacred divorce work fashioned strategies to appeal to Jews from a range of movements and ritual observance. My respondents led me to several resources that I have drawn from for this volume, including voices from: the National Center for Jewish Healing's magazine, *Outstretched Arm* (2004 edition, *The Crisis of Divorce: From Darkness to Light*); Rabbi Vicki Hollander's "Weathering the Passage: Jewish Divorce," in *Lifecycles* (1994), edited by Rabbi Debra Orenstein; Rabbi Alan Lew's pamphlet *Looking Back on Divorce and Letting Go* (2000), which I found displayed at a Conservative synagogue; Rabbi Perry Netter's *Divorce Is a Mitzvah* (2002); and the website http://www.ritual.org. These religious architects represent feminist, Reconstructionist, and Conservative Jewish movements, as well as the communal welfare sphere of American Jewry.[2]

CATHOLIC CASE

I interviewed respondents primarily from the Roman Catholic tradition, although I did interview one priest from the American Catholic tradition who taught seminars for CDM events. I interviewed three Catholic priests and four lay leaders. I formally interviewed ten divorced Catholics and informally interviewed six during conferences and follow-up phone calls and meetings. I located CDM respondents largely through snowball sampling and contacts made during CDM conference events. Twelve of my Catholic respondents were associated with CDM or had gone to CDM events; the other four had not attended a CDM event, and two were not aware that such a ministry existed. Laurie's Catholic divorce group, for example, was not officially associated with CDM; I was drawn to her congregation after reading about how her parish was known for providing community support for parish families.

My focus on CDM began with an interview with a founding member of Catholic Divorce Ministries. One of my colleagues who knew that I was researching the subject of divorce and religion ran across a brochure for a CDM support group while traveling in Massachusetts. She brought me the brochure, and I called the woman who ran the group. Over one year, I interviewed this woman twice and heard her speak at a CDM conference in a mid-Atlantic state. She had kept cassette tapes of regional CDM conferences throughout the 1980s and 1990s and, after our second interview session together and a long lunch, she gifted me with these tapes. In addition, she had saved a large box filled with newsletters she had written over the years, training materials for support group leaders, and handouts from her support groups. She trusted me with the box of printed materials for a few hours, and I ran to the nearest Staples to copy them. Listening over and over again to these tapes of James Young speaking to crowds of divorced Catholics, and hearing the voice of Paula Ripple, formed an unexpected ethnographic treat.

I analyzed the CDM website as well as texts by CDM leaders and others published by Catholic presses. The following books and article displayed at events and CDM-affiliated books were analyzed: Paula Ripple (1982), "The Spiritual Journey of the Divorcing Catholic," in James Young (1982); James Young (1984); Geoffrey Robinson (1984); John Hosie (1991); Barbara Leahy Shlemon (1992); Vincent Marquis (1997); Medard Laz (1998); Foster (1999); William E. Rabior and Vicki W. Bedard (2004); Antoinette Bosco (2006); Kathy Brewer Gorham (2006); John Catoir (2007).

BLACK CHURCH CASES

I knew that I wanted to provide racial/ethnic diversity in my sample, and I had been struck by the lack of research on the relationship between religion and family gender dynamics in black church settings. The first contact I made was a phone call to an African Methodist Episcopal (AME) Church ministry organization, during which I spoke at length with a minister who identified a major concern in the black community as marriage, and noted how he and others were trying to get black couples in the church to get married. He sent me several books about ministering to married couples and about ministry that reinforces marriage as a sacred union. I was fascinated by his emphasis on marriage, given that my question was about divorce ministries and whether the AME church might have resources for those ending marriages. At the time, I did not know that this emphasis on saving marriages would become a pattern in many interviews with clergy in the black church cases and across traditions.

My decision to concentrate on black Baptist and Pentecostal cases was based largely on access to these congregations through friends and students. Most of my Baptist respondents were from churches within three hours of my home in Virginia. The same was true for black Pentecostal respondents and congregations. Black Baptist divorced respondents were found through snowball sampling and targeted interviews with black Baptist ministers. As a white woman, I felt racial boundaries in accessing some congregations and events. I had a difficult time getting interviews with black pastors. A number did not return my messages, and those who did sometimes had to cancel because of pressing pastoral duties. I sent electronic messages and made phone calls in an effort to attend a larger National Baptist Convention, USA, Inc.(NBC) singles group event, but never heard back from organizers.

My respondents in the black church cases were primarily from two types of congregations, those associated with the NBC, the largest black church organization in the United States, and the Church of God in Christ (COGIC) founded in the United States at the turn of the twentieth century in the wake of the Holiness Pentecostal movement, now the second largest of all black Christian churches. I include these black church cases together as one case, given that some were hard to distinguish in worship style and as the members sometimes crossed categories. There were also distinctions between particular congregations in each tradition, as in the evangelical and Protestant cases. For example, respondents noted differences between attitudes toward divorce in "full gospel Pentecostal" versus what they called more "traditional COGIC Pentecostal" churches.

The NBC website notes the divorced as a focal concern of the organization's formal Singles Ministries, and in 2006 the ministry held its Inaugural National Baptist Singles Conference in Richmond, Virginia. This conference became the ground for a subsequent book, *Singles: Strengthened, Secured, and Spirit-Filled*, a text that I analyzed. Some COGIC congregations have singles' ministries, although my respondents' churches did not.

Black friends and students introduced me to pastors and divorced Baptists and COGIC individuals. Two of my students worked as my research assistants and interviewed (alone and with me) about half of the respondents in the black church case. The other half, I interviewed alone. Pentecostal respondents (nine divorced individuals, one clergy member) were located through snowball sampling. One student's interest in family dynamics and religion brought me deeper into this case: I attended Pentecostal services with Danielle Wingfield, who had also been raised in the COGIC Pentecostal tradition. Danielle and I interviewed the pastor of the small rural family Pentecostal church that several of our respondents had attended; we tried to interview the women in charge of our respondents' regional COGIC women's organization, and she agreed to an interview, but her busy schedule kept us from meeting despite our attempts over several months.

All but one black Baptist respondent (an American Baptist minister) attended churches associated with the NBC. There were a total of thirteen black Baptist respondents (four clergy, nine divorced). One of the divorced respondents (Jeff) was also an associate pastor. Only one clergy was a woman. Two of the divorced respondents were men. I tried numerous times (phone calls, e-mails, messages through informants) to interview more women involved in the singles ministries, but without success. One woman agreed to be interviewed, but in the end her busy work schedule kept us from meeting. One of the black Baptist clergy members I interviewed was a woman who, with two other female pastors, started a local women's conference in her hometown. I was drawn to these women through a black Baptist woman whom I interviewed who was in the process of separating from her husband and had attended one of her conferences. I attended services several times in three black Baptist congregations. One church was in a poor urban section of a large city; another was a newly renovated black Baptist church with a large (approximately 2,000 people) congregation; and the third housed a medium-sized older congregation in a small town. The largest, although affiliated with the NBC, sustained a more Pentecostal "praise" worship style. Three of the divorced individuals in the black church cases had crossed traditions at some point in their lives—one left the Pentecostal community and moved to a Baptist church after his divorce (see the discussion of Lenny in chapter 1).

In each of the many cases mentioned in this appendix, I had difficulty identifying and getting people to talk about divorce. This was true both for those who had been divorced and for clergy. Individual circumstances in congregations and gender dynamics likely kept some away. As I noted in the introduction, in one case a pastoral counselor told me that men would not want to talk with a woman about their divorce. I tried on numerous occasions to speak with Alice's pastor but he did not respond. Perhaps this was because divorce had been such an issue at his church and such a taboo topic that he did not want to discuss it with a sociologist. Overall, finding religious people to agree to be interviewed about divorce was hard, and the private nature of both divorce and religious experience no doubt added to the difficulty. Further, as I make clear in this book, divorce is often a traumatic experience marked by major transitions in social roles and status and continues to hold social shame, and this made the interview process itself challenging.

INTERVIEWING ABOUT LOSS AND GRIEF

Interviewing people who are working through profound life transitions requires respecting meaning created through silences. I reminded Elaine, after several silent pauses, her eyelids fighting tears, and deep breaths that she did not have to answer my questions, and I slowly came to understand that she wanted to talk about music as guiding a lifelong spiritual path, but that she had to move through these physical-emotional responses at her own pace to tell her story. There were times when I had to let interview questions go—for example, when Jill shook her head and became teary-eyed, indicating she did not want to talk in depth about how she felt during synagogue services. Conducting interviews about extreme loss can bring the interviewer to a vulnerable place, where one questions one's research motives and wonders if one should be asking research participants to talk about experiences that may cause pain or heightened emotion through remembrance and expression (Behar 1996). Narratives of illness or significant life disruption can also bring unfinished stories filled with gaps, inconsistencies, and contradictions.[3] When silence presented, I made sure to record emotional markers in my field notes.

My interview guide began with background questions—where the respondent was from, how she or he was raised, occupation, and education. I then moved to a broad question, "Tell me about the divorce." This prompt almost always gave way to long stories that inevitably hit other questions on my interview guide. I followed with questions like "Tell me about your religious community" and "Did you attend services while you were going through the divorce?" These prompts brought longer stories. Toward the end of the interview, I asked the interviewee to reflect on the positive and negative ways that religion and religious communities may have been active during their divorce.

Given that interviewees knew I was interested in their experience of religion and divorce, probably the stories they told me were different from how they would have presented themselves in other social interactions. My interpretations of respondents' stories are, then, coconstructed recollections and performances of self, but they still provide a valuable lens for determining respondents' understanding of emotional life and religious beliefs and practice.[4] Robert Orsi (2005, 3) writes that we must acknowledge the "intersubjective nature of research on religion. . . . Our lives and our stories are not simply implicated in our work; they are among the media through which we scholars of religion encounter and engage the religious worlds of others."

My respondents' moral presentations of self were influenced by my asking questions about how religion may or may not have played a role as their relationship ended. When I asked my research participants to tell me about divorce, family, and religious experience, I played a role in shaping the moral stories they told, by creating a space where they could relate religious narratives. I also introduced myself as a scholar of religion who was also a religious practitioner. They knew I was ready to listen respectfully to their experience of relationship with spirituality, the divine, and religious community. They also knew I had been divorced, which brought a level of trust. Lenny, for example, told me the interview was the first time he had talked to anyone in depth about the divorce: "I'm glad I could say it to you without somebody saying, 'Are you crazy! Are you crazy! What that person did to you and you can't forget her!'"

All of the people I interviewed at Shelby called the interview therapeutic. Oliver, Elaine's husband, in fact began our interview by naming our time together a kind of "talk therapy." Sandy commented on the collective interest: "It's funny that, in a congregation like this, . . . typically Unitarian, we would be pleased to become research subjects. It's a way of talking about it, but it's slightly less dangerous than talking about it in a service or in a group that meets at the church. So we leave, go out and talk about it, and then come back." The minister affirmed my listening to members' stories as a collective effort to bring voice to a topic that many felt had become a congregational taboo. My presence in the congregation was understood as the community addressing its issues.

Narrative coherence is not a given, especially in stories people tell about traumatic life events. When working with narratives about private and disruptive experiences, researchers must look outside of stories bounded by interview dialogue and pay attention not only to silences, but also to other social spaces where people might "perform" their endings, such as photographs, media, and other texts or images. "Many experiences cannot be spoken," and so are communicated in alternate ways (Salmon and Riessman 2008, 83). For example, Janet gave me a copy of an interview she had done for a local paper in relation to her involvement with a parents' grief group outside of church. During our interview she talked of her son's "passing," but left the task of filling in the detail of suicide to the article. I listened carefully to the sources and mediums through which people constructed and voiced their stories. As a coconstructor of their accounts, I accepted narrative significance in their silences and in the songs, books, articles, journal entries, music, and choreographed physical prayer movements performed during interviews. Before they gave me these songs, stories, and poetry, I asked if I could use them in the book, given the risk of breeching confidentiality, and each agreed without hesitation.

NOTES

INTRODUCTION

1. Whyte draws from a 1983 U.S. Department of Health and Human Services study that demonstrates 75.9 percent of marriage ceremonies were religious. If we include contemporary ceremonies structured around spiritual and religious ideas outside of traditional congregations, the number likely grows.

2. In 2008, 71 percent of respondents to the Pew Forum's U.S. Religion Landscape Survey said that they were absolutely certain that they believed in God or a Universal Spirit, and 17 percent were fairly certain. See also the 2006 General Social Survey (GSS), where 63.1 percent of respondents said that they "know God exists," 16.7 percent said they "believe but have doubts," 4.2 percent "believe sometimes," and 9.6 percent believed in "some higher power." In 2006, 7.1 percent of GSS respondents said that they attended religious services more than once a week, 19.0 percent said they attended every week, 5.0 percent said nearly every week, 8.4 percent said two to three times a month, 6.8 percent said once a month, and 11.6 percent said several times a year. For more detail regarding U.S. adults' religious affiliations, see page 3 of chapter 1 of the Pew Forum's 2008 U.S. Religion Landscape Survey, http://religions.pewforum.org/pdf/report-religious-landscape-study-chapter-1.pdf. For details regarding adults' turning to congregations for help in family challenges, see Sullivan (2011) and Ammerman (2005, 2).

3. See Frank Furedi (2004); Eva Illouz (2007); James Nolan (1998); Philip Rieff (1966).

4. See Kathleen Gerson (2010). In chapter 1, subsection *Facing the Future,* she describes her interviewees as all hoping to "create lasting, egalitarian partnerships" yet doubtful about their "chances of reaching this goal. . . . Far from rejecting the value of commitment," she found, almost all wanted to create "a lasting marriage or marriage-like relationship."

5. See Gerson (2010); Annette Lareau (2003); and Nicholas Townsend (2002).

6. Examples include Robert S. Weiss (1975); Diane Vaughan (1986); Catherine Riessman (1990); Terry Arendell (1995; 1986).

7. See Scott Coltrane and Michele Adams (2003) and Paul R. Amato (2010) for a review of literature on divorce and outcomes for children and parents. See also Coltrane and Adams; Amato (2003; 2000).

8. See Margaret Vaaler, Christopher Ellison, and Daniel A. Powers (2009), and Norval Glenn and Michael Supancic (1984). See also research conducted by the Barna Group in 2008 (https://www.barna.org/barna-update/article/15-familykids/42-new-marriage-and-divorce-statistics-released) regarding divorce statistics and religion. The National Jewish Population Survey, 2000–2001, reported 9 percent of Jewish adults as currently divorced, slightly below national numbers. Quantitative studies fail to capture the complexity of religious identity; even more, statistics are lacking on the relationship between religion

and those life partnerships not recognized by the state, as a broader category—the subject of this book.

9. See Andrew Cherlin (2009).

10. See Coltrane and Adams (2003).

11. See Leeat Granek (2010).

12. For two edited volumes that highlight differences in cultural practices of death and mourning, and the influence of social factors, see David Field, Jennifer Hockey, and Neill Small (1997) and Colin Parkes, Pittu Laungani, and Bill Young (1997).

13. See for example Sharon Bolton (2005) and Arlie Hochschild (1983).

14. For example, Juniper Wiley (1990) and Michelle Wolkomir (2001).

15. See special edition of *Sexualities* for review of debates around same-sex marriage, in particular Elizabeth Peel and Rosie Harding (2008, 659–666).

16. Same-sex marriage activism in the late 1960s and 1970s occurred primarily in nascent Metropolitan Community Churches. See George Chauncey, *Why Marriage? The History of Shaping Today's Debate Over Gay Equality* (Basic Books, 2004). Contemporary activists have also founded organizations that both advocate for LGBT equality and have roots in religious beliefs, such as the Human Rights Campaign's Religion and Faith Program; California Faith for Equality, an interfaith organization founded after the passage of the state's Proposition 8; and the Unitarian Universalist Legislative Ministry.

17. For explanation of theoretical sampling, see Anselm Strauss and Juliet M. Corbin (1990, 176–193).

CHAPTER 1   SOCIAL SHAME AND RELIGIOUS TOOLS

1. In *Elementary Forms of the Religious Life*, Emile Durkheim (1996 [1912]) notes: "Mourning is not the natural response of a private sensibility hurt by a cruel loss. It is an obligation imposed by the group" (400). For contemporary theorizing regarding the social nature of grief, see Kenneth Doka (1989); Lorraine Green and Victoria Grant (2008); Sarah Goodrum (2008); Thomas J. Scheff (2000).

2. Thomas J. Scheff, in "Shame and the Social Bond" (2000, 96–97), building on the work of Erving Goffman (1963; 1959) and other pioneers in the sociology of emotions, names shame as a core social emotion, a "threat to the social bond," involving a "large family of emotions," including many forms, "most notably embarrassment, humiliation, and related feelings such as shyness that involve reactions to rejection or feelings of failure or inadequacy."

3. The people I interviewed were "storytellers," meaning they spoke "from a moral stance" and their narratives contained some kind of "evaluative orientation" (Phillida Salmon and Catherine Riessman 2008, 78). As Wade Clark Roof (1993, 294) argues, "Narrative is motivated by the drive for coherence," and "stories have a great capacity to bring things together, to sharpen the focus, to see things differently." Robert Weiss (1975, 15) argues that someone's development of an "account" of his or her divorce is extremely significant because it "organizes the events into a conceptual, manageable unity."

4. Numerous medical sociologists have noted the social benefits of seeking and acquiring diagnosis. For example, see Dorothy Broom and Roslyn Woodward (1996) for a discussion of chronic fatigue syndrome and legitimation. See also Peter Conrad (2007).

5. See E. M. Hetherington and John Kelly (2002).

6. See Erving Goffman (1959) and George Herbert Mead (1956).

7. See core liberation theology texts: Gustavo Gutiérrez (1973); Leonardo Boff (1991). On Catholic social traditions, see Judith Merkle (2004). For sociological analysis, see Christian Smith (1991).

8. In the Christian tradition, the Paschal Mystery refers to the mysterious nature of the death, suffering, and then resurrection of Jesus Christ, a central basis and process in salvation; in death, Christ frees individuals from sin, and in his resurrection he brings new life.

9. Vatican II introduced major changes regarding Catholicism and modern culture, opening doors for marginal groups like CDM to shape a unique identity. Of consequence to the birth of CDM was Vatican II's emphasis on laity as the church, efforts to relate faith and church to contemporary global circumstances, and respect of individual subjectivity and religious freedom.

10. Widely attributed to Friedrich Nietzsche, "Why I Am So Wise," in *Ecce Homo*. Written in 1888, it was translated and published posthumously in 1908 by Anthony M. Ludovici. Original quote: "Now, how are we to recognize Nature's most excellent human products? They are recognized by the fact that an excellent man of this sort gladdens our senses; he is carved from a single block, which is hard, sweet, and fragrant. He enjoys only what is good for him; his pleasure, his desire, ceases when the limits of what is good for him are overstepped. He divines remedies against injuries; he knows how to turn serious accidents to his own advantage; whatever does not kill him makes him stronger" (13).

11. See Randall Collins (2004), 38–39. Working from Emile Durkheim (1912), Collins talks about "participation in a ritual" as giving "the individual a special kind of energy," which he calls "emotional energy."

CHAPTER 2   DIVORCE WORK AS CULTURAL STRATEGY

1. The concept of a social script is found in Erving Goffman (1959; 1974). Goffman's dramaturgical analysis is highly significant in cultural studies of discourse, narrative, and organizational framing. Scripts represent particular socially objectified actions, words, and ideas that come together in individual, group, or institutional social performances. Cultural scripts can support formal "discourse repertoires," as suggested in William Gamson, David Croteau, William Hoynes, and Theodore Sasson (1992, 373–393) and David Snow and Robert Benford (1992, 133–155).

2. In discussing the social power of familiar religious emotional routines and practices I draw implicitly from the work of Ole Riis and Linda Woodhead (2010) and of Randall Collins (2004).

3. See Barbara Whitehead (1997, 107–128), for her attention to the growth of literature for children and parents. I analyzed the followed popular divorce self-help books:

Matthew McKay, Peter Rogers, Joan Blades, and Richard Gosse (1999); Bruce Fischer and Robert Alberti (2008 [1981]); Mel Krantzler (1974), and Mel and Pat Krantzler (1999); journalist Abigail Trafford (1992).

4. See Jay Atkinson (2000, 385–426).

5. See Gayraud Wilmore (2000 447–468); C. E. Lincoln and Lawrence H. Mamiya (1990). For womanist theology, see Toinette M. Eugene (2000, 434–443).

6. See for example Michèle Chaban (2000).

7. See Robert N. Bellah, Richard Madsen, William M. Sullivan, Ann Swidler, and Steven M. Tipton (1985). For prominence of small groups and religious wellness/healing, see Robert Wuthnow (1994b).

8. Such individualism reflects processes and social power at work in the increasing medicalization of society, where more and more individual problems and conditions are seen through a medical model. See Peter Conrad (2007).

9. *Let's Talk* was produced by the UUA Family Matters Task Force, http://www.uua .org/documents/mcdonaldcolleen/divorce.pdf, whose stated mission is to transform Unitarian Universalism into a community of families empowered through faith, celebration, support, education, advocacy, and service.

10. See James D. Hunter (1983); Christian Smith, Michael Emerson, Sally Gallagher, and Paul Kennedy (1998); Douglas Sweeney (2005).

11. See John Bartkowski (2001); Kathleen Jenkins (2005).

12. See for example Corinthians 6:19–20 for reference to the body as a temple of the Holy Spirit. See R. Marie Griffith (2004) for a history of Protestant ideas about the body and shaping/controlling the body.

13. See David R. Shumway (2003); also John D'Emilio and Estelle B. Freedman (1988, 75–76); and Tatiana Schnell (2000).

14. See for example Barbara Ehrenreich (1987), for discussion of changes in men's family and relationship roles, and their relationship to feminist movements and therapeutic culture.

15. See Scott Coltrane (2001) for discussion of conservative Christian forces in the construction of programs that privilege normative family structures.

CHAPTER 3   SOLITARY WORK THROUGH COMMUNITY

1. See Ole Riis and Linda Woodhead (2010, 33) for further discussion of religion and how "obedience to emotional scripts allays guilt, deflects disapproval, and sustains a positive self-image."

2. See Kathleen Jenkins (2010).

3. Tia DeNora (2000); Robin Sylvan (2002). See also Robert Wuthnow (2003, 384–385), where he writes that art and religion "seem ancient or even primordial companions, and it seems abundantly clear that representations appearing in ritual may evoke emotion and may affect cognition through their aesthetic qualities." Music as art is one such emotion evoker with cognitive powers.

4. See Kathleen Jenkins (2005) and Sally K. Gallagher and Christian Smith (1999) for dynamics of female submission in conservative Christian traditions.

5. The prayer has been attributed to Protestant theologian Reinhold Niebuhr and was later adopted in similar and shorter form by Alcoholics Anonymous (AA): "God grant me the serenity to accept the things I cannot change, courage to change the things I can, and wisdom to know the difference." See Laurie Goodstein (2008) for controversy over its origins.

6. Researchers have used these categories to uncover patterns, contradictions, and gendered differences in marriage exit narratives. See for example Joseph Hopper (2001); Diane Vaughan (1986); and Susan Walzer and Thomas Oles (2003).

7. Robert Wuthow (1994a, 6) found that 40 percent of adult Americans were involved in small groups that met on a regular basis and that 60 percent of those small group members belonged to groups formally associated with a church or synagogue.

8. See for example Natalie Searl, "The Women's Bible Study: A Thriving Evangelical Support Group," in Robert Wuthnow (1994a, 97–124).

9. See Robert Wuthnow (1994b, 289–314).

10. For example, Nancy Ammerman and Arthur E. Farnsley (1997); Gerardo Marti (2008); Darren E. Sherkat and Christopher G. Ellison (1999); Robert Wuthnow (2003).

11. (Collins 2004, 38–39).

12. When communities are small, concern that criticism and gossip may erode congregational networks is likely warranted. See Christopher G. Ellison, Neil M. Krause, Bryan C. Shepherd, and Mark A. Chaves (2009, 3).

CHAPTER 4   CAUTIOUS CLERGY

1. See Jackson W. Carroll (2006, 100), regarding how clergy in Catholic, mainline Protestant, conservative Protestant, and historic black churches spend their time. "The medium, [hours at work every week] regardless of denomination and whether full- or part-time, is forty-eight." For clergy who worked full-time (defined as thirty-five or more hours per week), the median was 51 hours. Fifteen percent of the clergy's weekly time was for "pastoral care (counseling, spiritual direction, and visitation)" and 30 percent went to preaching and worship leadership.

2. The Paschal Mystery refers to what Catholics see as the mysterious nature of the death, suffering, and resurrection of Jesus Christ, a central basis and process in Christian salvation; in death, Christ frees individuals from sin and, in his resurrection, he brings new life.

3. CDM leaders recommended Catholic press books like those by Michael S. Foster (1999), Geoffrey Robinson (1984), and Antoinette Bosco (2006). Bosco writes that, as divorced ministries took shape, "we started to hear a new phrase, the 'internal forum'"; this phrase meant: "Church law maintained that a canonically valid marriage was unbreakable—that was the 'external forum.' But if remarried divorced Catholics truly and honestly believed in their conscience that they were now free of the previous marriage bond, then they could receive the Eucharist—that was the 'internal forum.'"

4. See Emile Durkheim (1996) and Randall Collins (2004, 31).

5. Barbara Brown Zikmund, Adair T. Lummis, and Patricia M. Y. Chang (1998, 23) note: "Clergy often have a more difficult time than people in other occupations claiming private space for themselves away from the demands of the church job; . . . for many people, 'being in the ministry' is a way of life, not just a job."

6. For discussion of the declining authority of clergy in contemporary society, see Irving Zola (1972). See also Mark Chaves (1994). Michel Foucault (2003, 32) alludes to a shift of sacred power in *The Birth of the Clinic: An Archeology of Medical Perception*, in articulating the "medicalization of society, by way of a quasi-religious conversion and the establishment of a therapeutic clergy."

CHAPTER 5   RICH LIVED PRACTICE

1. Ole Riis and Linda Woodhead (*2010*, 38) point to both Emile Durkheim (1996) and Randall Collins (2004) regarding how religious symbols "can somehow 'store' emotions between ritual gatherings," as well as act as a "shared focus of that emotion within the group setting." Religious emotions are bound up with sacred places, temples, shrines, and landscapes," and "go beyond ordinary social relations to include relations with gods, goddesses, ancestors, and other symbolically mediated beings."

2. See Richard J. Foster (1992) and Kevin L. Ladd and Bernard Spilka (2006).

3. See Susan Crawford Sullivan (2011), for prayer in the lives of mothers living in poverty.

4. Sociologists and anthropologists have illustrated empirical uses of "Spiritual Warfare" as a Pentecostal tool of individual power and political resistance. See for example Rosalind Shaw (2007, 66–93).

5. See Nancy T. Ammerman (2010) and Christian Smith, Michael Emerson, Sally Gallagher, and Paul Kennedy (1998).

CHAPTER 6   RELIGIOUS EMOTION AND MULTIPLE FAMILY FORMS

1. See Erving Goffman (1959, 22–30).

2. See R. Stephen Warner (2005, 152) and Mark Chaves (2004, 2).

3. See Gerardo Marti (2012). Marti's work demonstrates how individuals often stay in congregations where worship coincides with their musical desires.

4. See Micki McGee (2005).

5. See Patricia Dixon (2009). See also Kris Marsh, William A. Darity Jr., Philip N. Cohen, Lynne M. Casper, and Danielle Salters (2007). Marsh and her colleagues argue that it is necessary to rethink studies of the black middle class, given a growing segment of the black middle class who are never-married singles and live alone. See also Megan M. Sweeney and Julie A. Phillips (2004). Regarding blacks and retreat from marriage, see R. Kelly Raley (2000, 19–39).

6. A striking contemporary example of this character of balancing can be found in a DVD produced in 2006 by Andrea Wiley, *Soulmates* (www.soulmatefilm.com), which

bemoans a lack of marriageable Christian black men and the high numbers of single black professional women, and promotes both marriage and singlehood as holy life choices.

7. Peter L. Berger (1967, 145) argues that "the crucial sociological and social-psychological characteristic of the pluralistic situation is that religion can no longer be imposed but must be marketed." See Stephen Warner (1993) for his discussion of U.S. religious history, pluralism, and implications of marketing, "Work in Progress toward a New Paradigm for the Sociological Study of Religion in the United States," where he notes the flexibility and structural adaptability of religious institutions. See also Smith et al. (1998) for creative engagement in evangelical subculture.

8. Penny Edgell (2006, 118) comments on the many similarities found in rhetoric in religious communities that belie liberal/conservative categorizations: "The willingness of many evangelical pastors to meet new family needs results in local congregations that are as welcoming of single parents, singles, childless couples, and dual-earner families as are many of their more liberal counterparts. The nostalgia in some mainline Protestant and Catholic congregations for the male-breadwinner lifestyle results in congregations that communicate a preference for the kind of 'domesticated patriarchy' that we often associate with evangelicals. And the pragmatism of many Catholic parishes means that, regardless of the priest's rhetoric, the reworking of family ministry programs has made a welcoming space for dual-earner families, blended families, and single parents."

9. See Jerome P. Baggett (2009, 156–168) on oppositional communities.

10. See CDM's history pages for information on restricting and financial history throughout the 1990s (http://www.nacsdc.org/about/nineties.html).

11. See Michelle Wolkomir (2006). See also Teodoro Maniaci and Francine M. Rzeznik (1993, film).

12. For history of discussions of men, masculinity, and the search for mental health, see Genevieve Creighton and John Oliffe (2010, 409–418).

13. For instance, Joseph Schneider (1988, 63–78); see also Nancy J. Herman and Charlene E. Miall (1990).

14. See Arthur Greil and David Rudy (1984, 260–278).

15. Research in the area of recent immigrants' encounters with medical and mental health institutions provide some window into the complexity of encounters and political power wielded. For example, Leo Chavez, Estevan T. Flores, and Marta Lopez-Garza (1992, 6–26). There is also a small literature on help-seeking behaviors and adherence to treatment plans, for example, Alenjandro Portes, David Kyle, and William Eaton (1992, 283–298).

16. See Nancy T. Ammerman (2005, 69–114) for discussion of use of media resources in congregations.

17. See Kelly A. Joyce (2008) for an example of visual authority in medical monitoring through MRI. See also Birgit Meyer (2006), whose edited volume offers several case studies that speak to the power of visual media, religious authority, and belonging across the globe.

18. See Kevin D. Dougherty and Andrew L. Whitehead (2011, 91): "We believe that they [small groups] represent a potent source of vitality in congregations big and small."

See also Robert Wuthnow (1994b) on the historical development of the small-group movement as a reaction to rising interests in spirituality and diminishing forms of traditional kinds of communities and kinship networks. He argues as well that participation in small groups relates to more involvement in other congregational activities, friendship networks, and financial commitment.

19. Randall Collins (2004: chapter 3, 39) defines "socially derived emotional energy" as "a feeling of confidence, courage to take action, [and] boldness in taking initiative." This energy is "morally suffused" in that "it makes the individual feel not only good, but exalted, with the sense of doing what is most important and most valuable."

20. See *Time* magazine (http://business.time.com/2012/10/15/the-booming-business -of-divorce-parties/).

21. For example: (http://christianmediationservicesllc.com/); (http://catholiccharities gainesville.org/?page_id=60); Jewish family services (e.g., http://www.jcfs.org/node/ 389, and other Jewish family services pages).

22. Barbara D. Whitehead (1997) speaks to literature on emotional divorce vs. legal divorce.

23. See Carol Bruch (2001, 385). Bruch addresses the history of alienation syndrome and suggests that the label has power that "reminds parents, therapists, lawyers, mediators, and judges" of caution as it stresses allegedly dangerous divorce emotions like anger.

APPENDIX ON METHODS

1. Sociologists have attempted to articulate such processes as systematic qualitative sociological inquiry. For example, Barney Glaser and Anselm Strauss (1967) and Anselm Strauss and Juliet Corbin (1990) name "grounded theory," developing their own methodological language for points in systematic processes of qualitative data analysis. They include types of coding "open" versus "axial" and systematic theory-based approaches to sampling under "theoretical sampling." Michael Burawoy (1998) developed the "extended case method" that entails attention to how macro theory applies to findings at the micro (case) level and how ongoing analysis of micro-level data builds new and useful macro theories. Both grounded theory and the extended case method are inductive approaches that involve analyzing and theoretical engagement while collecting data.

2. Most of the support groups I located took place outside of the synagogue. This reflects a Jewish structure in the United States distinguished by a "religious-congregational" sphere separate from a "communal-welfare" one. See Daniel Elazar (1999).

3. See Catherine Riessman (1998); Arthur Frank (1995); and Kathy Charmaz (2002).

4. See David Yamane (2000); Nancy T. Ammerman and Arthur E. Farnsley (2003); Catherine K. Riessman (1993); Catherine K. Riessman (2008, 80–85).

REFERENCES

Amato, Paul R. 2000. "The Consequence of Divorce for Adults and Children." *Journal of Marriage and the Family* 62(4): 1269–1287.

———. 2003. "Reconciling Divergent Perspectives: Judith Wallerstein, Quantitative Family Research, and Children of Divorce." *Family Relations* 52(4): 332–339.

———. 2007. *Alone Together: How Marriage in America Is Changing.* Cambridge, MA: Harvard University Press.

———. 2010. "Research on Divorce: Continuing Trends and New Developments." *Journal of Marriage and Family* 72(3): 650–666.

Ammerman, Nancy T. 2003. "Religious Identities and Religious Institutions." In *Handbook of the Sociology of Religion,* edited by Michele Dillon. New York: Cambridge University Press.

———. 2005. *Pillars of Faith: American Congregations and Their Partners.* Berkeley: University of California Press.

———. 2007. *Everyday Religion: Observing Modern Religious Lives.* New York: Oxford University Press.

———. 2010. "The Challenges of Pluralism: Locating Religion in a World of Diversity." *Social Compass* 57(2): 154–167.

———. 2014. *Sacred Stories, Spiritual Tribes: Finding Religion in Everyday Life.* New York: Oxford University Press.

Ammerman, Nancy T., Wendy Cadge, Milagros Pena, Robert D. Woodberry, and Omar M. McRoberts. 2006. "2005 SSSR Presidential Address: On Being a Community of Scholars—Practicing the Study of Religion." *Journal for the Scientific Study of Religion* 45(2): 137–148.

Ammerman, Nancy T., with Arthur E. Farnsley II et al. 1997. *Congregation and Community.* New Brunswick, NJ: Rutgers University Press.

Andrews, Molly, Corinne Squire, and Maria Tamboukou, eds. 2008. *Doing Narrative Research.* Los Angeles; London: SAGE.

Arendell, Terry. 1986. *Mothers and Divorce: Legal, Economic, and Social Issues.* Berkeley: University of California Press.

———. 1995. *Fathers and Divorce.* Thousand Oaks, CA: Sage.

Atkinson, Jay. 2000. "Religious Tolerance and Social Concord in the Unitarian and Universalist Traditions." *Research in Human Social Conflict* 2: 385–426.

Baggett, Jerome P. 2009. *Sense of the Faithful: How American Catholics Live Their Faith.* New York: Oxford University Press.

Bartkowski, John. 2001. *Remaking the Godly Marriage: Gender Negotiation in Evangelical Families.* New Brunswick, NJ: Rutgers University Press.

Battle, Michael. 2006. *The Black Church in America: African American Christian Spirituality.* Malden, MA: Blackwell Publishing.

Behar, Ruth. 1996. *The Vulnerable Observer: Anthropology That Breaks Your Heart.* Boston: Beacon Press.

Bellah, Robert N., Richard Madsen, William M. Sullivan, Ann Swidler, and Steven M. Tipton. 1985. *Habits of the Heart: Individualism and Commitment in American Life.* Berkeley: University of California Press.

Berger, Peter L. 1967. *The Sacred Canopy: Elements of a Sociological Theory of Religion.* Garden City, NY: Anchor Books.

Berzon. Betty. 1990. *Permanent Partners: Building Gay and Lesbian Relationships That Last.* New York: Plume Printing.

———. 1996. *The Intimacy Dance.* New York: Penguin.

Boff, Leonardo. 1991. *Faith on the Edge: Religion and Marginalized Existence.* Maryknoll, NY: Orbis.

Bolton, Sharon C. 2005. *Emotion Management in the Workplace.* New York: Palgrave Macmillan.

Boris, Eileen, and Rhacel Salazar Parreñas, eds. 2010. *Intimate Labors: Cultures, Technologies, and the Politics of Care.* Stanford, CA: Stanford University Press.

Bosco, Antoinette. 2006. *Growing in Faith When a Catholic Marriage Fails: For Divorced or Separated Catholics and Those Who Minister with Them.* Totowa, NJ: Resurrection Press.

Brasher, Brenda E. 1997. *Godly Women: Fundamentalism and Female Power.* New Brunswick, NJ: Rutgers University Press.

Broom, Dorothy H., and Roslyn V. Woodward. 1996. "Medicalization Reconsidered: Toward a Collaborative Approach to Care." *Sociology of Health and Illness* 18: 357–378.

Bruch, Carol S. 2001. "Parental Alienation Syndrome: Junk Science in Child Custody Determinations." *European Journal of Law Reform* 3(3): 385.

Burawoy, Michael. 1998. "The Extended Case Method." *Sociological Theory* 16(1): 1–33.

Butler, Anthea D. 2007. *Women in the Church of God in Christ: Making a Sanctified World.* Chapel Hill: University of North Carolina Press.

Cardin, Nina B. 1994. "A Ritual Acknowledging Separation." In *Lifecycles: Jewish Women on Life Passages and Personal Milestones.* Vol. 1, edited by D. Orenstein, 206–210. Woodstock, NY: Jewish Lights Publishing.

Carroll, Jackson W. 2006. *God's Potters: Pastoral Leadership and the Shaping of Congregations.* Grand Rapids, MI: William B. Eerdmans Publishing.

Catoir, John. 2007. *The Dilemma of Divorced Catholics: Where Do You Stand with the Church? What is the Internal Forum?* Ottawa: Catholic Book Publishing/Resurrection Press.

Celello, Kristin. 2009. *Making Marriage Work: A History of Marriage and Divorce in the Twentieth-Century United States.* Chapel Hill: University of North Carolina Press.

Chaban, Michèle C. G. 2000. *The Life Work of Dr. Elisabeth Kübler-Ross and Its Impact on the Death Awareness Movement.* Lewiston, ME: E. Mellen Press.

Chalfant, H. P. 1992. "Stepping to Redemption: Twelve Step Groups as Implicit Religion." *Free Inquiry in Creative Sociology* 20(2): 115–120.

Charmaz, Kathy. 2002. "Stories and Silences: Disclosures and Self in Chronic Illness." *Qualitative Inquiry* 8(3): 302–328.

Chauncey, George. 2004. *Why Marriage? The History Shaping Today's Debate Over Gay Equality*. New York: Basic Books.

Chaves, Mark. 1994. "Secularization as Declining Religious Authority." *Social Forces* 72: 749–774.

———. 2004. *Congregations in America*. Cambridge, MA: Harvard University Press.

Chavez, Leo, Estevan T. Flores, and Marta Lopez-Garza. 1992. "Undocumented Latin American Immigrants and U.S. Health Services: An Approach to a Political Economy of Utilization." *Medical Anthropology Quarterly* 6(1): 6–26.

Cherlin, Andrew J. 2004. "The Deinstitutionalization of American Marriage." *Journal of Marriage and Family* 66(4): 848–861.

———. 2009. *The Marriage-Go-Round: The State of Marriage and the Family in America Today*. 1st ed. New York: Alfred A. Knopf.

Chiswick, Carmel U., and Evelyn L. Lehrer. 1991. "Religious Intermarriage: An Economic Perspective." *Contemporary Jewry* 12(1): 21–34.

Christiano, Kevin J., William H. Swatos, and Peter Kivisto. 2008. *Sociology of Religion: Contemporary Developments*. Lanham, MD: Rowman & Littlefield.

Christopher, Karen. 2012. "Employed Mothers' Constructions of the Good Mother." *Gender & Society* 26(1): 73–96.

Clark, Candace. 1997. *Misery and Company: Sympathy in Everyday Life*. Chicago: University of Chicago Press.

Clunis, Merilee, and G. Dorsey Green. 2005. *Lesbian Couples: A Guide to Creating Healthy Relationships*. 4th ed. Berkeley, CA: Seal Press.

Cohen, Steven M. 1989. *Alternative Families in the Jewish Community: Singles, Single Parents, Childless Couples, and Mixed-Marrieds*. American Jewish Committee.

Collins, Randall. 2004. *Interaction Ritual Chains*. Princeton, NJ: Princeton University Press.

Coltrane, Scott. 2001. "Marketing the Marriage 'Solution': Misplaced Simplicity in the Politics of Fatherhood." *Sociological Perspectives* 44(4): 387–418.

Coltrane, Scott, and Michele Adams. 2003. "The Social Construction of the Divorce 'Problem': Morality, Child Victims, and the Politics of Gender." *Family Relations* 52(4): 363–372.

Conrad, Peter. 2007. *The Medicalization of Society: On the Transformation of Human Conditions into Treatable Disorders*. Baltimore: Johns Hopkins University Press.

Conrad, Peter, and Deborah Potter. 2000. "From Hyperactive Children to ADHD Adults: Observations on the Expansion of Medical Categories." *Social Problems* 47(4): 559–582.

Coontz, Stephanie. 2005. *Marriage, a History: From Obedience to Intimacy or How Love Conquered Marriage*. New York: Viking.

Creighton, Genevieve, and John L. Oliffe. 2010. "Theorising Masculinities and Men's Health: A Brief History with a View to Practice." *Health Sociology Review* 19(4): 409–418.

Davidman, Lynn. 1991. *Tradition in a Rootless World: Women Turn to Orthodox Judaism*. Berkeley: University of California Press.

D'Emilio, John, and Estelle B. Freedman. 1988. *Intimate Matters: A History of Sexuality in America*. 1st ed. New York: Harper & Row.

DeNora, Tia. 2000. *Music in Everyday Life*. Cambridge; New York: Cambridge University Press.

Dillon, Michele. 1999. *Catholic Identity: Balancing Reason, Faith, and Power*. Cambridge; New York: Cambridge University Press.

Dixon, Patricia. 2009. "Marriage among African Americans: What Does the Research Reveal?" *Journal of African American Studies* 13(1): 29–46.

Dodson, Jualynne E. 2002. *Engendering Church: Women, Power, and the AME Church*. Lanham, MD: Rowman & Littlefield.

Doherty, William J. 2001. *Take Back Your Marriage: Sticking Together in a World That Pulls Us Apart*. New York: Guilford Press.

Doka, Kenneth J. 1989. *Disenfranchised Grief: Recognizing Hidden Sorrow*. Lexington, MA: Lexington Books.

Dougherty, Kevin D., and Andrew L. Whitehead. 2011. "A Place to Belong: Small Group Involvement in Religious Congregations." *Sociology of Religion* 72(1): 91–111.

Durkheim, Émile. 1996. *The Elementary Forms of the Religious Life*. Translated by Karen E. Fields. New York: Free Press.

Edgell, Penny. 2005. *Religion and Family in a Changing Society*. Princeton, NJ: Princeton University Press.

Ehrenreich, Barbara. 1987. *The Hearts of Men: American Dreams and the Flight from Commitment*. New York: Anchor Books.

Elazar, Daniel L. 1999. "The Organization of the American Jewish Community." In *Jewish in America: A Contemporary Reader*, edited by R. Rosenberg and C. I. Waxman. Hanover, NH: Brandeis University Press.

Ellison, Christopher G., Neal M. Krause, Bryan C. Shepherd, and Mark A. Chaves. 2009. "Size, Conflict, and Opportunities for Interaction: Congregational Effects on Members' Anticipated Support and Negative Interaction." *Journal for the Scientific Study of Religion* 48(1): 1–15.

Eugene, Toinette M. 2000. "'Lifting as We Climb': Womanist Theorizing about Religion and the Family." In *Down by the Riverside: Readings in African American Religion*, edited by L. G. Murphy, 434–443. New York: New York University Press.

Evangelisti, Silvia. 2007. *Nuns: A History of Convent Life, 1450–1700*. Oxford; New York: Oxford University Press.

Field, David, Jennifer L. Hockey, and Neil Small, eds. 1997. *Death, Gender, and Ethnicity*. London; New York: Routledge.

Fischer, Bruce, and Robert Alberti. 2006. *Rebuilding When Your Relationship Ends*. 3d ed. Atascadero, CA: Impact Publishers.

Foster, Michael S. 1999. *Annulment, the Wedding That Was: How the Church Can Declare a Marriage Null*. New York: Paulist Press.

Foster, Richard J. 1992. *Prayer: Finding the Heart's True Home*. 1st ed. San Francisco: Harper.

Foucault, Michel. 2003. *The Birth of the Clinic: An Archaeology of Medical Perception.* Routledge: Taylor and Francis e-library.

Furedi, Frank. 2004. *Therapy Culture: Cultivating Vulnerability in an Uncertain Age.* New York: Routledge.

Frank, Arthur W. 1995. *The Wounded Storyteller: Body, Illness, and Ethics.* Chicago: University of Chicago Press.

Freeman, Carla. 2011. "Neoliberalism: Embodying and Affecting Neoliberalism." In *A Companion to the Anthropology of the Body and Embodiment,* edited by Francis E. Mascia-Lees, 353–369. Malden, MA: Wiley-Blackwell.

Gallagher, Sally K., and Christian Smith. 1999. "Symbolic Traditionalism and Pragmatic Egalitarianism: Contemporary Evangelicals, Families, and Gender." *Gender and Society* 13(2): 211–233.

Gamson, William A., David Croteau, William Hoynes, and Theodore Sasson. 1992. "Media Images and the Social Construction of Reality." *Annual Review of Sociology* 18: 373–393.

Garey, Anita Ilta. 1999. *Weaving Work and Motherhood.* Philadelphia: Temple University Press.

Geertz, Clifford. 1973. "Religion as Cultural System." In *Interpretation of Cultures,* 87–125. New York: Basic Books.

Gennep, Arnold V. 1960. *The Rites of Passage.* Chicago: University of Chicago Press.

Gerson, Kathleen. 2010. *The Unfinished Revolution: How a New Generation Is Reshaping Family, Work, and Gender in America.* New York: Oxford University Press.

Gerson, Kathleen, and Jerry A. Jacobs. 2004. "The Work-Home Crunch." *Contexts* 3(4): 29–37.

Gerstel, Naomi. 1987. "Divorce and Stigma." *Social Problems* 34(2): 172–186.

Giddens, Anthony. 1991. *Modernity and Self-Identity: Self and Society in the Late Modern Age.* Stanford, CA: Stanford University Press.

Gilbert, Elizabeth. 2007. *Eat, Pray, Love: One Woman's Search for Everything Across Italy, India, and Indonesia.* New York: Penguin.

Gilkes, Cheryl Townsend. 2001. *If It Wasn't for the Women: Black Women's Experience and Womanist Culture in Church and Community.* Maryknoll, NY: Orbis Books.

Glaser, Barney G., and Anselm L. Strauss. 1967. *The Discovery of Grounded Theory: Strategies for Qualitative Research.* Chicago: Aldine.

Glenn, Norval D., and Michael Supancic. 1984. "The Social and Demographic Correlates of Divorce and Separation in the United States: An Update and Reconsideration." *Journal of Marriage and the Family* 46(3): 563–575.

Goffman, Erving. 1959. *The Presentation of Self in Everyday Life.* New York: Doubleday.
———. 1963. *Stigma: Notes on the Management of Spoiled Identity.* New York: Simon & Schuster.
———. 1974. *Frame Analysis: An Essay on the Organization of Experience.* New York: Harper & Row.

Goodrum, Sarah. 2008. "When the Management of Grief Becomes Everyday Life: The Aftermath of Murder." *Symbolic Interaction* 31(4): 422–442.

Goodstein, Laurie. 2008. "Serenity Prayer Stirs Up Doubt: Who Wrote It?" *New York Times,* July 11. Accessed December 8, 2012. http://www.nytimes.com/2008/07/11/us/11prayer.html.

Gorham, Kathy B. 2006. *Finding Your Way through Divorce.* Notre Dame, IN: Ave Maria Press.

Gottman, John M., and Nan Silver. 1999. *The Seven Principles for Making Marriage Work.* New York: Three Rivers Press.

Granek, Leeat. 2010. "Grief as Pathology: The Evolution of Grief Theory in Psychology from Freud to the Present." *History of Psychology* 13(1): 46–73.

Green, Lorraine, and Victoria Grant. 2008. "'Gagged Grief and Beleaguered Bereavements?' An Analysis of Multidisciplinary Theory and Research Relating to Same Sex Partnership Bereavement." *Sexualities* 11(3): 275–300.

Greil, Arthur, and David Rudy. 1984. "Social Cocoons: Encapsulation and Identity Transformation Institutions." *Sociological Inquiry* 54(3): 260–278.

Griffith, R. Marie. 2004. *Born Again Bodies: Flesh and Spirit in American Christianity.* Berkeley: University of California Press.

Grimes, Ronald L. 2006. *Rite Out of Place: Ritual, Media, and the Arts.* Oxford; New York: Oxford University Press.

Gutiérrez, Gustavo. 1973. *A Theology of Liberation: History, Politics, and Salvation. Uniform Title: Teologia de la Liberación. English.* Maryknoll, NY: Orbis Books.

Hackstaff, Karla B. 1999. *Marriage in a Culture of Divorce.* Philadelphia: Temple University Press.

Hays, Sharon. 1996. *Cultural Contradictions of Motherhood.* New Haven: Yale University Press.

Herman, Nancy J., and Charlene E. Miall. 1990. "The Positive Consequences of Stigma: Two Case Studies in Mental and Physical Disability." *Qualitative Sociology* 13(3): 251–269.

Hetherington, E. M., and John Kelly. 2002. *For Better or for Worse: Divorce Reconsidered.* New York: W. W. Norton.

Hill, Shirley A. 2006. "Marriage among African American Women: A Gender Perspective." *Journal of Comparative Family Studies* 37(3): 421–440.

Hilgartner, Stephen. 2000. *Science on Stage: Expert Advice as Public Drama.* Stanford, CA: Stanford University Press.

Hinson, Glenn. 2000. *Fire in My Bones: Transcendence and the Holy Spirit in African American Gospel.* Philadelphia: University of Pennsylvania Press.

Hochschild, Arlie R. 1979. "Emotion Work, Feeling Rules, and Social Structure." *American Journal of Sociology* 85(3): 551–575.

———. 1983. *The Managed Heart: Commercialization of Human Feeling.* Berkeley: University of California Press.

Hollander, Vicki. 1994. "Weathering the Passage: Jewish Divorce." In *Lifecycles: Jewish Women on Life Passages and Personal Milestones,* edited by Rabbi Debra Orenstein, 201–207. Woodstock, NY: Jewish Lights Publishing.

Hopper, Joseph. 2001. "The Symbolic Origins of Conflict in Divorce." *Journal of Marriage and the Family* 63(2): 430–445.

Hosie, John. 1995. *With Open Arms: Catholics, Divorce, and Remarriage.* Rev. ed. Liguori, MO: Liguori Publications.

Hout, Michael, and Andrew M. Greeley. 1987. "The Center Doesn't Hold: Church Attendance in the United States, 1940–1984." *American Sociological Review* 52(3): 325–345.

Hunter, James D. 1983. *American Evangelicalism: Conservative Religion and the Quandary of Modernity.* New Brunswick, NJ: Rutgers University Press.

Huston, Ted L., and Heidi Melz. 2004. "The Case for (Promoting) Marriage: The Devil Is in the Details." *Journal of Marriage and Family* 66(4): 943–958.

Illouz, Eva. 2007. *Cold Intimacies: The Making of Emotional Capitalism.* Malden, MA: Polity Press.

Ingersoll, Julie. 2003. *Evangelical Christian Women: War Stories in the Gender Battles.* New York: New York University Press.

Jenkins, Kathleen E. 2005. *Awesome Families: The Promise of Healing Relationships in the International Churches of Christ.* New Brunswick, NJ: Rutgers University Press.

———. 2010. "In Concert and Alone: Divorce and Congregational Experience." *Journal for the Scientific Study of Religion* 49(2): 278–292.

Joyce, Kelly A. 2008. *Magnetic Appeal: MRI and the Myth of Transparency.* Ithaca, NY: Cornell University Press.

Krantzler, Mel. 1974. *Creative Divorce: A New Opportunity for Personal Growth.* New York: Signet.

Krantzler, Mel, and Pat Krantzler. 1998. *The New Creative Divorce: How to Create a Happier, More Rewarding Life during—and after—Your Divorce.* Holbrook: Adams Media Corporation.

Kübler-Ross, Elisabeth. 1969. *On Death and Dying.* New York: Macmillan.

Kübler-Ross, Elisabeth, and David Kessler. 2005. *On Grief and Grieving: Finding the Meaning of Grief through the Five Stages of Loss.* New York: Scribner.

Ladd, Kevin L., and Bernard Spilka. 2006. "Inward, Outward, Upward Prayer: Scale Reliability and Validation." *Journal for the Scientific Study of Religion* 45(2): 233–251.

Lareau, Annette. 2003. *Unequal Childhoods: Class, Race, and Family Life.* Berkeley: University of California Press.

Laz, Medard. 1998. *Life after the Divorce: Practical Advice for Starting Over.* Liguori, MO: Liguori Publications.

Lee, Richard W. 1995. "Strained Bedfellows: Pagans, New Agers, and 'Starchy Humanists' in Unitarian Universalism." *Sociology of Religion* 56(4): 379–396.

Lehrer, Evelyn L., and Carmel U. Chiswick. 1993. "Religion as a Determinant of Marital Stability." *Demography* 30(3): 385–404.

Lew, Alan. 2000. *Looking Back on Divorce and Letting Go.* Woodstock, NY: Jewish Lights Publishing.

Lincoln, C. E., and Lawrence H. Mamiya. 1990. *The Black Church in the African-American Experience.* Durham, NC: Duke University Press.

Lowney, Kathleen S. 1999. *Baring Our Souls: TV Talk Shows and the Religion of Recovery.* New York: Aldine de Gruyter.

Macfarlane, Julie. 2012. *Islamic Divorce in North America: A Shari'a Path in a Secular Society*. New York: Oxford University Press.

MacRobert, Iain. 1988. *The Black Roots and White Racism of Early Pentecostalism in the USA*. New York: Palgrave Macmillan.

Maniaci, Teodoro, and Francine M. Rzeznik. 1993. *One Nation under God: The Religious Right and Their Crusade to "Cure" Gay People in America*. Film.

Markman, Howard J., Scott M. Stanley, and Susan L. Blumberg. 2010. *Fighting for Your Marriage*. Rev. ed. San Francisco: Jossey-Bass.

Marquis, Vincent. 1997. *A Mortal on the Mend: A Passage to Healing*. Kearney, NE: Morris Publishing.

Marsh, Kris, William A. Darity Jr., Philip N. Cohen, Lynne M. Casper, and Danielle Salters. 2007. "The Emerging Black Middle Class: Single and Living Alone." *Social Forces* 86(2): 735–762.

Marti, Gerardo. 2005. *A Mosaic of Believers: Diversity and Innovation in a Multiethnic Church*. Bloomington: Indiana University Press.

———. 2008. *Hollywood Faith: Holiness, Prosperity, and Ambition in a Los Angeles Church*. New Brunswick, NJ: Rutgers University Press.

———. 2012. *Worship across the Racial Divide: Religious Music and the Multiracial Congregation*. New York: Oxford University Press.

Martin, Emily. 2007. *Bipolar Expeditions: Mania and Depression in American Culture*. Princeton, NJ: Princeton University Press.

McDonald, Colleen. "Let's Talk about Divorce and Broken Relationships." UU Family Matters Task Force. Accessed January 13, 2013. http://www.uua.org/documents/mcdonaldcolleen/divorce.pdf.

McGee, Micki. 2005. *Self-Help, Inc.: Makeover Culture in American Life*. Oxford; New York: Oxford University Press.

McGrew, Edith L. 2008. *The Pain of Death When There Is No Funeral: It's Called Divorce*. Decatur, GA: Daybreak Consultant Services.

McGuire, Meredith B. 2008. *Lived Religion: Faith and Practice in Everyday Life*. Oxford; New York: Oxford University Press.

McKay, Matthew, Peter Rogers, Joan Blades, and Richard Gosse. 1999. *The Divorce Book: A Practical and Compassionate Guide*. New York: MJF Books.

Mead, George Herbert. 1956, revised edition 1964. *On Social Psychology*. Chicago: University of Chicago Press.

Merkle, Judith A. 2004. *From the Heart of the Church: The Catholic Social Tradition*. Collegeville, MD: Liturgical Press.

Meyer, Birgit, and Annalies Moors, eds. 2006. *Religion, Media, and the Public Sphere*. Bloomington: Indiana University Press.

Murphy, Larry G., ed. 2000. *Down by the Riverside: Readings in African American Religion*. New York: New York University Press.

National Baptist Congress of Christian Education. 2007. *Sacred Singles: Strengthened, Secured, and Spirit-Filled*. Compilation Based on the Inaugural National Baptist Singles Conference. Tallahassee, FL: National Baptist Congress of Christian Education.

National Center for Jewish Healing. 2004. *The Outstretched Arm* 5(1). New York: Jewish Board of Family and Children's Services.

Nelson, Timothy J. 2005. *Every Time I Feel the Spirit: Religious Experience and Ritual in an African American Church.* New York: New York University Press.

Nemser, Rudolph W. 1998. "A Rite of Divorce." In *Great Occasions: Readings for the Celebration of Birth, Coming-of-Age, Marriage and Death,* edited by C. Seaburg. Boston: Skinner House Books.

Netter, Perry. 2002. *Divorce Is a Mitzvah: A Practical Guide to Finding Wholeness and Holiness When Your Marriage Dies.* Woodstock, NY: Jewish Lights Publishing.

Nietzsche, Friedrich W., translated by Anthony M. Ludovici. 2004. *Ecce Homo.* Dover ed. Mineola, NY: Dover Publications. Orig. 1908.

Nolan, James L., Jr. 1998. *The Therapeutic State: Justifying Government at Century's End.* New York: New York University Press.

Oppenheimer, Mark. 1996. "'The Inherent Worth and Dignity': Gay Unitarians and the Birth of Sexual Tolerance in Liberal Religion." *Journal of the History of Sexuality* 7(1): 73–101.

Orenstein, Debra, ed. 1994. *Lifecycles.* Vol. 1: *Jewish Women on Life Passages and Personal Milestones.* Woodstock, NY: Jewish Lights Publishing.

Orsi, Robert A. 2005. *Between Heaven and Earth: The Religious Worlds People Make and the Scholars Who Study Them.* Princeton, NJ: Princeton University Press.

Otto, Rudolf. 1958. *The Idea of the Holy; an Inquiry into the Non-Rational Factor in the Idea of the Divine and Its Relation to the Rational. Uniform Title: Heilige. English.* New York: Oxford University Press.

Parkes, Colin M., Pittu Laungani, and Bill Young, eds. 1997. *Death and Bereavement across Cultures.* London; New York: Routledge.

Parsons, Talcott, and Robert F. Bales. 1955. *Family, Socialization, and Interaction Process.* Glencoe, IL: Free Press.

Pattillo-McCoy, Mary. 1998. "Church Culture as a Strategy of Action in the Black Community." *American Sociological Review* 63(6): 767–784.

Peel, Elizabeth, and Rosie Harding. 2008. "Editorial Introduction: Recognizing and Celebrating Same-Sex Relationships: Beyond the Normative Debate." *Sexualities* 11(6).

Peña, Milagros. 1995. *Theologies and Liberation in Peru: The Role of Ideas in Social Movements.* Philadelphia: Temple University Press.

Penningroth, Phil, and Barbara Penningroth. 2001. *A Healing Divorce: Transforming the End of Your Relationship with Ritual and Ceremony.* AuthorHouse.

Portes, Alejandro, David Kyle, and William Eaton. 1992. "Mental Illness and Help-Seeking Behavior among Mariel Cuban and Haitian Refugees in South Florida." *Journal of Health and Social Behavior* 33(4): 283–298.

Rabior, William E., and Vicki W. Bedard. 1991. *Catholics Experiencing Divorce: Grieving, Healing, and Learning to Live Again.* Liguori, MO: Liguori Publications.

Raley, R. Kelly. 2000. "Recent Trends and Differentials in Marriage and Cohabitation: The United States." In *The Ties that Bind: Perspectives on Marriage and Cohabitation,* edited by Linda Waite and Christine Bachrach, 19–39. New York: Aldine de Gruyter.

Rayner, John D. 1998. "From Unilateralism to Reciprocity: A Short History of Jewish Divorce." *Journal of Progressive Judaism* 11: 47–68.

Rieff, Philip. 1966. *The Triumph of the Therapeutic: Uses of Faith After Freud.* 1st ed. New York: Harper & Row.

Riessman, Catherine K. 1990. *Divorce Talk: Women and Men Make Sense of Personal Relationships.* New Brunswick, NJ: Rutgers University Press.

———. 1993. *Narrative Analysis.* Newbury Park, CA: Sage Publications.

Riis, Ole, and Linda Woodhead. 2010. *A Sociology of Religious Emotion.* New York: Oxford University Press.

Robinson, Geoffrey. 1984. *Marriage, Divorce, and Nullity: A Guide to the Annulment Process in the Catholic Church.* Melbourne: Dove Communications.

Roof, Wade C. 1993. *A Generation of Seekers: The Spiritual Journeys of the Baby Boom Generation.* 1st ed. San Francisco: Harper.

Salmon, Phillida, and Catherine K. Riessman. 2008. "Looking Back on Narrative Research." In *Doing Narrative Research,* edited by M. Andrews, C. Squire, and M. Tamboukou, 78–85. Thousand Oaks, CA: Sage Publications.

Sarbin, Theodore R. 1995. "Emotional Life, Rhetoric, and Roles." *Journal of Narrative and Life History* 5(3): 213–220.

Scheff, Thomas J. 2000. "Shame and the Social Bond: A Sociological Theory." *Sociological Theory* 18(1): 84–99.

Schneider, Joseph. 1988. "Disability as Moral Experience: Epilepsy and Self in Routine Relationships," *Journal of Social Issues* 44(1): 63–78.

Schnell, Tatjana. 2000. "I Believe in Love." *Implicit Religion* 3(2): 111–122.

Schütz, Alfred. 1964. "Making Music Together: A Study in Social Relationship." In *Collected Papers 2, Studies in Social Theory,* edited by A. Broderson, 159–178. The Hague: M. Nijhoff.

Searl, Natalie. 1994. "The Women's Bible Study: A Thriving Evangelical Support Group." In *"I Come Away Stronger": How Small Groups Are Shaping American Religion,* edited by Robert Wuthnow, 97–124. Grand Rapids, MI: William B. Eerdmans Publishing.

Shaw, Rosalind. 2007. "Displacing Violence: Making Pentecostal Memory in Postwar Sierra Leone." *Cultural Anthropology* 22(1): 66–93.

Sherkat, Darren E., and Christopher G. Ellison. 1999. "Recent Developments and Current Controversies in the Sociology of Religion." *Annual Review of Sociology* 25: 363–394.

Shlemon, Barbara L. 1992. *Healing the Wounds of Divorce: A Spiritual Guide to Recovery.* Notre Dame, IN: Ave Maria Press.

Shumway, David R. 2003. *Modern Love: Romance, Intimacy, and the Marriage Crisis.* New York: New York University Press.

Smith, Christian. 1991. *The Emergence of Liberation Theology: Radical Religion and Social Movement Theory.* Chicago: University of Chicago Press.

Smith, Christian, Michael Emerson, Sally Gallagher, and Paul Kennedy. 1998. *American Evangelicalism: Embattled and Thriving.* Chicago: University of Chicago Press.

Snow, David, and Robert Benford. 1992. "Master Frames and Cycles of Protest." In *Frontiers in Social Movement Theory,* edited by A. D. Morris and C. M. Mueller, 133–155. New Haven: Yale University Press.

Stolzenberg, Ross M., Mary Blair-Loy, and Linda J. Waite. 1995. "Religious Participation in Early Adulthood: Age and Family Life Cycle Effects on Church Membership." *American Sociological Review* 60(1): 84–103.

Strauss, Anselm L., and Juliet M. Corbin. 1990. *Basics of Qualitative Research: Grounded Theory Procedures and Techniques*. Newbury Park, CA: Sage Publications.

Sullivan, Susan Crawford. 2011. *Living Faith: Everyday Religion and Mothers in Poverty*. Chicago: Chicago University Press.

Summit, Jeffrey A. 2000. *The Lord's Song in a Strange Land: Music and Identity in Contemporary Jewish Worship*. New York: Oxford University Press.

Sweeney, Douglas A. 2005. *The American Evangelical Story: A History of the Movement*. Grand Rapids, MI: Baker Academic.

Sweeney, Megan M., and Julie A. Phillips. 2004. "Understanding Racial Differences in Marital Disruption: Recent Trends and Explanations." *Journal of Marriage and Family* 66(3): 639–650.

Swidler, Ann. 1986. "Culture in Action: Symbols and Strategies." *American Sociological Review* 51(2): 273–286.

———. 2001. *Talk of Love: How Culture Matters*. Chicago: University of Chicago Press.

Sylvan, Robin. 2002. *Traces of the Spirit: The Religious Dimensions of Popular Music*. New York: New York University Press.

Tamboukou, Maria, ed. 2008. "A Foucauldian Approach to Narratives." In *Doing Narrative Research*, edited by M. Andrews, C. Squire and M. Tamboukou, 102–120. Thousand Oaks, CA: Sage Publications.

Townsend, Nicholas W. 2002. *The Package Deal: Marriage, Work, and Fatherhood in Men's Lives*. Philadelphia: Temple University Press.

Trafford, Abigail. 1992. *Crazy Time: Surviving Divorce and Building a New Life*. Rev. ed. New York: Harper Perennial.

Turner, Victor W. 1969. *The Ritual Process: Structure and Anti-Structure*. Chicago: Aldine.

Vaaler, Margaret L., Christopher G. Ellison, and Daniel A. Powers. 2009. "Religious Influences on the Risk of Marital Dissolution." *Journal of Marriage and Family* 71(4): 917–934.

Vaughan, Diane. 1986. *Uncoupling: Turning Points in Intimate Relationships*. New York: Oxford University Press.

Wallerstein, Judith S., and Sandra Blakeslee. 1989. *Second Chances: Men, Women, and Children a Decade after Divorce*. New York: Ticknor & Fields.

Wallerstein, Judith S., Julia Lewis, and Sandra Blakeslee. 2000. *The Unexpected Legacy of Divorce: A 25 Year Landmark Study*. 1st ed. New York: Hyperion.

Walzer, Susan, and Thomas P. Oles. 2003. "Accounting for Divorce: Gender and Uncoupling Narratives." *Qualitative Sociology* 26(3): 331–349.

Warner, R. Stephen. 1993. "Work in Progress toward a New Paradigm for the Sociological Study of Religion in the United States." *American Journal of Sociology* 98(5): 1044–1093.

———. 1997. "Religion, Boundaries, and Bridges." *Sociology of Religion* 58(3): 217–238.

———. 2005. *A Church of Our Own: Disestablishment and Diversity in American Religion.* New Brunswick, NJ: Rutgers University Press.

Weber, Max. 1958. *The Protestant Ethic and the Spirit of Capitalism.* Translated by Talcott Parsons. New York: Charles Scribner's Sons.

Weiss, Robert S. 1975. *Marital Separation.* New York: Basic Books.

Whitehead, Barbara D. 1997. *The Divorce Culture.* 1st ed. New York: Alfred A. Knopf.

Whyte, Martin K. 1990. *Dating, Mating, and Marriage.* New York: De Gruyter.

Wilcox, W. Bradford. 1998. "Conservative Protestant Childrearing: Authoritarian or Authoritative?" *American Sociological Review* 63(6): 769–809.

Wilcox, W. Bradford, Mark Chaves, and David Franz. 2004. "Focused on the Family? Religious Traditions, Family Discourse, and Pastoral Practice." *Journal for the Scientific Study of Religion* 43(4): 491–504.

Wilde, Melissa J. 2007. *Vatican II: A Sociological Analysis of Religious Change.* Princeton, NJ: Princeton University Press.

Wiley, Andrea. 2006. "Soulmate: Every Woman's Journey to Finding True Love." Clean Heart Productions.

Wiley, Juniper. 1990. "The Dramatisation of Emotions in Practice and Theory: Emotion Work and Emotion Roles in a Therapeutic Community." *Sociology of Health and Illness* 12(2): 127–150.

Williams, Roman R. 2010. "Space for God: Lived Religion at Work, Home, and Play." *Sociology of Religion* 71(3): 257–279.

Wilmore, Gayraud S. 2000. "Survival, Elevation, and Liberation in Black Religion." In *Down by the Riverside: Readings in African American Religion,* edited by L. G. Murphy, 447–468. New York: New York University Press.

Wiseman, Reva. 1975. "Crisis Theory and the Process of Divorce." *Social Casework* 56: 205–212.

Wolkomir, Michelle. 2001. "Emotion Work, Commitment, and the Authentication of the Self: The Case of Gay and Ex-Gay Christian Support Groups." *Journal of Contemporary Ethnography* 30(3): 305–334.

———. 2006. *Be Not Deceived: The Sacred and Sexual Struggles of Gay and Ex-gay Christian Men.* New Brunswick, NJ: Rutgers University Press.

Wuthnow, Robert, ed. 1994a. *"I Come Away Stronger": How Small Groups Are Shaping American Religion.* Grand Rapids, MI: W. B. Eerdmans.

———. 1994b. *Sharing the Journey: Support Groups and America's New Quest for Community.* New York: Free Press.

———. 1998. *After Heaven: Spirituality in America since the 1950s.* Berkeley: University of California Press.

———. 2000. "How Religious Groups Promote Forgiving: A National Study." *Journal for the Scientific Study of Religion* 39(2): 125–139.

———. 2003. *All in Sync: How Music and Art Are Revitalizing American Religion.* Berkeley: University of California Press.

Yamane, David. 2000. "Narrative and Religious Experience." *Sociology of Religion* 61(2): 171–189.

Young, James J. 1982. *Divorce Ministry and the Marriage Tribunal.* New York: Paulist Press.

———. 1984. *Divorcing, Believing, Belonging.* New York: Paulist Press.

Zikmund, Barbara Brown, Adair T. Lummis, and Patricia M. Y. Chang. 1998. *Clergy Women: An Uphill Calling.* Louisville, KY: Westminster John Knox Press.

Zola, Irving Kenneth. 1972. "Medicine as an Institution of Social Control." *Sociological Review* 20: 487–504.

INDEX

ABOUT THE AUTHOR

KATHLEEN JENKINS is an associate professor and chair of the Sociology Department at the College of William and Mary. She holds a BA and MA in religious studies from Brown University and a PhD in sociology from Brandeis University. Her first book, *Awesome Families: The Promise of Healing Relationships in the International Churches of Christ,* was published by Rutgers University Press in 2005.